W9-BRR-495

FREUD
& JUNG

ANTHONY STORR

FREUD & JUNG
A DUAL INTRODUCTION

ANTHONY STEVENS

BARNES
&NOBLE
BOOKS
NEW YORK

FREUD

by

ANTHONY STORR

Acknowledgements

Sir Keith Thomas made valuable comments on the text, and Catherine Clarke has proved an expert editor. I am particularly grateful to Dr Charles Rycroft, who drew my attention to some omissions, and made other useful suggestions. I owe a considerable debt to his books, as well as to his critical appraisal of the present text.

Contents

1 Life and character   1

2 From trauma to phantasy   11

3 Exploring the past   20

4 Free association, dreams, and transference   30

5 Ego, super-ego, and id   43

6 Aggression, depression, and paranoia   54

7 Jokes and *The Psycho-Pathology of Everyday
   Life*   65

8 Art and literature   73

9 Culture and religion   84

10 Freud as therapist   95

11 Psycho-analysis today   108

12 The appeal of psycho-analysis   118

    Further reading   129

    Index   132

1 Life and character

Sigmund Freud was born on 6 May 1856 in the Moravian town of Freiberg, now Pribor in Czechoslovakia. His mother Amalie was the third wife of Jacob Freud, a Jewish wool merchant, some twenty years younger than her husband. In 1859, when Sigmund Freud was 3 years old, the family moved to Vienna. For the next seventy-nine years Freud continued to live and work in this city, for which he recurrently professed distaste, but which he was extremely reluctant to leave. In 1938, he was compelled to take refuge from the Nazis, and spent the last year of his life in England, dying on 23 September 1939, shortly after the beginning of the Second World War.

Freud's mother, a vivacious and charming lady who survived until the age of 95, was only 21 when Freud was born. She went on to bear seven other children; but Sigmund, referred to by her as 'mein goldener Sigi', remained her indisputable favourite, one circumstance to which Freud attributed his inner confidence. Freud also believed that his later success was directly related to his being a Jew. Although Freud never practised the Jewish religion and dismissed all religious belief as illusory, he was very conscious of being Jewish, made few friends who were not Jews, regularly attended the meetings of B'nai B'rith, his local Jewish society, and declined royalties from those of his books which were translated into Yiddish and Hebrew. He attributed his intellectual autonomy to his being Jewish, writing that, when he first encountered anti-Semitism at the University of Vienna, his lack of acceptance by the community drove him into opposition and fostered his independence of judgement.

As a boy, Freud was intellectually precocious and an extremely hard worker. For six successive years, Freud was first in his class at school; and, by the time he left, had not only obtained a thorough knowledge of Greek, Latin, German and Hebrew, but had learned French and English, and had also taught himself the rudiments of Spanish and Italian. He began to read Shakespeare at the age of 8. Shakespeare and Goethe remained his favourite authors. From his earliest years, Freud was a serious, dedicated student who was evidently expected by his family and teachers to make his mark in the world, and who himself acquired a conviction that he was destined to make some important contribution to knowledge. Family life revolved around his studies. He took his evening meal apart from the rest of the family and, because the sound of her practising disturbed him, his sister Anna's piano was removed from the apartment by his parents.

Freud enrolled in the medical department of the University of Vienna in the autumn of 1873, but did not graduate until 30 March 1881. His initial interest was in zoological research. From 1876 to 1882 he carried out research in the Physiological Institute of Ernst Brücke, an authority whom he greatly admired and who exercised a considerable influence upon his thinking. Brücke and his co-workers were dedicated to the idea, then not widely accepted, that all vital processes could ultimately be explained in terms of physics and chemistry, thus eliminating religious and vitalist concepts from biology. Freud remained a determinist throughout his life, believing that all vital phenomena, including psychological phenomena like thoughts, feelings and phantasies, are rigidly determined by the principle of cause and effect.

Freud was reluctant to practise medicine, and would have been content to spend his life in research. But, in 1882, he fell in love and became engaged to Martha Bernays. Since there was no possibility of his earning enough to support a wife and family if he remained in Brücke's laboratory, Freud reluctantly abandoned his research career, and spent the next three years gaining medical experience in the Vienna General Hospital, preparatory to embarking upon medical practice. In 1885 he was appointed a lecturer in neuropathology at the University of Vienna. From October 1885 to February 1886 he worked at the Salpêtrière Hospital in Paris under the great neurologist Charcot, whose teaching on hysteria awoke his interest in the problems of the neuroses, as opposed to organic diseases of the nervous system. In April 1886 Freud opened his medical practice in Vienna, and, on 13 September, at last married his fiancée.

Their first child, Mathilde, was born in October 1887. Five more children were to follow; the last being Anna Freud, born in 1895, the only one of Freud's children to become a psychoanalyst. His wife Martha was content to devote herself entirely to his welfare and to that of their six children throughout their long and tranquil married life. We know from letters that their sexual life declined comparatively early; but their family life remained harmonious. After his death, she wrote to a friend:

And yet how terribly difficult it is to have to do without him. To continue to live without so much kindness and wisdom beside one! It is small comfort for me to know that in the fifty-three years of our married life not one angry word fell between us and that I always sought as much as possible to remove from his path the misery of everyday life.

From the mid-1890s onward, Freud's life becomes the history of the development of psycho-analysis. *Studies on Hysteria*, written jointly with Josef Breuer, appeared in 1895. If one considers the influence which Freud has had upon contemporary thought, and the fact that his own contributions to psycho-analysis are so extensive as to require twenty-four volumes, it is extraordinary that the first psycho-analytic publication did not appear until he was 39 years old.

What kind of personality is able to achieve so much within the span of only half a lifetime? Most people of outstanding intellectual achievement exhibit traits of personality which psychiatrists label obsessional; that is, they are meticulous, scrupulous, accurate, reliable, honest, and much concerned with cleanliness, control and order. Only when these admirable traits become exaggerated do we speak of obsessional neurosis, a disorder which ranges in severity from mild compulsions to check and re-check to a state of total disablement in which the sufferer's existence is so dominated by rituals that normal life becomes impossible.

Freud himself recognized that his personality was obsessional, and told Jung that, if he were to suffer from neurosis, it would be of the obsessional type. His intellectual precocity, and his dedication to work, which remained compulsive from boyhood onwards, are characteristic. He wrote to his friend Fliess that he needed a 'dominating passion'. He claimed that he could not contemplate a life without work, and that, for him, the creative imagination and work went together. He was an enormously productive writer. Most of his writing was done on Sundays, or late at night after a day in which he might have spent eight or nine demanding hours seeing analytic patients. Although he took long summer holidays, during which he was an energetic walker, he allowed himself little time for relaxation during the working week.

Like most people with this type of personality, Freud was extremely neat in dress and appearance, even when early poverty made this difficult. A letter to Wilhelm Fliess reveals that a barber attended him daily. He exhibited all the most valuable traits characteristic of this variety of personality, being scrupulous, self-controlled, honest and passionately concerned with the pursuit of truth. Freud himself described obsessional personalities as being 'especially *orderly, parsimonious* and *obstinate'* (*SE*, IX.169). He was certainly orderly and obstinate; and may have appeared parsimonious in his early days, when he was extremely poor and dependent on the financial help of friends like Josef Breuer. His tastes remained simple, and Ernest Jones tells us that he never owned more than three suits, three pairs of shoes, and three sets of underclothes. In later years, he could not tolerate owing money to anyone; and, although charging high fees to those who could afford them, gave generous financial help to those in need, including some patients, his own relatives, and poverty-stricken students.

He also suffered from some of the tensions which are inseparable from the valuable traits found in obsessional personalities. He was superstitious about numbers. In a letter to Jung (16 April 1909), he reveals that, for many years, he was convinced that he would die between the ages of 61 and 62. In 1904, he went to Greece with his brother, and writes that it

4

was 'really uncanny' how often the number 61 or 60 kept on cropping up in connection with 1 or 2. His hotel room in Athens was numbered 31; that is, half of 62. He tells Jung that this obsession first appeared in 1899.

> At that time two events occurred. First, I wrote 'The Interpretation of Dreams' (which appeared postdated 1900), second, I received a new telephone number which I still have today: 14362. It is easy to find a factor common to these two events. In 1899 when I wrote 'The Interpretation of Dreams' I was 43 years old. Thus it was plausible to suppose that the other figures signified the end of my life, hence 61 or 62 (*The Freud-Jung Letters*, 219).

Such superstitions, often combined with compulsive rituals and with a preoccupation with death, are commonly found in cases of obsessional neurosis. Ernest Jones has drawn attention to the fact that, like many other creative men of genius, Freud exhibited a peculiar oscillation between scepticism and credulity. Although Freud did not subscribe to the belief in mediums and 'spiritualism' which seduced so many scientists towards the end of the nineteenth century, he did retain an irrational conviction about the occult significance of numbers and a more than half-hearted belief in telepathy.

Freud exhibited a number of other obsessional habits and traits. For example, he was a compulsive smoker of cigars. When, during the years 1893 to 1896, he suffered from a recurrent cardiac arrhythmia which may have been partly attributable to smoking, he found it impossible to abstain for long. At the age of 67, he developed a cancerous condition of the palate which recurred throughout the rest of his life, requiring more than thirty operations. Although he knew that smoking was an agent which provoked recurrence by the irritation which it caused, he was unable to abandon the habit. Obsessional personalities usually exhibit self-control to the point of appearing inhibited and lacking in spontaneity, and Freud was no exception. But smoking was his Achilles' heel; a compulsive part of his behaviour which he was unable to master.

His collecting habits were also characteristic. Freud had a passion for antiquities, stimulated by his classical studies, his romantic longing for Rome, and his interest in the remoter aspects of human history. Photographs of his apartment in Vienna, and the reconstruction of that apartment in his study at 20 Maresfield Gardens, Hampstead, now the Freud Museum, show his collection of antique statuettes. These crowd the shelves and the top of his desk so closely that not one can be appreciated as an aesthetic object in its own right. This display is not that of a connoisseur but that of an obsessional collector whose interest is in accumulation rather than in beauty. Freud himself realized that his interest in such objects, like his interest in sculpture, depended upon the historical associations of the object and its emotional and intellectual meaning rather than upon its aesthetic form. He frankly admits as much in his essay on 'The Moses of Michelangelo'; a piece which also exhibits Freud's meticulous attention to small details which would escape the scrutiny of most observers. This close attention to detail also showed itself in his clinical interpretations of his patients' symptoms, dreams, and other psychological material.

Freud had a lively appreciation of literature. The excellence of Freud's own literary style was recognized when he was still a schoolboy. In 1930, he became the fourth recipient of the Goethe prize for literature awarded by the City of Frankfurt. In Freud's collected works there are more references to Goethe and to Shakespeare than there are to the writings of any psychiatrist. His appreciation of music was confined to opera, the type of musical performance which most appeals to the unmusical. A nephew describes him as despising music.

Freud's inhibited, controlled nature extended to his autobiography, which concentrates almost entirely upon the development of psycho-analysis and tells us next to nothing about his personal life. As early as 1885, he wrote to his fiancée telling her that he had destroyed his notes, letters and manuscripts of the last fourteen years, presciently adding that he had no desire to make it easy for his future biographers. Freud, the man who spent his life investigating the kind of intimate secrets which people strive to conceal from themselves as well as from others, was extremely reluctant to reveal his own.

In his clinical work, Freud was kind and tolerant, as psychoanalysts have to be. However, his kindness was not based upon any great expectations of the human race, whom he regarded with distaste or with detachment rather than with love.

I have found little that is 'good' about human beings on the whole. In my experience, most of them are trash . . .

(Psychoanalysis and Faith, 61–2)

he wrote in one letter.

One analysand records that his interest was

curiously impersonal . . . He was so concentrated on the inquiry he was pursuing that his self functioned only as an instrument.

Those who were close to him admired him, not only for his intelligence and breadth of culture, but also for his integrity and courage. Perhaps he lacked something in immediate warmth. In a letter to Jung (2 September 1907) Freud wrote:

I have always felt that there is something about my personality, my ideas and manner of speaking, that people find strange and repellent, whereas all hearts open to you. If a healthy man like you regards himself as an hysterical type, I can only claim for myself the 'obsessional' type, each specimen of which vegetates in a sealed-off world of his own.

(The Freud-Jung Letters, 82)

Freud's honesty compelled him substantially to modify or revise his ideas on a number of occasions throughout his long life; but this always seems to have been brought about by new insights of his own rather than by any response to the criticism of others. When Freud had reached a particular conclusion, he was intolerant of disagreement, and this rigidity led to the long series of defections among his collaborators and disciples which is such a regrettable feature of psycho-analytic history.

Freud treated such defections as betrayals rather than as intellectual divergences. Breuer, the first collaborator to become estranged, wrote to Forel:

> Freud is a man given to absolute and exclusive formulations: this is a psychical need which, in my opinion, leads to excessive generalization.

Breuer was right on both counts. Where human frailty was concerned, Freud exhibited a quite unusual tolerance. This, because it has led to a more civilized attitude towards neurosis, sexual deviation and other forms of emotional maladaptation, is one of Freud's most valuable legacies. But, in the early days of psycho-analysis, he could not allow those close to him to dispute what he claimed to be the fundamental, absolute tenets of the new science of the mind which he had originated; and this led not only to the breaches with Breuer and Fliess, but to the departure of Adler, Stekel, Jung, Rank, and others from the psycho-analytic movement.

Breuer's remark about 'excessive generalization' is also well founded. Freud was a bold and original thinker; but the nature and length of the psycho-analytic procedure which he invented meant that he based his conclusions about human nature on a very small sample of the human race. Freud's patients belonged predominantly to the upper or upper-middle classes. Moreover, the type of case upon which early psycho-analytic theory was originally based, namely, severe conversion hysteria in women, is seldom seen today.

Excessive generalization is a temptation for all original thinkers, who are usually in love with their own ideas and who therefore over-value them. Perhaps novel and unpopular ideas would never win a hearing unless their originators were entirely convinced that they were right. Freud was not only sure that he had discovered new aspects of the truth about human beings, but he was also a persuasive writer who endeavoured to meet all possible criticisms which his readers might advance in the course of his own exposition; a technique which is deliberately 'disarming'. He expected hostility and incredulity and often experienced both. But his literary skill and his absolute conviction of his own rightness eventually made psycho-analysis a force to be reckoned with throughout the Western world.

There is also another reason for over-generalization which springs not from over-valuation of the new ideas, but from a desire or need which is very characteristic of thinkers with obsessional personalities. Because their psychology is based on the need to order and control, they tend to look for, and be attracted by, comprehensive systems of thought which promise near-complete explanations of human existence, and which therefore hold out the hope that the individual can master both his own nature and external reality by means of his new understanding. Many of the greatest philosophers, including Kant and Wittgenstein, were people of this kind, creating their own systems, impervious to the ideas of others, often unable to read the works of other philosophers with profit or pleasure.

Freud claimed to be a scientist, and was certainly not a philosopher in the technical sense, nor particularly interested in the subject, although, as a young man, he had translated a book by John Stuart Mill. Nevertheless, he resembled some philosophers in being a system-builder. Very early in its history, psycho-analysis left the narrow confines of the consulting room and made incursions into anthropology, sociology, religion, literature, art, and the occult. It became, if not a philosophical system, at least a *Weltanschauung*; and this extraordinary expansion of a method of treating neurotics into a new way of regarding human nature had its origin in the psychological needs of its founder. Freud repudiated religion as an illusion, yet needed some systematic approach to making coherent sense out of the world. He called the system which he invented a science; but psycho-analysis is not, and could never have been, a science in the sense in which physics or chemistry are sciences, since its hypotheses are retrospective and cannot be used for prediction, and most are insusceptible of final proof. Freud's deterministic stance, and his insistence that psycho-analysis was a science, have discredited his discoveries in the eyes of philosophers like Popper, and of scientists like

9

Medawar, with the consequence that they have failed to appreciate the importance of psycho-analysis as a hermeneutic system and as a way of looking at human nature. A short book cannot attempt an account of everything that Freud wrote. What follows is an attempt to evaluate his more important theories in the light of modern knowledge.

2 From trauma to phantasy

Freud's brief sojourn in Paris during the winter of 1885–6 had a profound effect upon his thinking. Charcot had, for some years, been investigating hypnosis, with the object of discovering a diagnostic technique which would distinguish between paralyses which were the consequence of organic disease of the central nervous system and paralyses which were hysterical, that is, 'neurotic' in origin. Charcot demonstrated to Freud that *ideas*, although intangible, could nevertheless be causal agents in neurosis. When a patient developed a hysterical paralysis, the form which the paralysis took was not determined by the facts of anatomy, but by the patient's faulty *idea* of anatomy. Instead of developing a paralysis which could be explained by a lesion of a particular peripheral nerve, he exhibited a paralysis of a limb which corresponded to his idea of where his leg or arm began and ended. Charcot demonstrated that such paralyses could be cured, and then artificially produced again, by hypnotic suggestion.

Freud learned from Charcot that, in order to understand hysteria, he had to look to psychology rather than to neurology. Since patients awaking from the trance-like state induced by hypnosis could not recall what had been suggested to them whilst hypnotized, hypnotic experiments also taught Freud that mental processes which took place unconsciously could have a powerful effect upon behaviour.

Freud therefore employed hypnosis in the treatment of neurotic patients and continued to do so until 1896. But he did not use hypnosis solely as a means of implanting suggestions of positive health. A second and more important aspect derived from the observations of Freud's friend and colleague, Josef Breuer. When treating his famous case, Anna O. (Bertha Pappenheim), with hypnosis, Breuer discovered that, if she could recall the first moment at which a particular hysterical symptom appeared, and re-experience the emotion accompanying this, the symptom disappeared. Breuer named this method of treatment 'catharsis'. Hypnosis, therefore, came to be used as a method of enabling the patient to recall the forgotten origins of particular symptoms. Instead of being used as a direct attack upon symptoms by means of suggestion, it became a method of investigation.

Freud and Breuer came to hope that all neurotic symptoms could be abolished in this laborious, though essentially simple way. In their first paper in *Studies on Hysteria*, they wrote:

> For we found, to our great surprise at first, that *each individual hysterical symptom immediately and permanently disappeared when we had succeeded in bringing clearly to light the memory of the event by which it was provoked and in arousing the accompanying affect, and when the patient had described that event in the greatest possible detail and had put the affect into words.*

In a famous sentence, Breuer and Freud proclaimed:

Hysterics suffer mainly from reminiscences (*SE*, II.6, 7).

These reminiscences were of a special kind. First, they were not easily accessible to conscious recall. The patient could only recover them if hypnotized or if, as Freud later discovered, the patient was authoritatively told that the memories were there, could certainly be retrieved, and would return at the moment when the physician pressed the patient's forehead with his hand. Second, the reminiscences were invariably painful, shameful, or alarming. It followed that there must be some mental mechanism which tended to banish unpleasant memories from consciousness and make them relatively inaccessible. This mechanism Freud named *repression*; and repression, the first 'mechanism of defence', became the corner-stone of the psycho-analytic theory of neurosis. Already, he was postulating the existence of *conflict* within the mind; conflict between some emotion (affect) which was seeking to become conscious and to be discharged, and another part of the mind which refused to admit or face the existence of an emotion which it found repellent.

Freud postulated that the disowned affect which had become repressed, being unable to find direct expression and discharge, gave rise to neurotic symptoms. The mental state which Freud proposed is analogous to the physical condition of a 'blind' boil or abscess which, being unable to find a path to the surface of the body, cannot discharge the toxic matter which it contains. This 'surgical' view of neurosis is one which must have appealed to Freud as a medical scientist. It implied that the disowned affect which was causing the neurotic symptoms could be excised as if it were a foreign body; an intruder which was not part of the patient's personality as a whole.

In a case of hysteria, Freud affirmed that the affect became converted into a physical symptom; hence the term 'conversion hysteria'. In many instances, the physical symptom expressed the patient's feelings in symbolic fashion. Thus, constriction in the throat might express an inability to swallow an insult; or a pain in the region of the heart might signify that the patient's heart had been metaphorically broken or damaged. In other types of neurosis, a variety of neurotic symptoms, like obsessions and phobias, resulted from the repressed affect struggling to express itself indirectly.

At first, Freud thought of the repressed affect as being always associated with trauma; that is, with some unpleasant event which the patient wished to forget. This observation is still valid today in cases of so-called 'traumatic neurosis', in which a patient has developed neurotic symptoms following a near escape from death, an accident, or some horrific experience like being tortured. Enabling such a patient to recover the memory of the experience, to go through it in detail, and to discharge or 'abreact' the emotions of fear and horror which accompanied the experience does indeed have beneficial results, as those who treated wartime neuroses have repeatedly demonstrated.

Later, Freud extended the notion to include instinctual impulses seeking discharge which might either be aroused by some external stimulus, or might simply arise spontaneously within the person. An early example which illustrates this is the case of a girl who found it impossible to leave her room or

13

receive visitors without having urinated a number of times. Freud traced the origin of the symptom to an occasion on which the girl had been in a theatre and had found herself so strongly attracted by a particular man that she had experienced genital sensations which had led to her wanting to urinate and to being compelled to leave the theatre. Since that occasion, she had feared a repetition of the sensation, and had replaced the fear of her erotic impulses with a fear of being unable to control her bladder. Recovery of the memory of the origin of her symptom together with, one may suppose, recognition and acceptance of her sexuality, effected a cure.

At this time, Freud also proposed that there was a special group of neuroses which were directly caused by unsatisfactory or incomplete discharge of sexual impulses. Such incomplete discharge was brought about by practices like masturbation or *coitus interruptus*, or simply by sexual abstinence. Freud called such states 'actual neuroses', from the German *aktuelle*, meaning 'current'. Substitution of normal sexual activity for the previous practice was enough to cure such cases.

Even at this very early stage in the development of psycho-analysis, one can recognize certain ideas which were to influence Freud throughout the rest of his life. The first is that, except in the cases of 'actual neurosis', past emotions are the cause of present problems; the second, that such emotions are invariably shameful or painful or frightening, and therefore repudiated and repressed. Freud always believed that a dominating principle of mental life was the need of the organism to reach a state of tranquillity by completely discharging all tensions (this was later named the Nirvana principle). This basic assumption tends to treat all powerful emotions in a negative fashion, as disturbances which must be got rid of, rather than as pleasures to be sought. Bliss, in the Freudian scheme, is attained when needs have been satisfied and passions spent. There is no place for 'stimulus hunger', the need which human beings have to seek out emotional and intellectual stimuli when they are placed in a monotonous environment with little input from the outside world, or when they have been in a state of tranquillity for so long that they suffer from *ennui*.

Freud's next step was to assert that, in many cases of hysteria, the trauma which ostensibly provoked the onset of symptoms was often too trivial to be an adequate determinant. In such cases, Freud alleged, the ostensible trauma had awoken memories of an earlier trauma, and it was this combination of present with past trauma which constituted the true provocation. In an early paper, based on a lecture which he delivered in Vienna in 1896, Freud affirmed that:

> *no hysterical symptom can arise from a real experience alone, but that in every case the memory of earlier experiences awakened in association to it plays a part in causing the symptom* (*SE*, III.197).

Freud then made a momentous statement. On the basis of eighteen cases of hysteria he asserted:

> Whatever case and whatever symptom we take as our point of departure, *in the end we infallibly come to the field of sexual experience* (*SE*, III.199).

In the same paper, Freud continues:

> I therefore put forward the thesis that at the bottom of every case of hysteria there are *one or more occurrences of premature sexual experience*, occurrences which belong to the earliest years of childhood but which can be reproduced through the work of psycho-analysis in spite of the intervening decades. I believe that this is an important finding, the discovery of a *caput Nili* in neuropathology (*SE*, III.203).

Roger Brown, a professor of psychology at Harvard, has drawn attention to the fact that this was Freud's last attempt to give figures concerning aetiology, and that, even in this instance, there were no controls. In spite of this, Freud continued to claim that he was a scientist.

Freud's findings made sexual emotions the key emotions which, if repressed, were the cause of neurotic symptoms.

Although he recognized that other emotions could be implicated in hysterical symptoms, for example, resentment at an insult which could not be 'swallowed' causing constriction in the throat, sexuality, rather than aggression, became Freud's central preoccupation and remained so for many years. The popular perception that psycho-analysis is chiefly concerned with sex is largely justified, although there is a good deal more to psycho-analysis than popular perception recognizes. For Freud, sex was especially suitable as a linchpin around which psycho-analytic theory could circle and coalesce. For sex not only gives rise to powerful emotions which are often repudiated and therefore repressed, but it also bridges the gap between mind and body, in that it is responsible for a great many purely psychological manifestations like thoughts, phantasies, and dreams, and yet is obviously physical, both in its hormonal origin and in its ultimate expression. Freud, faithful to his training in Brücke's laboratories, continued to hope that neurosis could ultimately be shown to be physical in origin, although he had abandoned his own attempt to link neurotic mechanisms with cerebral anatomy and physiology (the so-called 'Project for a Scientific Psychology') by 1897. In a letter to Jung dated 19 April 1908, he wrote:

> In the sexual processes we have the indispensable 'organic foundation' without which a medical man can only feel ill at ease in the life of the psyche (*The Freud-Jung Letters*, 140–1).

Freud became more and more convinced that the chief characteristic of the neurotic person was lack of a normal sex life and that sexual satisfaction was the key to happiness. This implied that the healthy person was fully able to discharge the tensions caused by his sexual impulses in repeated, satisfying orgasm, thus recurrently experiencing the state of tensionless Nirvana referred to above.

Freud at first concluded that, in cases of hysteria, the premature sexual experience which constituted the core of the neurosis in early childhood was seduction of the child by an adult. This was often seduction of a daughter by a father, as in

16

the case of Katharina, which Freud described in *Studies on Hysteria*, though originally disguising 'father' as 'uncle'. Freud realized that not all those who had been seduced as children became neurotic; but maintained that this was because they had retained *conscious* access to the traumatic experience, whereas those who later became neurotic had repressed it. Freud's tendency to generalization made him conclude that all his patients had suffered sexual seduction in early childhood, a conclusion which, in a number of instances, his patients were eager to confirm, but which, as Freud himself realized, he might have forced on them because of the strength of his own conviction.

There were three reasons for Freud's subsequent abandonment of the seduction theory. The first was that, although sexual seduction of young children by adults undoubtedly occurred, Freud could not believe that this happened quite so frequently as his growing practice suggested. The second was that, if actual seduction was an invariable precursor to the development of hysterical symptoms, Freud would have been forced to conclude that his own father had been guilty of such acts, since he had noted the existence of some hysterical symptoms in his brother and sisters. The third reason was that, in the course of his own self-analysis, Freud had become more and more impressed with the importance of sexual phantasy. He had, for example, recognized that in his own early childhood he had experienced erotic feelings towards his mother when he saw her naked. He concluded that many of his patients were recounting sexual phantasies of being seduced by a parent rather than recalling actual events.

This was a significant change in Freud's thinking. As he put it himself, it led to the conclusion

> that the neurotic symptoms were not related directly to actual events but to wishful phantasies, and that as far as the neurosis was concerned psychical reality was of more importance than material reality (*SE*, XX.34).

From this time onward, psycho-analysis changed from being an attempt to disclose a causal series of events culminating in the outbreak of a neurosis to an exploration of the patient's imaginative world, especially as that world manifested itself in the early years of childhood. The medical model of neurosis had almost disappeared, although Freud still believed that symptoms were related to the 'damming-up' of sexual tensions which were not properly discharged.

To face the collapse of a hypothesis so painstakingly constructed is daunting, and Freud's abandonment of the seduction theory was originally hailed as an example of his integrity and his uncompromising adherence to truth. J. M. Masson, editor and translator of Freud's letters to Fliess, has questioned Freud's honesty in a book in which he claims that Freud deliberately suppressed his findings about the sexual seduction of children in order not to outrage psychiatric opinion more than he had done already. This is so out of character with what we know of Freud's personality from those who were close to him that Masson's accusations can be dismissed. Nevertheless, in recent years, psychatrists and others have realized that sexual seduction of children is far more prevalent than they had hitherto supposed; and although such seduction is not necessarily followed by the development of hysterical symptoms in the way that Freud originally postulated, it does often have dire consequences for the subsequent emotional adjustment of the individual concerned.

It is quite possible that psycho-analysts have underestimated the occurrence of actual sexual seduction, and that they have treated as phantasies memories recalled by their patients which were accurate reports of real events. No one knows the actual prevalence of sexual seduction in childhood; but there is no doubt that increasing public tolerance of discussion of such matters, and the provision of facilities for children to report sexual abuse privately to understanding adults outside the family, has brought to light a great many cases which had previously been unreported.

Concentration upon the patient's inner world of phantasy has sometimes caused psycho-analysts to neglect, not only sexual seduction, but other real events and circumstances which influence people's lives. As we shall see, this is one of the criticisms levelled at 'classical' psycho-analysis by such critics as John Bowlby. But Freud's realization of the importance of phantasy is a corner-stone in the construction of psycho-analytic theory. He came to see that what was subjected to repression was not usually the memories of actual traumatic incidents (though these might certainly occur), but instinctual impulses manifesting themselves as phantasies. On this basis rest Freud's theories of infantile sexuality and libidinal development, and also his view of dreams.

3 Exploring the past

Infantile sexual development

Freud's rejection of the seduction theory did not shake his conviction that neurosis was connected with disturbances of the sexual function, nor his belief that neurosis originated in the earliest years of childhood. But instead of continuing to concentrate his attention upon traumatic incidents, he turned to studying the sexual and emotional development of children, and advanced the idea that neurosis in later life came about because the child's sexual development had been partly arrested at some immature stage. As he himself put it:

> A formula begins to take shape which lays it down that the sexuality of neurotics has remained in, or been brought back to, an infantile state (*SE*, VII.172).

In line with his requirement that psychological processes should, wherever possible, be formulated in terms of their 'indispensable organic foundation'. Freud couched his stages of infantile sexual development in terms of parts of the body rather than in terms of perception, cognition, learning, or attachment. During the first year of life, the infant's capacity for physical gratification is centred upon the mouth; this is the 'oral' stage. From around 1 to 3 years old, the anal region takes over. This is followed by the 'phallic' stage, in which the penis or clitoris becomes the focus of libidinal investment and masturbatory activity, although the child remains incapable of genital fulfilment with another person. The final 'genital' stage, in which the individual becomes capable of fully satisfying sexual relations with the opposite sex, is not reached until after puberty; and, even in the most maturely developed characters, traces of earlier stages of libidinal development can always be detected.

In Freud's original account of the infant's sexual development the emphasis is upon *auto-erotism*; that is, upon changes taking place in the infant's own body, rather than in its relationships. Freud thought that the infant was transiently attached to the mother's breast in the oral stage, but that the oral component instinct then detached itself and found satisfaction in such activities as thumb-sucking and chewing. Although Freud continued to be aware of trauma as a cause of disturbance, he pictured the infant's development as an internal process only tenuously connected with interaction with the mother or other care-takers. It was not until near the end of Freud's life that he began to appreciate the signal importance of the infant's relationship with the mother. Before this, mothers were considered chiefly as agents who answered the infant's needs by relieving accumulated tensions which the infant feared as dangerous. Mothers were not perceived as persons with whom the infant interacted emotionally and who provided stimulation and opportunities for learning as well as the relief of tension.

Freud pictured the infant's sexuality as 'polymorphously perverse': that is, as diffusely composed of component instincts which at first are separate tendencies, but which finally coalesce at a later stage to form the adult sexual drive. Amongst these component instincts are sadistic and masochistic impulses, homosexual interests, exhibitionistic and voyeuristic tendencies, and fetishistic preoccupations. Traces of all these components can be found in the normal person, but they are particularly emphasized in neurotics. Freud now suggested that neurotic symptoms were the consequence of the repression of *perverse* sexual impulses dating from the earliest years. Because of this early repression, the neurotic's sexuality remained partly undeveloped. When one or other component instinct had become exaggerated, but had not been repressed, the person concerned became a sexual pervert: that is, he acted out his perverse tendency in real life. Both neurotics and perverts, therefore, were fixated at early stages of sexual development, but dealt with this fixation differently. It was this observation which led to Freud's well-known statement that

> *neuroses are, so to say, the negative of perversions*
> (*SE*, VII.165).

At the end of the nineteenth century, many investigators were interested in the vagaries of human sexuality; but Freud was the most influential in persuading both doctors and the general public that sexual perversions are disorders of psycho-sexual development, not 'hereditary taints' or manifestations of 'degeneration'. He particularly emphasized the bisexuality of both men and women.

In some persons, traces of early stages of libidinal development were so persistent that it became customary to refer to 'oral' or to 'anal' characters. Oral traits of character were largely worked out by Freud's disciple, Karl Abraham. Freud himself, as one might expect from the character sketch given in the first chapter of this book, concentrated upon anal traits. No one paid much attention to describing phallic traits of character; but Rycroft, in his dictionary of psycho-analysis, refers to the phallic character as

> a person who conceives of sexual behaviour as a display of potency, in contrast to the genital character, who conceives of it as participation in a relationship.

Of a variety of oral characteristics described, passivity, dependency, and doubts about one's own competence are those most often linked. These traits are commonly found together in persons prone to recurrent depression. Some people exhibiting these features of personality are also given to 'oral' habits, like thumb-sucking, overeating, and over-indulgence in alcohol and tobacco; patterns of behaviour which have been considered by psycho-analysts as compensatory for an original sense of deprivation at the breast. In the case of sexual perverts, a particular preoccupation with *cunnilingus* and *fellatio*, or even with kissing, to the detriment of coitus, would be deemed evidence of persisting oral psychopathology. But the research evidence linking actual deprivation with the later development of oral behaviour or character is weak. It is best to regard orality as a useful piece of clinical observation without being specific about its cause.

The same holds good for the 'anal' character. Preoccupation with orderliness and cleanliness was considered to be a 'reaction-formation' against a particularly marked concern with the messiness and dirt associated with defecation. Obstinacy was interpreted as deriving from rebellion against parental insistence that excretion should take place only in particular circumstances. Parsimony was related to the infant's desire to obtain pleasure by holding on to its faeces for as long as possible; for, as Freud demonstrated from myths, fairy tales, and popular speech, money and faeces are often associated in phrases like 'filthy lucre', and 'tight-arsed'. In perverts, rather than neurotics, preoccupation with excretion and with the anal orifice is easily demonstrated as, for example, in de Sade's *Les 120 Journées de Sodome*.

Research designed to discover whether or not obsessional neurosis and 'anal' traits of character are the consequence of severe or eccentric methods of toilet-training has not found any consistent causal connection. But the traits which Freud described as being associated are in fact found together quite frequently. Although Freud's causal explanation receives little support, his clinical observation and descriptions are accurate.

The Oedipus complex

We come now to the vexed questions of the Oedipus complex, childhood amnesia, and the so-called latency period which is supposed to follow the Oedipal phase. Freud's formulation of the Oedipus complex originated from his self-analysis. In a letter to Fliess dated 15 October 1897, Freud wrote:

> My self-analysis is in fact the most essential thing I have at present and promises to become of the greatest value to me if it reaches its end. . . . It is by no means easy. Being totally honest with oneself is a good exercise. A single idea of general value dawned on me. I have found, in my own case too, [the phenomenon of] being in love with my mother and jealous of my father, and I now consider it a universal event in early childhood, even if not so early in children who have been made hysterical. (Similar to the invention of parentage

[family romance] in paranoia – heroes, founders of religion). If this is so, we can understand the gripping power of *Oedipus Rex*, in spite of all the objections that reason raises against the presupposition of fate; and we can understand why the later 'drama of fate' was bound to fail so miserably (*The Freud-Fliess Letters*, 271–2).

Freud came to assume that, by the time he has reached the 'phallic' stage of development, at around the age of 4 or 5, the small boy is sexually interested in his mother, wishes to gain exclusive possession of her, and therefore harbours hostile impulses towards his father. However, the hostility arouses fear that the father will retaliate, and the form which this retaliation is likely to take is that of castration. The 'castration complex' is activated partly by threats of castration from adults who have observed him masturbating, and partly by the little boy's assumption that, because girls are without a penis, they must have suffered castration. Confronted by what he perceives as a horrifying threat to the most precious part of his body, the small boy unconsciously abandons his hopes of sexual union with his mother, identifies himself with his potentially aggressive father, and finally turns his attention towards securing sexual satisfaction from other feminine sources.

The female version of the Oedipus complex is less clearly worked out, in line with the fact that Freud continued to find women a puzzle throughout his life. However, Freud concluded that, while the little girl is also at first involved emotionally with her mother, her discovery that she lacks a penis, and is therefore an inferior being, leads her to become disillusioned with her mother whom she blames for her condition. This turns her towards her father as a love object, and she begins to phantasize that he will impregnate her. The resulting child, Freud supposes, will compensate the girl for her lack of a penis, and, in this sense, might be said to be a substitute for the missing organ. What brings this stage of emotional development to a conclusion is the girl's growing perception of other men as potential impregnators who will enable her to have a baby and thus overcome her continuing sense of being an inferior kind of human being.

Stated in so bald a fashion, Freud's perception of the Oedipus complex as constituting the central emotional stage through which every human being has to pass if she or he is to achieve adult stability and happiness sounds crude indeed. We have already observed that Freud invariably strove to reduce the psychological and emotional to the physical. To allege that all small boys fear castration at the hands of their fathers sounds ridiculous when taken literally. But, if we were to phrase it differently, and affirm that small boys are greatly concerned with establishing their identity as male persons, feel rivalry with their fathers, and are easily made to feel humiliated or threatened by disparaging remarks about their size, weakness, incapacity, and lack of experience, most people would concur.

Moreover, both small boys and men do feel that their genitals are an especially vulnerable part of their anatomy. Freud's contention that castration anxiety is greater in men, whilst fear of loss of love is greater in women, is supported by research. Females fear penetration, but because their sexual organs are less exposed, are not so prone to fear actual injury. Male genitals are not only unprotected, but also exquisitely sensitive to pain, as the torturers of the world have long appreciated. Enquiry among children attending a paediatric clinic revealed that a substantial minority had supposed that girls originally possessed a penis, but had lost it in one way or another. Castration anxiety has become part of day-to-day speech. Those familiar with psycho-analytic jargon often use it as a kind of shorthand. Thus, a man might say, 'I feel castrated', if, for some reason, he was unable to drive his car or carry on with his work. Freud's persistent attempt to abolish the metaphorical in favour of the literal has contributed to a widespread misunderstanding of what he had to say.

The same comments apply to the notion of 'penis envy'. In Freud's era, male dominance was even more evident than it is today. Because men hold most of the power, many women consider themselves inferior, unappreciated, despised, or weak. Producing babies is one way in which women can feel equal or superior to men. If we express Freud's idea in psychological, rather than anatomical, terms, very few people would take issue with it. As Jung is supposed to have remarked, 'After all, the penis is only a phallic symbol.'

In putting forward his ideas about infantile sexuality and the Oedipus complex, Freud was responsible for underlining the concept that the child is father to the man, emotionally and sexually, as well as in other ways. Freud was writing before zoologists had carried out the kind of experiments with subhuman primates which demonstrate that, for example, prolonged isolation in infancy renders the adult animal incapable of mating or forming normal social relationships. Today, we take it for granted that a child's intimate relationship with each parent, including physical closeness, is likely to affect its future capacity for making warm, affectionate relationships with its peers when it grows up; and the fact that we make such an assumption is largely due to Freud, even though we may not now agree with everything which he had to say about childhood.

Freud thought of the Oedipus complex as a universal; but it can be argued that it is very much a Western concept which particularly applies to the small, 'nuclear' family. Do children brought up in extended families, in which polygamy is the norm, experience the jealousy, possessiveness, and fear which Freud found in his patients? We do not know; but anecdotal evidence suggests the contrary. A Nigerian analyst told me that, during his training analysis, it took him over a year to make his analyst understand the entirely different emotional climate which obtains in a family in which the father has several wives.

We have already observed that Freud, at least in the early stages of his thought, was more concerned with the child's relation with the father than with its relation with the mother. Moreover, the father was also portrayed as authoritarian and severe; the source of prohibitions and threats; and the origin of what later became called the 'super-ego'. Modern research supports Freud's idea of a stage of male development in which the boy feels rivalry with the father; but indicates that the boy's subsequent identification with the father is not 'identification with the aggressor' but because the father makes friendly, loving overtures. As Fisher and Greenberg put it:

It would appear that he [the boy] gives up his acute competitive stance vis-à-vis father because father transmits
friendly positive messages inviting him to join up rather than
fight . . . He invites his son to draw close, to form an alliance,
to adopt his identity, and to accept his values (p. 222).

Infantile amnesia

Most human beings can recall very little of their earliest
childhood. Enquiry has demonstrated that 'first memories'
date from about 3.2 years. Freud attributed infantile amnesia to
repression, assuming that everyone would prefer to banish to
the unconscious their earliest sexual impulses and experiences.
This seems improbable, especially in cultures in which sexual
play between children evokes amusement rather than horror.
There are more likely reasons. Research shows that the growth
of memory is a gradual process. Registration, retention, and
recall are all less efficient before the development of language.
No one knows how well children of, say, 3 or 4 recall events
from still earlier periods, memory for which will disappear.
But, even in adults, memory for recent events is transient
unless it is refreshed by rehearsal. Without a capacity for
language, rehearsal does not occur; and so it is not surprising
that, before language is fairly well developed, memories are not
well retained.

The latency period

Freud believed that the Oedipal phase was succeeded by a
'latency period', lasting from about 5 until puberty, in which
sexual impulses and behaviour, though not abolished, were
much less in evidence. Research does not support this latter
supposition. In sexually permissive cultures, sex play is common throughout the years of middle childhood; and even in
cultures in which sex play is frowned upon, and hence concealed, the evidence is that masturbation, heterosexual play,
and homosexual play all increase with every year that passes.

However, Freud was right in his perception that human growth and development are diphasic. From birth to 5, the pace is rapid. Then comes a phase in which the growth curve rises less steeply, to be succeeded by another spurt just before puberty. Human adaptation largely depends upon learning and the transmission of culture. For these to take place effectively, the period of childhood dependency has to be prolonged, and it is probably for this reason that a phase of slower development, corresponding to the latency period, has been interposed between the two rapid phases. Many common human problems can justifiably be related to the prolongation of immaturity and dependence on parents. Freud's perception that the parent of the opposite sex constituted the child's first sexual object goes some way towards explaining a number of sexual difficulties experienced by adults. A man or woman who has not broken free of emotional ties with parents is likely to perceive potential sexual partners partly as if they were parents. This complicates the relationship, both sexually and in other ways. According to Freud, the Oedipal attachment to the parent of the opposite sex (at least in the male) is accompanied by the threat of castration. Men who continue to perceive women chiefly or partly as mothers may, therefore, regard them as potentially dangerous as well as sexually attractive; and this perception is likely to cause a variety of sexual difficulties, including turning away from women altogether, partial or complete impotence, or the need for reassuring devices like sado-masochistic rituals or fetishes before intercourse is possible. Various details of the Oedipal theory are open to question, but the general outline stands as powerfully explanatory of a variety of sexual difficulties and ways of behaving which had previously appeared inexplicable.

Where Freud was wrong was in making psychosexual development so central that all other forms of social and emotional development were conceived as being derived from it. In his essay on Leonardo, Freud even derives curiosity and the desire for knowledge from sexuality. He must have been aware that many animals exhibit exploratory behaviour which is obviously adaptive in providing information about the environment. Such behaviour seems more closely analogous to human intellectual curiosity; but Freud so insists upon sex as the prime mover that he regards sublimated *infantile sexual researches* as providing the motive power for a subsequent passion for knowledge. Today, most students of childhood development regard sexual development as only one link in the chain, not as a prime cause. Difficulties in interpersonal relationships may be derived from early insecurities which have nothing to do with sex, but which may cause later sexual problems. Similarly, difficulties in sexual development may cause subsequent social problems.

4 Free association, dreams, and transference

Free association

Pari passu with the development of his theory of neurosis, Freud was altering his technique of treatment. From 1892 onwards, he gradually abandoned hypnosis in favour of free association. The patient was still required to recline on a couch, with Freud sitting out of sight at its head; but attempts at urging the patient to recover memories by hypnosis or by using pressure on the forehead were given up. Instead, the patient was required to put into words without censorship whatever thoughts or phantasies spontaneously occurred to her. This change in technique had consequences which have had a lasting influence, not only upon psycho-analysis, but upon most subsequent forms of psychotherapy, and upon many other situations in which one human being is endeavouring to help another. The employment of free association compels the patient to take the initiative, and makes the psycho-analyst assume a much more passive attitude than that conventionally expected of a doctor. Hypnosis is a treatment which is principally dependent upon the patient's compliance and the doctor's authority. Free association requires the patient to retain a larger measure of autonomy. Thus, psycho-analysis became a technique of helping the patient to help him or herself. Instead of looking to the psycho-analyst for direct advice, positive suggestions, or specific instructions, the patient had to learn to use psycho-analysis as a means of understanding herself better. It was hoped that, armed with new insight, she would then be able to solve her own problems.

Dreams

If a patient lying on the couch engages in free association, she is likely, from time to time, to tell the psycho-analyst about her dreams, since dreams are often impressive or disturbing mental phenomena. Although there was an extensive literature on the subject of dreams before Freud turned his attention to it, Freud is justly famous for pulling the threads together, for making the dream into a legitimate object of scrutiny, and for creating a theory of dreams and a technique for interpreting them.

The Interpretation of Dreams was first published in November 1899. While staying at the Schloss Bellevue, outside Vienna, in July 1895, Freud had dreamed his famous dream of 'Irma's injection'. The details of this dream, which has provoked a vast literature, need not concern us. Freud's reading of the dream was that it was an attempt to absolve him from the responsibility of mishandling the treatment of a particular patient, and thus represented the fulfilment of a wish. In 1900, he was staying there again, and on 12 June wrote to Fliess:

> Do you suppose that someday one will read on a marble tablet on this house:
>
> > Here, on July 24, 1895,
> > the secret of the dream
> > revealed itself to Dr. Sigm. Freud
> >
> > *(The Freud-Fliess Letters,* 417)

Freud's phantasy became reality on 6 May 1977, when such a plaque was placed there.

In 1931 Freud wrote a preface to the third English edition of *The Interpretation of Dreams* in which he said:

> This book, with the new contribution to psychology which surprised the world when it was published (1900), remains essentially unaltered. It contains, even according to my present-day judgement, the most valuable of all the discoveries it has been my good fortune to make. Insight such as this falls to one's lot but once in a lifetime.
>
> *(SE,* IV.xxxii)

Creative innovators are not always the best judges of their own works. Freud's theory of dreams, although still influential, has not stood the test of time unmodified, as Freud believed it would. His final theory was incubating for a long period, for Freud had been interested in dreams when he was a medical student, years before the birth of psycho-analysis. We need not record the stages through which the theory passed; but simply state it in its final form.

Freud affirmed that, with very few exceptions, dreams were disguised, hallucinatory fulfilments of repressed wishes. He also asserted that dreams not only represented current wishes, but were also invariably expressions of wish-fulfilments dating from early childhood. This theory is clearly derived from, or comparable with, Freud's early statement about hysteria quoted in Chapter 2, in which he supposed that the trauma which provoked the current symptoms did so only because it awoke memories of traumata in childhood. Freud regarded dreams as if they were neurotic symptoms. Since normal people dream, Freud's theory of dreams supported the idea that neurotic and normal cannot be sharply distinguished, and paved the way for establishing psycho-analysis as a general theory of the mind which applied to everyone.

It also ingeniously reinforced his fundamental conviction that nearly all neurotic problems originated in early childhood. Dreams, he believed, gave indirect expression to infantile sexual wishes which had been repressed and which, if expressed in undisguised form, would so disturb the dreamer that he would wake up.

> Our theory of dreams regards wishes originating in infancy as the indispensable motive force for the formation of dreams.
>
> (*SE*, V.589)

Because these wishes are unacceptable and potentially disturbing, they are censored and disguised. The emergent dream, like a neurotic symptom, is a compromise between censorship and direct expression. The events of the previous day, which often enter into dreams, are important only because they resonate with, and therefore activate, the repressed infantile impulse.

Freud described the mental processes, or 'dream-work', by which the dream was modified and rendered less disturbing. These processes included condensation, the fusing together of different ideas and images into a single image; displacement, in which a potentially disturbing image or idea is replaced by something connected but less disturbing; representation, the process by which thoughts are converted into visual images; and symbolization, in which some neutral object stands for, or alludes to, some aspect of sexual life or those persons connected with it which the dreamer would prefer not to recognize. In addition, Freud referred to secondary revision; a process which strives to make the dream intelligible by converting it into a coherent story and, in doing so, probably distorts it still further.

This view implies that the dream as recalled by the dreamer had previously been subjected to a complex process of disguise which concealed its real meaning. Freud introduced the term 'manifest content' to describe what the dreamer recalled. In contrast, the 'latent content' was the hidden, true meaning of the dream, which could be ascertained only when the dreamer's associations to the images in the dream had been subjected to psycho-analytical scrutiny and interpretation.

Freud's dream theory reflects both his single-mindedness and his tendency to generalization. He was sure that he was right in asserting that infantile sexual wishes were the root cause of neurosis. Dreams, in Freud's view, were primitive, irrational mental phenomena which ignored logic, syntax, and the consciously accepted criteria defining time and space. But ˊ

The interpretation of dreams is the royal road to a knowledge of the unconscious activities of the mind (SE, V.608).

Dreams, therefore, must needs be primarily concerned with infantile sexuality, the single 'indispensable organic foundation' of psycho-analytic theory, even if, at first sight, many of them appeared to be concerned with quite other matters.

Freud's technique of dream interpretation is notably ingenious; but even he had to admit that certain types of dream did not fit his theory. First, there are dreams which do not require interpretation. A hungry person dreams of food; a thirsty person dreams of drinking. These so-called 'convenience' dreams certainly express wishes, but refer only to the present state of the dreamer and not to his infancy.

Secondly, there are 'traumatic' dreams which repeat, in undisguised form, some unexpected, shocking event like a car accident, a bomb incident, or an unprovoked attack like rape or other physical assault. Freud eventually admitted that such dreams could not be regarded as fulfilling wishes. He believed that they occurred when the trauma had been so sudden that the mind of the individual had had no opportunity to shield itself against shock by anxious preparation. He wrote:

> These dreams are endeavouring to master the stimulus retrospectively, by developing the anxiety whose omission was the cause of the traumatic neurosis (*SE*, XVIII.32).

Freud, although concerned with the 'compulsion to repeat' in this paper, does not mention the fact that individuals who have been exposed to trauma consciously behave in the same way as their dreams indicate: that is, they strive to come to terms with, or master, their shock by repeatedly telling the story of their trauma to anyone who will listen. 'Bomb stories' following air raids in the Second World War often became tedious.

Thirdly, anxiety dreams, sometimes amounting to nightmares, appear to contradict Freud's theory of wish-fulfilment. Freud explained such dreams in two ways. First, it might be that anxiety pertained to the manifest content only. Analysis would surely demonstrate that the latent content contained a wish-fulfilment. Or it might be that repression and the dream-work had partially failed, thus allowing some of the anxiety connected with forbidden impulses to manifest itself. In this case, the dreamer usually awoke, for such dreams also fail to fulfil their function as guardians of sleep. It should be added that, at the time when Freud formulated his theory of dreams, he thought that anxiety was simply a manifestation of undischarged sexual energy. Later, in his book *Inhibitions, Symptoms and Anxiety*, he came to regard anxiety as a signal pointing to a possible danger threatening the ego, which made the individual feel helpless. For example, a child might feel incapable of discharging, or otherwise coping with, aggressive or sexual impulses arising from within. Or he might feel threatened from without by the loss of a parent who provided both love and protection. Freud did not modify his dream theory to include this new interpretation of anxiety.

Fourthly, both men and women not infrequently have sexual dreams which culminate in orgasm. The imagery in such dreams may either be symbolic or else undisguised. Freudians have attempted to explain this by alleging that the sexual wishes which appear overtly are those which are acceptable to the dreamer, whilst those which appear in symbolic form are unacceptable; but this does not explain dreams in which sexual impulses are both openly expressed and also distressing to the dreamer. The idea that dreams invariably conceal repressed wishes is not tenable.

Although Freud tenaciously maintained that repressed infantile wishes were the main instigators of dreams, most of the clinical examples which he furnishes are concerned with the emotions of adult life: with rivalry, inappropriate sexual desires, or, as in the case of his own dream about Irma, with the wish to be absolved from blame. Today, very few psychoanalysts support Freud's theory in its original form. Although some dreams are certainly concerned with unfulfilled or disreputable wishes, this is not true of all dreams. Moreover, if dreams were all expressions of repressed infantile impulses which found an indirect way past the censor, one would expect that the proportion of sleep spent in dreaming would increase with age. In reality, electroencephalographic studies show that infants spend more time dreaming than do adults; information which was not available to Freud. Dreams are not couched in the language of everyday speech, but it does not follow that they are necessarily concealing something unacceptable. Poetry is a kind of human utterance in which symbol and metaphor play a predominant role. Poetry may often be hard to understand, but we do not usually think of it as wilfully obscure on this account.

A symbol may be defined as 'whatever stands for something, or has representative function'. A banal example is a national flag. 'Freudian symbols' are popularly supposed to be objects occurring in dreams or phantasies which represent the genitals. Thus, hollow containers, like caves or handbags, may symbolize the female genitals; while swords, umbrellas, or pencils may be taken as indicating the penis. As Rycroft has pointed out in his essay, 'Is Freudian Symbolism a Myth?', Freud did not at first attach great significance to sexual symbolism, and only came to do so because of the work of Wilhelm Stekel. Having recognized the importance of symbolization, Freud treated it in typically reductive fashion. That is, he stated that:

The very great majority of symbols in dreams are sexual symbols (*SE*, XV. 153).

and goes on to list a large number of objects of the kind referred to above. In other words, symbols are treated by Freud as predominantly serving the function of concealment, or of making the anatomical aspects of sexuality more acceptable. As we shall see in Chapter 8, which is concerned with Freud's views on art and literature, Freud took a similarly negative view of phantasy, which he regarded as primarily escapist.

If, unlike Freud, we regard the development of an inner world of the imagination and the development of the capacity for symbolization as adaptive functions which march hand in hand and which are especially highly developed in man, it is possible to see that symbols can have the positive function of bridging the gap between the inner world and the external world and of giving objects in the external world emotional significance. The 'transitional objects' described by Winnicott in his paper of 1951 in *Through Paediatrics to Psychoanalysis* (1975) are typical examples. Very young children develop powerful attachments to inanimate objects from which they are reluctant to be parted, like teddy bears or bits of blanket. Such objects originally symbolize the mother. But, since these symbolic objects actually exist, they cannot be dismissed as merely imaginary. Nor can the process of symbolization which gives these objects significance be regarded as escapist, since a transitional object acts as a real comforter. As we shall see in subsequent chapters, Freud's rigid division of mental activities into rational and irrational, or 'secondary process', and 'primary process', causes endless difficulties.

Freud's theory of dreams seems to be based upon the supposition that, because repression is the mechanism for banishing what is unacceptable to the unconscious, everything unconscious carries a negative sign. In a paper on 'The Unconscious', written in 1915, Freud states that 'the repressed does not cover everything that is unconscious' (SE, XIV.166); but there is little sign of this in his original dream theory. There are many reasons for thinking that what is unconscious is not exclusively, or even predominantly, the consequence of repression, including the fact that some dreams are clearly creative or provide answers to problems. Modern theorists are inclined to think of dreams in terms of information processing; perhaps something to do with comparing the experiences of the day with similar experiences which are stored in the long-term memory. But, in spite of the deficiencies in Freud's theory of dreams, it is important to recognize that it was Freud who reinstated the dream as a phenomenon deserving study.

Transference

The other notable consequence which followed Freud's adoption of free association was his discovery of transference. Transference was originally defined as the process by which a patient attributes to his analyst attitudes and ideas that derive from previous figures in his life, especially from his parents. The term has now been extended to include the patient's total emotional attitude towards the analyst. If a patient is encouraged to say everything which comes into her mind without censorship, she will talk not only about her neurotic symptoms and early childhood memories, but about her hopes and fears, her successes and failures, and also about her current relationships, including her relationship, or lack of relationship, with the psycho-analyst.

As a scientist and medical man, Freud's original hope was that he had discovered both the cause of neurotic symptoms and also a treatment which would abolish them. By enabling the patient to circumvent repression and recall the vicissitudes of her infantile development, the blocks which were preventing the proper discharge of instinctual impulses would be overcome, and the symptoms, which were the result of a compromise between repression and discharge, would disappear. According to this view, the treatment of neurosis was comparable with the treatment of physical illness. Just as tubercle bacilli might be regarded as the cause of pulmonary tuberculosis, and abolished by a strict regime of treatment, so neuroses were caused by repressed infantile impulses, and abolished by recall and abreaction of those impulses, thus overcoming the blocks which had obstructed the patient's progress towards sexual maturity. Psycho-analysis could therefore be regarded as a technique which could be learned like the technique of any other medical treatment; and the psycho-analyst could assume the traditional role of a skilled medical practitioner: benevolent, considerate, but essentially detached.

This is certainly the model which Freud originally attempted to follow; one in which the relationship between patient and doctor was professional and objective rather than personal, although personal elements like gratitude might be in evidence to a limited extent. Freud himself compared his role to that of a mountain guide. As we saw in Chapter 1, Freud was a particularly detached individual, regarded by at least one analysand as 'curiously impersonal'. When Freud abandoned hypnosis or using pressure on the forehead in favour of free association, it was no longer strictly necessary to enjoin patients to lie prone upon a couch. But Freud kept the couch and his own position out of sight of the patient, partly in order to facilitate the flow of the patient's associations, but partly, as he admitted, because he did not like being stared at for so many hours a day. His insistence upon his own anonymity and his refusal to answer questions about himself may also have had personal origins. We noted in Chapter 1 that Freud was extremely reluctant to reveal anything about himself. However, this reluctance proved in the end to be a powerful means of evoking phantasies from patients which would never have appeared if Freud had been more forthcoming. It is still an important aspect of contemporary techniques of psychotherapy. It was Freud's detachment and refusal to become personally involved with his patients that both promoted the phenomena of transference and made those phenomena apparent.

When Freud found that he became emotionally important to his patients, his initial response was negative, although he quickly recognized that transference was a vital and unavoidable part of the psycho-analytic process. Freud at first thought of transference as an erotic attachment to the psychoanalyst, as indeed it can be. However deplorable this might be, it was, so Freud believed, a useful way of overcoming the resistances of the patient. Later, Freud came to think of transference as an artificially induced neurosis in which the patient repeated all the attitudes which she had held towards her parents. By means of interpretation, Freud strove to convert this repetition into recollection, thus reducing the intensity of the patient's present emotions by affirming that they really belonged to the past.

As late as 5 June 1910, Freud was still exhibiting distaste for transference, in spite of recognizing its importance. In a letter to Pfister, he wrote:

As for the transference, it is altogether a curse. The intractable and fierce impulses in the illness, on account of which I renounced both indirect and hypnotic suggestion, cannot be altogether abolished even through psycho-analysis; they can only be restrained, and what remains expresses itself in the transference. That is often a considerable amount.

One can understand Freud's feelings. He had hoped that his patients would accept him simply as a skilled physician who could, by means of his technique, expose the origins and abolish the symptoms of their neuroses. Instead, they made him into an idealized lover, a father-figure, or a saviour. What they wanted was not his science, but his love.

It is surely because Freud was by nature an impersonal investigator that he interpreted his patients' emotional impulses towards him as being entirely repetitions from the past, and discounted the possibility that they might be experiencing genuine feelings in the here-and-now.

> The patient, that is to say, directs toward the physician a degree of affectionate feeling (mingled, often enough, with hostility) which is based on no real relationship between them and which—as is shown by every detail of its emergence—can only be traced back to old wishful phantasies of the patient's which have become unconscious.
>
> (SE, XI.51)

In fact, it is perfectly natural that patients should genuinely value the psycho-analyst, however much their picture of him or her may be distorted by past experience. Many patients seeking psycho-analysis have never experienced from anyone else the kind of long-term concern which is offered in psycho-analysis. There is no other situation in life in which one can count on a devoted listener for so many hours. What many patients experience is an awakening of emotions which they have never had, rather than a repetition of phantasies from the past. The majority of contemporary psycho-analysts believe that neurosis is not so much a matter of inhibited or underdeveloped sexuality as of a wider failure to make satisfying human relationships on equal terms. Interpretation of transference, therefore, depends upon the psycho-analyst detecting and commenting upon the way in which the patient is relating to him in the present: whether he is fearful, compliant, aggressive, competitive, and so on. Such attitudes have their history, which needs to be explored; but the emphasis is on understanding in what way the patient's attitude to others is distorted through perceiving in what way his attitude to the analyst is distorted. To do this effectively requires that the psycho-analyst is not concerned solely with the events of early childhood, but also recognizes that there is a real relationship in the here-and-now.

It soon became obvious to Freud that the psycho-analyst was not, and could not be, the kind of detached observer who was no more affected by his patient than if the latter was a chemical solution. In 1910 Freud wrote:

> Other innovations in technique relate to the physician himself. We have become aware of the 'counter-transference', which arises in him as a result of the patient's influence on his unconscious feelings, and we are almost inclined to insist that he shall recognize the counter-transference in himself and overcome it (*SE*, XI.144–5).

Freud originally hoped that this could be accomplished by a self-analysis comparable with his own. He later recognized that self-analysis should be replaced by a training analysis conducted by another person. In fact, Jung was the first of the early psycho-analysts to insist that the analyst must himself be analysed. The psycho-analyst must monitor his own emotional responses by means of introspection, since his own, subjective response to the patient's discourse is an inescapable part of understanding him.

This is a far cry from the mental set demanded of a scientist, who must on no account allow his emotions to affect any experiment which he is conducting. Although the psycho-analyst must, to some extent, regard his patient objectively, he will only be able to understand the patient as a person if he is also able to use his own, subjective reactions. The total detachment which Freud aimed at, but which, as we know from contemporary accounts of his behaviour as an analyst, he never achieved, would have cut him off from sources of information that we all need if we are to comprehend persons as opposed to comprehending the external world. In spite of his recognition of transference and counter-transference, Freud continued to maintain that he was a scientist until his death. His psychoanalytic endeavours might be more justly compared with those of a historian. Historians also try to reconstruct the past, but no one supposes that a totally objective vision of the past can ever be achieved, or that a history which attempted this would be anything but unreadable. A historian's understanding of the past and of the motives of the people who make history is bound to be influenced by his own experience and by his capacity for understanding human beings. This is why neither history nor psycho-analysis can be assigned to the exact sciences.

5 Ego, super-ego, and id

Although Freud generally resisted modifications of his ideas when suggested by others, he constantly revised them himself, and retained his capacity for creative innovation until the end of his long life. During the latter part of the First World War and the early 1920s, Freud made extensive additions to, and revisions of psycho-analytic theory. The most important of these concern narcissism, the structure of the mental apparatus, and recognition of the significance of aggressive impulses in addition to sexual ones.

Narcissism

This is a term originally used to describe a sexual perversion in which the subject is in love with himself rather than with another person. It was later extended to include any form of self-love. Since self-esteem is necessary to psychic health, some degree of narcissism is considered normal. Freud thought that everyone directed libido both toward the self (ego-libido), and towards others (object-libido). When a person is in love, the greater part of his libido is invested in his beloved. When a person is ill, either physically or mentally, he becomes more self-absorbed, and less capable of emotional involvement with others. Extreme forms of narcissism are exhibited in the type of schizophrenia in which everything that happens in the world is interpreted by the sufferer as referring to himself; in manic states in which the subject considers himself omnipotent; and in states of depression in which the subject may be hypochondriacally preoccupied with his own state of body and mind to the exclusion of all else. Freud postulated a narcissistic stage of emotional development, or primary narcissism, which precedes any investment of libido in objects other than the self. He described this stage as one in which the sexual instincts find auto-erotic satisfaction. Mental or physical illness,

43

therefore, may be considered as instituting regression to an early stage of infantile development.

Hitherto, Freud had assumed two sets of instincts: the self-preservative instincts, which pertained to the ego; and the sexual instincts, which pertained to objects. Now he concluded that self-preservation and self-love were really the same thing, and that what mattered was the degree to which libido was directed towards objects as compared with the degree to which it was directed towards the self.

As Ernest Jones commented in the second volume of his biography of Freud, Freud's paper 'On Narcissism: An Introduction' (*SE*, XIV.73–102) played into the hands of those critics who accused Freud of reducing everything to sex. Originally, Freud had assumed that the self-preservative instincts were distinct from the sexual instincts, and could be in conflict with them. By affirming that love of others was self-love turned outward, Freud appeared to be stating that sexual impulses were indeed the sole source of psychic energy. This position was soon to be modified.

Freud was essentially a dualist who habitually explained mental phenomena in terms of the interaction of, or conflict between, opposites. As he would have been the first to recognize, the tendency to think in this way is characteristic of obsessional personalities, who are notably 'ambivalent' towards the people with whom they are involved, and who often have difficulty in making decisions because they cannot reconcile opposing considerations. Love and hate are opposites which can be clearly discerned in any intense relationship between people; and when such a relationship is ruptured, love often appears to be transmuted into hatred. Freud came to the conclusion that hate was closely connected with the ego's struggle for self-preservation. He went on to state that:

> Hate, as a relation to objects, is older than love. It derives from the narcissistic ego's primordial repudiation of the external world with its outpouring of stimuli. As an expression of the reaction of unpleasure evoked by objects, it always remains in an intimate relation with the self-

preservative instincts; so that sexual and ego-instincts can readily develop an antithesis which repeats that of love and hate (*SE*, XIV.139).

The reference to 'the external world with its outpouring of stimuli' may appear obscure unless it is recalled that one of Freud's fundamental ideas was that the organism is always seeking to rid itself of disturbing stimuli, whether these impinge upon it from the external world, or originate as instinctual tensions from within. In Chapter 2 reference was made to 'the need of the organism to reach a state of tranquillity by completely discharging all tensions'. Freud continued to maintain that:

the nervous system is an apparatus which has the function of getting rid of the stimuli which reach it, or of reducing them to the lowest possible level; or which, if it were feasible, would maintain itself in an altogether unstimulated condition (*SE*, XIV.120).

Freud's original studies of hysteria and obsessional neurosis required a bipartite division of mind into conscious and unconscious. This simple model assumed that the unconscious was chiefly, if not entirely, derived from repression, and therefore consisted of impulses, thoughts and feelings which were unacceptable to the conscious ego. During the first twenty years of the twentieth century, Freud came to realize that this model was inadequate. For example, the agency instituting repression must be derived from the ego, the conscious part of the mind. Yet, patients on the couch behaved as if this agency was unconscious by manifesting *resistance*. That is, when dangerous or distasteful topics began to emerge during free association, the patient would cease to talk freely, claim that no thoughts occurred to him, say that he had forgotten what was being discussed, or in other ways become evasive. Freud said that the

force which instituted the repression and maintains it is perceived as *resistance* during the work of analysis (*SE*, XIX.14).

But this implied that part of the ego, hitherto associated only with consciousness, could itself be unconscious. Freud recognized that the term 'unconscious' was better used as a descriptive adjective rather than as a topographical noun. Although everything which was repressed was unconscious, not everything unconscious was repressed.

Structure of the mental apparatus

Freud's new model of the mind which was the consequence of these and other reflections consisted of three parts: ego, id, and super-ego. The id is defined as the oldest part of the mind from which the other structures are derived.

> It contains everything that is inherited, that is present at birth, that is laid down in the constitution – above all, therefore, the instincts which originate from the somatic organization and which find a first psychical expression here in forms unknown to us (*SE*, XXIII.145).

The id is primitive, unorganized, and emotional: 'the realm of the illogical'.

> It is the dark, inaccessible part of our personality; what little we know of it we have learnt from our study of the dream-work and of the construction of neurotic symptoms, and most of that is of a negative character and can be described only as a contrast to the ego. We approach the id with analogies: we call it a chaos, a cauldron full of seething excitations . . . It is filled with energy reaching it from the instincts, but it has no organization, produces no collective will, but only a striving to bring about the satisfaction of instinctive needs subject to the observance of the pleasure principle (*SE*, XXII.73).

Freud made a sharp distinction between two varieties of mental functioning which he called *primary process* and *secondary process*. The id uses primary process, which employs the mechanisms of condensation, displacement, symbolization, and hallucinatory wish-fulfilment to which we referred in Chapter 4 when discussing dreams. It also ignores the categories of time and space, and treats contraries like dark/light or high/deep as if they were identical. As indicated in Freud's description, the id is governed only by the most basic, primitive principle of mental dynamics: avoidance of 'unpleasure' caused by instinctual tension, which can only be achieved by satisfaction of instinctual needs accompanied by pleasure.

It is characteristic of Freud's predominantly pessimistic view of human nature that the so-called 'pleasure principle', upon which so much of his thought depends, is much more concerned with the avoidance of pain than with the pursuit of pleasure. In Chapter 2, we noted that powerful emotions were treated by Freud as disturbances which must be got rid of, not as pleasures to be sought.

The ego is that part of the mind representing consciousness. It employs secondary process: that is, reason, common sense, and the power to delay immediate responses to external stimuli or to internal instinctive promptings. It is originally derived from the id. Freud pictured the ego as a 'special organization' which is closely connected with the organs of perception, since it first develops as a result of stimuli from the external world impinging upon the senses.

'The ego is first and foremost a bodily ego' (*SE*, XIX.26).

Freud means by this that the ego, being originally derived from sensations springing from the surface of the body, is a projection of the surface of the body. The sense of 'I' depends upon the perception of one's own body as a separate entity. Once in existence, the ego 'acts as an intermediary between the id and the external world'. Because of the neural link between sensory perception and motor activity, the ego controls voluntary movement. The prime function of the ego is self-preservation.

As regards *external* events, it performs that task by becoming aware of stimuli, by storing up experiences about them (in

the memory), by avoiding excessively strong stimuli
(through flight), by dealing with moderate stimuli (through
adaptation) and finally by bringing about expedient changes
in the external world to its own advantage (through activity).
As regards *internal* events, in relation to the id, it performs
that task by gaining control over the demands of the
instincts, by deciding whether they are to be allowed
satisfaction, by postponing that satisfaction to times and
circumstances favourable to the external world or by
suppressing their excitations entirely (*SE*, XXIII.145–6).

Freud's third division of mind is described by him as
follows:

> The long period of childhood, during which the growing
> human being lives in dependence on his parents, leaves
> behind it as a precipitate the formation in his ego of a special
> agency in which this parental influence is prolonged. It has
> received the name of *super-ego*. In so far as this super-ego is
> differentiated from the ego or is opposed to it, it constitutes
> a third power which the ego must take into account.
>
> (*SE*, XXIII.146)

The origin of Freud's concept of the super-ego can be traced
to the paper on narcissism to which we referred earlier. Freud
thought that, as the child developed, his megalomanic primary
narcissism was gradually eclipsed: that is, he came no longer
to regard himself as the omnipotent 'King Baby', as centre of
the universe. As the child gradually acquires cultural and
ethical ideas, his libidinal instinctual impulses undergo repression. Because of this split within the psyche, the child comes
to realize that he can no longer idealize himself; that there is
an *ego-ideal* to which his own ego does not always conform.
Freud postulated an agency within the mind which devoted
itself to *self-observation*: which watched the ego, and decided
whether or not the ego was conforming to, or fell short of, the
ego-ideal. This agency was what Freud later named the super-
ego. As indicated in the last quotation, the super-ego originally
derived from parental prohibitions and criticism. Because of

the long period of childhood dependency, parental standards and subsequently the standards of society become introjected; that is, incorporated as part of the subject's own psyche with the consequence that the voice of conscience is heard whenever the ego falls short of the ego-ideal.

Freud might equally well have used Pavlovian terminology. The super-ego can be regarded as the product of repeated conditioning by parental injunctions and criticism: for example, 'You must clean your teeth after breakfast', may become so ingrained a command that the adult who has long ago left home continues to feel uncomfortable if he does not obey it.

The ego, therefore, is uneasily poised between three agencies: the external world, the id, and the super-ego, each of which may be urging a different course. It is not surprising that human actions sometimes appear vacillating or indecisive.

Aggression

Earlier in this chapter, we quoted Freud's conclusion that 'Hate, as a relation to objects, is older than love.' This sentence comes from a paper on 'Instincts and their Vicissitudes', written in 1915. It is Freud's first recognition of an 'aggressive instinct' as a constituent of the ego distinct from the sexual instinct. Before this period, Freud had regarded aggression as constituting a sadistic aspect of the sexual instinct; as 'an urge for mastery', a primitive form of striving for, and dominating, the sexual object.

> Love in this form and at this preliminary stage is hardly to be distinguished from hate in its attitude toward the object. Not until the genital organization is established does love become the opposite of hate (*SE*, XIV.139).

Very slowly, in a roundabout fashion, Freud came to accept that there was an 'aggressive instinct' which was entirely independent of anything sexual.

> I remember my own defensive attitude when the idea of an instinct of destruction first emerged in psycho-analytic

49

literature, and how long it took before I became receptive to it (*SE*, XXI.120).

Freud's frequent use of the word 'instinct' has an old-fashioned ring about it because modern psychologists and students of animal behaviour have largely abandoned the term. Instinct was originally used to describe aspects of behaviour which were thought to be innate and to develop independently of environmental influences. Today it is generally believed that all behaviour is influenced both by genetic constitution and by environmental conditions existing during development. Even relatively stereotyped forms of behaviour like bird-song may not manifest themselves unless the right environmental stimuli appear at the appropriate stage. There is a sense in which Freud was ahead of his time in postulating that the environment played such a large part in influencing sexual behaviour patterns. But there is no obvious reason other than his own preference for limiting 'instincts' to two. For example, sleep and eating are both largely determined by innate needs.

Freud's first full acknowledgement of an aggressive instinct appears in 'Beyond the Pleasure Principle', a speculative paper first published in 1920 (*SE*, XVIII.7–64). Although Freud continued to maintain that man was chiefly governed by the pleasure principle, modified, but not abolished, by the ego's acceptance of the reality principle, he concluded that another principle must also be in operation. As we saw in the last chapter, study of patients suffering from 'traumatic neurosis', that is, neuroses brought about by sudden accidents or shocks, revealed that their dreams often repeated the incident practically unmodified. Since the traumatic incident was, by definition, unpleasant, its repetition appeared to contravene the pleasure principle. Freud also noted that small children tended to repeat unpleasant experiences, like the departure of a parent, by making such happenings into a repetitive game which, in phantasy, gave them some control over the event. Freud concluded that both neurotics who had been exposed to shock and children who had been exposed to distress were attempting to master their unpleasant experiences by repeating them in dream and play.

At an earlier point in this chapter, we quoted Freud's view that hate was older than love, and connected with the ego's primordial rejection of objects as the origin of disturbing stimuli. Recalling this makes it comprehensible that Freud should link aggression with the mastery of shock and distress referred to above, and also with the tendency compulsively to repeat unpleasant experiences.

The manifestations of a compulsion to repeat . . . exhibit to a high degree an instinctual character and, when they act in opposition to the pleasure principle, give the appearance of some 'daemonic' force at work (*SE*, XVIII.35).

But Freud goes further. Remaining true to his conception that the function of the mental apparatus is to get rid of the stimuli which reach it, he concludes that this daemonic, instinctual compulsion to repeat is a universal attribute of instincts. He writes:

It seems, then, that an instinct is an urge inherent in organic life to restore an earlier stage of things which the living entity has been obliged to abandon under the pressure of external disturbing forces . . . (*SE*, XVIII.36).

And what is the earliest state of things which instinct is striving to restore? Since the inorganic precedes the organic in the history of our planet, it can only be a striving towards a state before life itself existed.

If we are to take it as a truth that knows no exception that everything living dies for *internal* reasons – becomes inorganic once again – then we shall be compelled to say that '*the aim of all life is death*' and, looking backwards, that '*inanimate things existed before living ones*' (*SE*, XVIII.38).

The death instinct

This is Freud's assertion of what he now calls the 'death

instinct': the ultimate expression of the Nirvana principle, of the organism's striving to reach Swinburne's 'The Garden of Proserpine', where no stimuli from either within or without disturb its everlasting peace.

> Then star nor sun shall waken,
> Nor any change of light:
> Nor sound of waters shaken,
> Nor any sound or sight:
> Nor wintry leaves nor vernal,
> Nor days nor things diurnal;
> Only the sleep eternal
> In an eternal night.

These highly abstract considerations gave Freud what he wanted: a dualistic scheme in which all the phenomena of mental life could be ultimately traced to the interaction of, or conflict between, two drives or instincts.

> After long hesitancies and vacillations we have decided to assume the existence of only two basic instincts, *Eros* and *the destructive instinct*. . . . The aim of the first of these basic instincts is to establish ever greater unities and to preserve them thus – in short, to bind together; the aim of the second is, on the contrary, to undo connections and so to destroy things. In the case of the destructive instinct we may suppose that its final aim is to lead what is living into an inorganic state. For this reason we also call it the *death instinct*.
> (*SE*, XXIII.148)

Freud considered that aggression was derived from the death instinct being redirected towards the external world. He wrote:

> The instinct of destruction, moderated and tamed, and, as it were, inhibited in its aim, must, when it is directed toward objects, provide the ego with the satisfaction of its vital needs and with control over nature (*SE*, XXI.121).

Freud goes on to conclude that the inclination towards aggression 'constitutes the greatest impediment to civilization'. He pictures civilization as a process in the service of Eros, whose purpose is to combine single human individuals, and after that families, then races, peoples and nations, into one great unity, the unity of mankind. But man's natural aggressive instinct, the hostility of each against all and all against each, oppose this programme of civilization. This aggressive instinct is the derivative and the main representative of the death instinct which we have found alongside of Eros and which shares world-dominion with it. And now, I think, the meaning of the evolution of civilization is no longer obscure to us. It must present the struggle between Eros and Death, between the instinct of life and the instinct of destruction as it works itself out in the human species. This struggle is what all life essentially consists of, and the evolution of civilization may therefore be simply described as the struggle for life of the human species. And it is this battle of the giants that our nurse-maids try to appease with their lullaby about Heaven (*SE*, XXI.122).

Who would have supposed that a doctor striving to comprehend the neuroses of the Viennese upper classes would have derived from his researches so majestic a concept of the human condition? Freud's pursuit of the byways of sex and aggression has become transmuted into a cosmic vision of opposing forces of good and evil. Freud wrote the passage just quoted some seventeen years after his parting with Jung. If the two pioneers had continued to collaborate, Freud might have recognized that his portrayal of Eros and Death as giants locked in perpetual combat is what Jung would have called an 'archetypal' vision. Whether or not such a vision is true is another matter. It has nothing to do with science.

6 Aggression, depression, and paranoia

Having determined the existence of an independent 'destructive instinct', Freud addressed the problem of how civilization imposed controls upon it. He concluded that the main way in which this took place was by 'introjection'; that is, by incorporating a substantial amount of aggression within the ego of the individual, thus turning aggression away from the external world against the self. Freud is thus postulating a double redirection of aggression. The death instinct is originally directed against the self and, because every individual dies in the end, is ultimately triumphant. But, during the individual's lifetime, the death instinct is to a large extent directed outward as aggression: first, against unwanted stimuli from the external world; second, as 'sadism' subserving the domination of sexual objects; and third, against individuals or circumstances which frustrate the desires of the ego. However, civilization ensures that part of this destructiveness is again turned inward; incorporated into the super-ego, and manifested as the sense of guilt giving rise to self-reproach, self-hatred, and self-punishment.

Civilization, therefore, obtains mastery over the individual's dangerous desire for aggression by weakening and disarming it and by setting up an agency within him to watch over it, like a garrison in a conquered city (SE, XXI.123–4).

Freud makes much of the irrational severity of the super-ego. He claims, with good reason, that a child who has been very leniently brought up may nevertheless develop a very strict conscience. His explanation of this is convincing. Freud believed that

every piece of aggression whose satisfaction the subject gives up is taken over by the super-ego and increases the latter's aggressiveness (against the ego) (SE, XXI.129).

In other words, the more anyone inhibits his aggression towards others, the more likely he is to be self-punitive. Freud had previously described a similar state of affairs in a famous paper, 'Mourning and Melancholia'.

Melancholia would today be described as a severe depressive illness. Freud accurately describes its distinguishing mental features as

> a profoundly painful dejection, cessation of interest in the outside world, loss of the capacity to love, inhibition of all activity, and a lowering of the self-regarding feelings to a degree that finds utterance in self-reproaches and self-revilings, and culminates in a delusional expectation of punishment (*SE*, XIV.244).

In mourning, loss of self-regard is not usually present to the same extent, although many who have lost someone close to them do blame themselves for their own failure to love and care for the departed. In other respects, the mental features of mourning and severe depression are closely similar. Freud notes that mourning is often a very prolonged process, and attributes this difficulty in withdrawing libido from the departed love object to the more general difficulty which everyone has in abandoning any libidinal position: for example, the difficulty which neurotics have in abandoning Oedipal ties to parents.

Freud points out that melancholia is also often provoked by the loss of a loved person, although the loss may be provoked by rejection or abandonment rather than by death. But why should the depressed person heap reproaches on himself? Freud points out that the accusations which the person suffering from depression levels at himself are generally reproaches which he might equally have directed against the loved object who is no longer available. 'I am a worthless person who does not deserve to live' is a displacement of '*You* are a worthless person who does not deserve to live, because you have left me.' This is an example of one way in which aggression which was originally directed outward becomes displaced inward, incorporated into the super-ego; and then manifests itself as self-reproach and self-hatred.

According to Freud, the difference between mourning and melancholia primarily consists in the fact that, in mourning, the loss is fully conscious, whereas in melancholia, the loss is partially unconscious. How is this related to the difference between mourning and melancholia which we have already noted: the much greater loss of self-esteem in the latter condition? Freud accepts that, in a certain sense, the melancholic is telling the truth about his loss of self-esteem.

> The analogy with mourning led us to conclude that he had suffered a loss in regard to an object; what he tells us points to a loss in regard to his ego (*SE*, XIV.247).

What Freud suggests is illuminating. People who react to loss of an object by loss of self-esteem are people who base their choice of objects on identification with the object, that is, upon a narcissistic choice of an object which in some way resembles themselves. Losing an object, therefore, is equivalent to losing part of the ego. In the important paper, 'On Narcissism', to which reference was made in the last chapter, Freud listed a variety of ways in which objects are chosen.

A person may love:—

1) According to the narcissistic type:
   a) what he himself is (i.e. himself),
   b) what he himself was,
   c) what he himself would like to be,
   d) someone who was once part of himself.
2) According to the anaclitic (attachment) type:
   a) the woman who feeds him,
   b) the man who protects him,
   and the succession of substitutes who take their place (*SE*, XIV.90)

('Anaclitic' literally means 'leaning-on'. Freud is thinking of the original situation between the child and its mother: two objects, each of which receive some of the child's libidinal investment.) Freud is suggesting that melancholics are either regressing to, or have never fully emerged from, a primitive stage of emotional development in which their object-choices are narcissistic rather than anaclitic. Thus, when they lose an object, they are losing a greater part of themselves than are those whose love is more determined by attachment to an object who is quite different from themselves.

Freud thought of such patients as being arrested in the 'oral' stage of emotional development (see Chapter 3). The reasons for this arrest are not clearly specified; but it was assumed that fixation at the oral stage might be the result of either deprivation or overgratification of the infant's oral needs. Freud's single-minded explanation of the depressive personality in terms of arrest at the 'oral' stage of emotional development may be seen as insufficient in the light of modern research, but does not detract from the accuracy and penetration of his clinical description. We noted in Chapter 3 that passivity, dependency and doubts about one's own competence are traits of character often found together.

Today, we might describe the person prone to melancholia rather differently. The person who is likely to develop serious depression in response to loss, rather than simply passing through a period of mourning, can be thought of as someone who has no abiding sense of his own worth, and who therefore has no inner resources to fall back upon when loss or deprivation assails him. Such a person remains entirely dependent upon external supplies to keep up his self-esteem; upon other people to love or admire him, or upon achievement to boost his ego. We think it probable that a child who has received the kind of irrational praise and adoration which loving parents habitually extend, gradually acquires a built-in sense of its own worth which may be unjustified in objective terms, but which becomes a source of inner strength when things go wrong. It is probable that such a process continues throughout the years of childhood rather than being linked especially with the first year of life, as Freud and his associate Karl Abraham believed.

There are a variety of reasons why such a process may not take place, thus leaving the subject especially vulnerable to depression. Perhaps the parents did not want the child, or did not love him. Perhaps they set such high standards that the child always felt that he was found wanting. Or perhaps some genetic factor (and there is good evidence for a genetic factor in cases of recurrent depression) rendered the child incapable of introjecting love and thus developing an inner sense of self-esteem however much love was offered.

Freud's concept of a narcissistic object-choice, that is, of object-choice through identification, is particularly interesting in this context. For 'depressive personalities', as I shall call those who are vulnerable to severe depression, are hungry for approval and anxious to avoid criticism or blame which might plunge them into depression. Their anxiety to please makes them hypersensitive to what others are feeling; a form of adaptation to the other which takes place by means of identification. Habitually fitting in with what others are feeling to this extent necessarily involves the suppression or repression of the depressive person's own opinions and feelings; more especially, the assertive or aggressive side of his personality.

Freud also had something to say about mania: the opposite state of mind to that of melancholia, but its well-recognized alternate in cases of manic-depressive psychosis or bipolar affective disorder, as it is often called today. Freud thought that states of 'joy, exultation or triumph' were the model for mania, and were characterized by the sudden availability of psychical energy which had hitherto been used for something else. An analogy might be suddenly taking off the brakes of an automobile, or, to use one of Freud's own examples, 'when a long and arduous struggle is finally crowned with success'. Whereas in states of depression, the subject reproaches himself for his shortcomings, in states of mania the individual not only appears to be well pleased with himself, but may attribute to himself almost magical powers; the 'omnipotence' which Freud thought characteristic of the infant's supposed state of primary narcissism. Freud considered that, in mania, the split between the ego-ideal and the ego was abolished. The super-ego, therefore, no longer concerned itself with pointing out in what ways the ego fell short of the ego-ideal, since there was no longer any division between the two entities.

On the basis of our analysis of the ego it cannot be doubted that in cases of mania the ego and the ego ideal have fused together, so that the person, in a mood of triumph and self-satisfaction, disturbed by no self-criticism, can enjoy the abolition of his inhibitions, his feelings of consideration for others, and his self-reproaches (*SE*, XVIII.132).

We commented earlier on the accuracy of Freud's description of severe depression, a variety of mental illness which may require admission to hospital but which, nevertheless, is often encountered in private practice. Freud's notes on states of mania are both briefer and less satisfactory, probably because he had little actual experience of the condition. Manic patients are rare in private psychiatric practice because they seldom seek medical help for themselves. They are admitted to mental hospitals and clinics either because their relatives arrange this, or because they behave antisocially and have to be restrained. Manic patients seldom exhibit the unmixed states of 'joy, exultation or triumph' which Freud described. In addition, they are usually irritable, aggressive, and distractible. Although mild states of hypomania are agreeable, and may include a rapid flow of ideas leading to intense creativity, the majority of manic patients are over-excited rather than happy, and, after recovery, describe their experience as intensely disturbing rather than joyful.

It is often forgotten that Freud had very little experience of patients suffering from severe mental illness. In 1885, while waiting to hear whether or not he had obtained a grant to study with Charcot in Paris, Freud worked as a locum tenens for three weeks in a private mental hospital in Oberdöbling on the outskirts of Vienna. He described the inmates to his fiancée as 'a mixture of feeble-minded and eccentric'. Apart from his period of work with Charcot at the Salpêtrière, which was chiefly concerned with hysteria, this three weeks at Oberdöbling was the sum of Freud's clinical experience with psychotic in-patients. As we shall see, his famous study of the paranoid Judge Schreber was based upon the patient's writings rather than upon any actual encounter with him. In his introduction to that study, Freud states that, like other psychiatrists, he sees 'plenty of cases of paranoia and of dementia praecox' (schizophrenia); but as Freud considered such cases unsuitable for psycho-analysis, he makes no claim to have studied them deeply. Jung worked as a psychiatrist in the Burghölzli mental hospital from 1900 to 1909 before giving up his post in favour of private practice. If Freud had had a similarly long experience of working closely with patients suffering from chronic schizophrenia, manic-depressive psychosis, and other forms of severe mental illness, he might have constructed a psychopathology based upon psychosis rather than upon neurosis. Such a psychopathology would probably be more concerned with the development of the individual's sense of reality than with the vicissitudes of his infantile sexuality. Freud's causal explanations of psychotic states are too narrowly based to satisfy most psychiatrists, but, as always, contain original clinical observations of great interest. The paper on the memoirs of Judge Daniel Paul Schreber referred to above is a telling example of both the acuity and the limitations of Freud's thinking.

Paranoid mental illnesses, of which there are several varieties, are principally characterized by the patient developing delusions of persecution. That is, he supposes that he is being pursued, attacked, poisoned, or injured by someone or some group of people with malign intentions. Very often, these beliefs are accompanied by a grandiose conviction of the sufferer's own importance, which may partly account for his being the subject of so much unwelcome attention. Perhaps he is really of royal descent, or possesses some vital secret which his foes are anxious to extract from him.

Schreber was an unusual case in several respects. Most paranoid psychoses are chronic rather than episodic, but Schreber had an initial mental illness lasting from October 1884 to June 1885 from which he made a good recovery. He returned to his profession as a judge, and remained well until 1893. At the age of 51, shortly after being promoted, he relapsed, became severely mentally ill, and had to remain in hospital until December 1902. His memoirs were published a year after his discharge. He never fully recovered from this second illness. In 1907 he was again admitted to a mental hospital in which he died on 14 April 1911.

During his second illness, Schreber believed that his body was being handled in all kinds of revolting ways, and that he was being persecuted and injured, especially by Professor Flechsig, the director of the clinic in which he was first confined. In time, Schreber's acute mental illness subsided, to be replaced by a chronic delusional system. Like other sufferers from paranoia, Schreber appeared perfectly normal unless the subject-matter of his delusions was touched upon. He obtained his release from hospital in 1902 in spite of the acknowledged persistence of his delusional system which was summarized as follows:

> He believed that he had a mission to redeem the world and to restore it to its lost state of bliss. This, however, he could only bring about if he were first transformed from a man into a woman (*SE*, XII.16).

In his own writings, Schreber announced his conviction that, when transformed into a woman, he would be impregnated by divine rays so that a new race of men might be created.

We do not know the content of Schreber's first illness; but Freud's interpretation of his second illness is that it was related to Schreber's fear of, and wish for, sexual relations with Flechsig.

> The exciting cause of his illness, then, was an outburst of homosexual libido; the object of this libido was probably from the very first his doctor, Flechsig; and his struggles against the libidinal impulse produced the conflict which gave rise to the symptoms (*SE*, XII.43).

Freud goes on to interpret Schreber's presumed homosexual feelings towards his psychiatrist as a transference of earlier unconscious homosexual feelings which had originally been directed towards his father. The later substitution of God as

61

impregnator for Flechsig as persecutor is traced back to a similar source. Freud states that

> the familiar principal forms of paranoia can all be represented as contradictions of the single proposition: '*I* (a man) *love him* (a man)', and indeed that they exhaust all the possible ways in which such contradictions could be formulated.
>
> (*SE*, XII.63)

Freud explains delusions of persecution by affirming that the patient's denial of his homosexual feelings first takes the form 'I do not *love* him – I *hate* him'; and second becomes transformed by projection into '*He hates* (persecutes) *me*, which will justify me in hating him.' Freud is convinced that the persecutor is always a person of the same sex who was once loved.

Freud made much of the fact that Schreber's father was a well-known physician and pedagogue whose views on physical education were widely recognized. He had died at the early age of 53 when Schreber himself was 19. Freud defends his interpretation that Schreber's delusions about God were ultimately derived from his feelings about his father by pointing out that such an eminent man would be even more likely than most fathers to arouse those feelings of 'reverent submission and mutinous insubordination' which Freud considered characteristic of boys' infantile attitudes towards their fathers.

Although Freud took the trouble to identify Judge Schreber's father as Dr Daniel Gottlob Moritz Schreber, and also to discover that Judge Schreber had an elder brother, he did not go any further in attempting to find out what Judge Schreber's childhood was actually like or what manner of man his father really was. Had he done so, he would have discovered that Dr Schreber was an authoritarian monster. His elder son shot himself at the age of 38; his younger son, Judge Schreber, became psychotic in the way described above. Lack of space prevents discussion of Dr Schreber's insistence on breaking a child's will, on keeping the child's body absolutely straight with various restrictive devices, on his use of enemas to prevent nocturnal emissions, and other horrors. A full account of

them can be found in Morton Schatzman's book *Soul Murder*
(New York, 1973).

In Chapter 2 I referred to the fact that Freud's insistence
upon the persistence or recrudescence of infantile sexual
phantasies as the causal agents of neurosis had sometimes
encouraged psycho-analysts to neglect the real events and
circumstances which influence people's lives. Freud's own
failure to discover anything about Schreber's father is a striking
example of this.

Freud does attempt to give an explanation of why Schreber's
second illness should have occurred when he was 51. Freud
assumes an increased liability to illness in both men and
women at this 'climacteric' period. He also points out that
Schreber had lost his father and brother, and that he had had no
children; more especially no sons 'upon whom he could have
drained off his unsatisfied homosexual affections'. And so
Schreber resuscitates the feminine wishes which Freud
assumes that he had had towards his father in early childhood.

Freud's contention that paranoia is based upon conflicts
concerning homosexual impulses has inspired a great deal
of research. Fisher and Greenberg, in their review of this
literature, conclude that experimental investigations do on the
whole support the idea that 'paranoids and nonparanoids
respond significantly differently to stimuli with homosexual
connotations'. However, Freud's contention that the persecutor is always of the same sex as the subject is not confirmed.

During the acute phase of his illness, Schreber, like many
other sufferers from similar illnesses, thought that a great
catastrophe was imminent, perhaps the end of the world. After
he had recovered sufficiently to be discharged from hospital,
Schreber still believed that a catastrophe had happened, but
realized, at any rate in part, that the disaster had been within
himself rather than in the external world. Freud postulates
that, in the acute stage of his illness, the paranoic's world has
indeed come to an end, since he is unable any longer to maintain his emotional ties with it. The mechanism of projection
makes him perceive this as pertaining to the external world
rather than to himself. Subsequently, he constructs a new

world based upon his delusional system. Freud makes the penetrating observation that a delusional system of this kind should be regarded as 'an attempt at recovery, a process of reconstruction'. At a time when the delusions of the insane were usually dismissed as pathological nonsense rather than as phenomena requiring investigation and understanding, Freud's remarks were startlingly original.

The paper on Schreber tells us a great deal about Freud's processes of thought and method of interpretation. It shows how important it is, in considering Freud's work, to sift the wheat from the chaff. Freud's comments on the course of Schreber's illness, on jealousy, on projection, and on the positive functions of delusional systems are often illuminating. But his failure to relate Schreber's character structure and the content of his delusions to the easily ascertained, dire paternal system in which he had been reared is a serious omission. And can anyone really suppose that the emergence of homosexual phantasies in middle life can be regarded as a sufficient cause for the outbreak of a psychotic illness of such severity? Even at the turn of the nineteenth century, an intelligent, educated judge, well used to the world and its ways, would hardly be unaware that men and women have a variety of sexual thoughts and phantasies which they might not like to acknowledge publicly but which are unlikely to be so shocking that they send them mad. Krafft-Ebing's *Psychopathia Sexualis*, with its wealth of information about every kind of sexual perversion, had been published in 1886. Sexuality and its variants were a contemporary topic of discussion in Vienna.

Freud's insistence that the persistence of infantile sexual phantasy was the root cause of mental illness has seldom been less convincingly displayed than in the case of Schreber. Even if all paranoid patients show a particular interest in, or aversion from, homosexual themes when psychologically tested, it does not follow that unresolved homosexual conflicts are the sole cause of paranoid mental illnesses. It is far more likely that this preoccupation is part of a much more profound and general disorder.

7 Jokes and *The Psycho-Pathology of Everyday Life*

The first part of this book has been chiefly concerned with Freud's investigation of the psycho-pathology of the neuroses and psychoses, because this formed the springboard from which psycho-analysis took off in its attempt to become a comprehensive psychology. As indicated in Chapter 1, Freud made speculative theoretical incursions into other fields from the earliest days of psycho-analysis. Had he confined himself to the study of the various forms of mental illness, psycho-analysis would hardly have exerted so wide an influence; but Freud was convinced that his discoveries about human motivation and the unconscious applied not only to neurotics but to every human endeavour.

The Psycho-Pathology of Everyday Life became one of Freud's most popular books. It is concerned with the famous 'Freudian slip'; that is, with slips of the tongue, slips of the pen, faulty recall of names, forgetting of intentions, and other errors. Freud strives to support his belief that all mental events are causally determined by demonstrating that such mistakes or 'parapraxes' are the result of interference by repressed, unconscious thoughts. A case reported by Jung will serve as a simple example.

A Herr Y. fell in love with a lady; but he met with no success, and shortly afterwards she married a Herr X. Thereafter, Herr Y., in spite of having known Herr X. for a long time and even having business dealings with him, forgot his name over and over again, so that several times he had to enquire what it was from other people when he wanted to correspond with Herr X. (*SE*, VI.25).

Obviously, his resentment of his successful rival made Y. want to ignore X.'s existence.

It is equally easy to interpret the following example of a slip of the pen:

> An American living in Europe who had left his wife on bad terms felt that he could now effect a reconciliation with her, and asked her to come across the Atlantic and join him on a certain date. 'It would be fine', he wrote, 'if you could come on the *Mauretania* as I did'. He did not however dare to send the sheet of paper which had this sentence on it. He preferred to write it out again. For he did not want her to notice how he had to correct the name of the ship. He had first written *Lusitania* (*SE*, VI.121–2).

The *Lusitania* was sunk off the coast of Ireland by a German submarine during the First World War.

Not all Freud's examples are equally straightforward. Some of his interpretations seem tortuous and contrived. As we noted when discussing dreams, Freud used considerable ingenuity when it was needed to support his theories. The very first example which he gives is a case in point. Freud found himself unable to remember the name of the artist who had painted some famous frescos in Orvieto cathedral. Instead of the correct name, 'Signorelli', the names of two other painters, Botticelli and Boltraffio, kept on occurring to him. Freud's explanation of this piece of forgetfulness occupies four pages of text and includes his reluctance to talk to a stranger about sex, his wish to forget the suicide of a former patient, and an account of how his repressed thoughts caused the name Signorelli to be split into two, while at the same time substituting the German 'Herr' for the Italian 'Signor'. 'Herr' is taken from Herzegovina, and the 'Bo' of Botticelli and Boltraffio from Bosnia. Herzegovina and Bosnia were occupied by the Turks, about whose sexual customs Freud was reluctant to talk to a mere acquaintance. While staying at Trafoi, Freud had heard the disturbing news of his former patient's suicide. Trafoi therefore contributes to his error of recall by furnishing part of the name 'Boltraffio'. Freud is trying to establish that two topics he had wished to avoid nevertheless manifested themselves in the names which substituted themselves for the name he had forgotten. It is the same kind of interpretation which he applied to obsessional rituals; namely, that the ritual is an indirect expression of an instinctual impulse which the sufferer had repressed and which therefore could not be discharged in a straightforward manner.

Freud's explanation is extremely ingenious; both difficult to fault and yet in the end unconvincing. It seems 'too clever by half' as do many of Freud's dream interpretations; an attribution to unconscious mental activity of over-elaborate means to conceal the essentially trivial. Many slips of the tongue and instances of forgetting are undoubtedly motivated in the ways suggested by Freud; but this may not be true of all. For example, most elderly people find the retrieval of names increasingly difficult. Names may be accurately registered, but it takes longer and longer to recall them. In Chapter 3 we doubted whether Freud was right in attributing infantile amnesia entirely to repression, and suggested alternative explanations. Similar doubts apply to Freud's theory of adult forgetting. For instance, Freud does not consider the social context in which the failure of memory takes place, nor the possibility that names may be originally registered with different degrees of intensity according to circumstances. One is more likely to recall the name of a new acquaintance with whom one has spent an evening than that of a person to whom one has been briefly introduced at a party. But, having decided that unconscious wishes and thoughts cause interference with recall in some instances, Freud makes the generalization that this must be so in every case.

Sebastiano Timpanaro wrote a book *The Freudian Slip* in which he criticized Freud for not taking into account that many slips are the kind of errors with which all writers are familiar: repeating words one has just used; omitting words because one's thought leaps ahead of one's pen, and so on. In his review of the book, the psycho-analyst Charles Rycroft adds a criticism that was first made by Jung in connection with free association. Many of Freud's interpretations of errors depend upon his obtaining the subject's associations to the circumstances surrounding the error. To be sure, Freud quickly reaches disturbing material by this means; not always sexual material, as one would expect from Freud's theories, but thoughts of jealousy, personal advancement, prejudice, or hostility which are unacceptable to the person furnishing the associations. As anyone who has honestly experimented with free association knows, the technique inevitably and rapidly brings to mind topics about which one is emotionally concerned. As Rycroft points out, 'the eventual arrival at "significant material" is not therefore evidence that the starting-point was in any sense caused by it'.

Freud's other early excursion from the consulting room into everyday life is concerned with humour. *Jokes and their Relation to the Unconscious* was first published in 1905. Freud had started to collect Jewish jokes as early as 1897; but his interest in the subject gained impetus when his friend Fliess, on reading the proofs of *The Interpretation of Dreams*, complained that dreams were too full of jokes. In his reply to Fliess's letter, Freud writes:

> All dreamers are equally insufferably witty, and they need to be because they are under pressure and the direct route is barred to them. . . . The ostensible wit of all unconscious processes is intimately related to the theory of the joke and the comic (*The Freud-Fliess Letters*, 371).

Freud wrote so clearly and persuasively that, even in translation, most of his work is a pleasure to read. The book on jokes is an exception. This is partly because jokes suffer grievously in translation, and partly because explaining jokes annihilates their humour.

Freud analyses what he calls the *technique* of jokes, and points out that some of the mechanisms employed are indeed to be found in dreams; in particular, condensation, and the substitution of one word for another. An English example is De Quincey's remark that old people are inclined to fall into their 'anecdotage', thus condensing 'anecdote' and 'dotage'. A similar example is a reference to the Christmas season as 'alcoholidays'. Freud goes on to list other mechanisms which appear in dreams and also in jokes: 'displacement, faulty reasoning, absurdity, indirect representation, representation by the opposite'. He then proceeds to classify jokes into two main classes: 'innocent' jokes and 'tendentious' jokes. The former are solely dependent upon verbal ingenuity; the latter upon the indirect expression of hostility or obscenity. It is the tendentious jokes which chiefly interest Freud. Indeed, as we shall see, he is hard put to it to explain why 'innocent' jokes give us such pleasure. No such difficulty attaches to the interpretation of 'tendentious' jokes. They easily fall into line with neurotic symptoms, slips of the tongue, and dreams.

> And here at last we can understand what it is that jokes achieve in the service of their purpose. They make possible the satisfaction of an instinct (whether lustful or hostile) in the face of an obstacle that stands in its way. They circumvent this obstacle and in that way draw pleasure from a source which the obstacle had made inaccessible.
>
> (*SE*, VII.100–1)

The obstacle may be either an internal inhibition or else social; that is, the presence of a person who might be shocked. In this early work, Freud is already picturing civilization as the enemy of instinct and an instigator of repression. Tendentious jokes are a way of bypassing the barriers against the direct expression of both obscenity and aggression which civilization has set up.

When considering Freud's interpretation of manic states in Chapter 6, we noted that he thought that states of 'joy, exultation or triumph' were characterized by the sudden availability of psychical energy, and we compared this with releasing the brakes of a car. The pleasure accompanying a joke is, Freud believed, of a similar nature. It is easy to see this in the case of a tendentious joke in which the joker, by dressing up his obscene thoughts or aggressive impulses in humorous guise, is circumventing his own internal inhibitions. But Freud also acknowledged that purely external factors, rather than internal inhibitions, might prevent the direct expression of such impulses. Freud quotes as an example of what he means the familiar story of the royal personage who sees a man in the crowd who closely resembles himself:

'Was your mother at one time in service in the Palace?'
'No, your Highness, but my father was.'

By making a joke, the man can express aggression toward the high and mighty prince which, because of the latter's power, he could not do directly. In this case, Freud affirmed that the pleasure obtained from the joke was because no barrier against expressing the man's true feelings had to be erected.

The cases of an external and an internal obstacle differ only in the fact that in the latter an already existing inhibition is lifted and that in the former the erection of a new one is avoided. That being so, we shall not be relying too much on speculation if we assert that both for erecting and for maintaining a psychical inhibition some 'psychical expenditure' is required. And, since we know that in both cases of the use of tendentious jokes pleasure is obtained, it is therefore plausible to suppose that *this yield of pleasure corresponds to the psychical expenditure that is saved* (*SE*, VIII.118).

This piece of ingenuity was necessary because Freud wanted an explanation which would apply to 'innocent' jokes as well as to tendentious ones. Innocent jokes depend upon verbal felicities, puns, play upon words, combining incongruous words, and so on. Freud writes of being 'driven to conclude that the techniques of jokes are themselves sources of pleasure', as if he was reluctant to admit that anything other than instinctual release could be pleasurable. Freud resolves his problem by postulating that the pleasure obtained from innocent jokes is also that of economy. When we rediscover something familiar, as often happens in jokes, or when we link together by verbal association two things which are not at first sight congruous, we are playing with words, avoiding the effort of critical thought, and by thus economizing our expenditure of psychic energy, obtaining pleasure.

Freud calls this minor pleasure deriving from economy a 'fore-pleasure', thus comparing it with the various fore-pleasures characteristic of sexual arousal, in which stimulation of parts of the body other than the genitals leads on to the real thing, involvement of the genitals themselves. For, finally, Freud disposes of the problem posed by the 'innocent' joke by alleging that:

> Jokes, even if the thought contained in them is non-tendentious and thus only serves theoretical intellectual interests, are in fact never non-tendentious (*SE*, VIII.132).

> The originally non-tendentious joke, which began as play, is *secondarily* brought into relation with purposes from which nothing that takes form in the mind can ultimately keep away (*SE*, VIII.133).

Freud states that a good joke makes a total impression; that it is often difficult to know whether pleasure is principally derived from the form of the joke, or from the thought contained in it. He thinks of form as a kind of wrapping which makes the underlying thought more acceptable, like sugar coating a pill. As we shall see, Freud uses the same analogy when discussing works of art. He writes of aesthetic form as a device by which artists both conceal their 'egoistic day-dreams' and also render them more acceptable to other people. In both cases, Freud is denying that true pleasure can be derived from form. Any pleasure which we get from the verbal ingenuity of a joke, or from the aesthetic order imposed by an artist, must be minor; a 'fore-pleasure' as opposed to a final pleasure, which must, in Freud's view, be sensual. This is not contradicted by Freud's recognition that tendentious jokes allow for the expression of aggression as well as sex since, at the time he was writing, he still regarded aggression as constituting a sadistic aspect of the sexual instinct.

What is perhaps surprising is Freud's failure to acknowledge that there is such a thing as pleasure in the exercise of power or mastery. When discussing play in this same book, Freud refers to a writer called C. Groos who, in his book on games, refers to 'joy in power' or joy in overcoming a difficulty. Freud at once dismisses this as secondary. Yet, we must surely accept that pleasure is to be obtained from exercising a skill, whether the skill be physical or mental. Jokes are usually variants upon some well-worn theme; but we do not object to this if the joke itself displays verbal ingenuity and economy of construction. In other words, what we appreciate, even in an obviously tendentious joke, is its form as much as its content. The form of the joke is not simply a bribe, an 'incentive bonus', as Freud calls it, but an essential part of what gives rise to pleasure. If we make a new joke, we are pleased with our own cleverness. If we hear a new joke, we appreciate the cleverness of its creator. The joke is concerned with form; with imposing an order upon material by linking incongruities. It is therefore an aesthetic product, albeit of a primitive variety.

The search for order, for explanatory principles, for common features which link disparate things together is an inescapable human endeavour. Freud himself, when he had solved a problem which had been perplexing him, must have known the pleasure which accompanies the 'eureka' experience. Yet he continued to regard such a pleasure as a sublimation, not as primary. As late as 1930, Freud wrote:

A satisfaction of this kind, such as an artist's joy in creating, in giving his phantasies body, or a scientist's in solving problems or discovering truths, has a special quality which we shall certainly one day be able to characterize in meta-psychological terms. At present we can only say figuratively that such satisfactions seem 'finer and higher'. But their intensity is mild as compared with that derived from the sating of crude and primary instinctual impulses; it does not convulse our physical being (*SE*, XXI.79–80).

In the next chapter, we shall review what Freud had to say about art and artists.

8 Art and literature

During the twentieth century, psycho-analysis has had a major effect upon both art and literature. Freud's concept of the unconscious, his use of free association, and his rediscovery of the importance of dreams encouraged painters, sculptors, and writers to experiment with the fortuitous and the irrational, to pay serious attention to their inner worlds of dream and day-dream, and to find significance in thoughts and images which they would previously have dismissed as absurd or illogical. Such movements as Dadaism and Surrealism owe much to Freud; and so do those works of literature which, like Virginia Woolf's *The Waves*, depend upon the employment of 'stream-of-consciousness' techniques. After psycho-analysis became established, biographers began to feel that, unless they had managed to uncover the emotional influences to which their subjects had been exposed during the earliest years of childhood, their portraits were incomplete. Revelations about sexual behaviour and preferences became almost obligatory, since Freud had laid it down that sexuality was the central driving force in human nature. It became generally accepted that even such figures as politicians could not be fully understood unless the psycho-analytic spotlight was brought to bear upon them. Freud himself collaborated with the American diplomat William C. Bullitt in writing a psycho-analytic study of Woodrow Wilson, the twenty-eighth President of the United States. Although a number of reputable historians have found psycho-analytic concepts valuable in understanding historical characters, this particular book has been generally regarded as disastrous, since both Freud and Bullitt were heavily pre-judiced against Wilson. For example, they call him 'a prime prig'; and go on to write: 'Sickly, spectacled, shy, guarded by father, mother and sisters, Tommy Wilson never had a fist fight in his life', as if having fist fights was a *sine qua non* of masculinity. They also pour scorn upon his religious beliefs and accuse him of identifying himself with Christ. This tendentious biography is an early example of using psycho-analysis as 'character assassination'.

Freud himself displayed a curiously ambivalent attitude to art and artists. As we noted in Chapter 1, he had a deep knowledge of, and love for, literature, which manifests itself in the elegance of his own writing. He was also responsive to sculpture and, in lesser degree, to painting. He himself wrote that he was almost incapable of obtaining pleasure from music. Freud wrote a number of books and papers on art and artists, of which the most famous are *Delusions and Dreams in Jensen's 'Gradiva'*; *Leonardo de Vinci and a Memory of his Childhood*; 'The Moses of Michelangelo'; and 'Dostoevsky and Parricide'.

Freud believed that sublimation of unsatisfied libido was responsible for producing all art and literature. That is, he thought that artists discharged their infantile sexuality by con-verting it into non-instinctual forms. As we saw in Chapter 3, Freud had suggested that repression of perverse, pre-genital components of the sexual instinct was responsible for the arrest of sexual development and consequent lack of sexual satisfaction which he regularly found in neurotics. If the impulses were not repressed, but for one reason or another exaggerated, the person concerned might become a sexual pervert rather than a neurotic.

A third way of dealing with the same material is open to those who are artistically gifted. Artists, in this view, are people who may avoid neurosis and perversion by sublimating their impulses in their work. Freud did not attempt to explain the nature of the artist's gift, any more than he tried to explain manual dexterity, intelligence, or any other of the cognitive and perceptual differences between people which experimental psychologists study. What Freud was concerned with was motivation; and in his view motivation, ultimately, could be derived only from the death instinct manifesting itself as aggression, or from the sexual instinct. Moreover, in the Freudian scheme, motivation had to be traced back to instinc-tual repressions in the earliest years of childhood. The limita-tions of such a view of 'instinct' are clearly demonstrable in

Freud's writings on art and artists. As we noted at the end of the last chapter, Freud did not admit that the human need to order our experience and make sense of it was anything but a secondary phenomenon, since it could not be directly linked with the pleasure principle. Yet both art and science, although very different types of human endeavour, are concerned with seeking order in complexity and unity in diversity; and the impulse to do this, which is biologically adaptive, could equally well be regarded as 'instinctive'.

This limitation meant that Freud abandoned any interest he may have had in the *form* of a work of art, and paid attention only to its *content*. He modestly admits as much in his paper on 'The Moses of Michelangelo'.

> I may say at once that I am no connoisseur in art, but simply a layman. I have often observed that the subject-matter of works of art has a stronger attraction for me than their formal and technical qualities, though to the artist their value lies first and foremost in these latter. I am unable rightly to appreciate many of the methods used and the effects obtained in art (*SE*, XIII.211).

Since content, rather than style, was the problem to which Freud addressed himself, it was natural that he should apply the same technique of interpretation to works of art as he did to dreams, phantasies, and neurotic symptoms. Granted his assumption that art is a sublimation, what he could do and did, with varying success, was to discover in the work of art evidence of the artist's presumed infantile conflicts.

Freud's essay on Leonardo da Vinci illustrates both the insights and the limitations of this approach. It is known from historical sources that Leonardo was homosexually inclined and also that he was an illegitimate child. During the course of the same year in which he was born, his father married another woman. His mother also married soon after the child's birth. Leonardo was later adopted by his father and brought up in his father's household. There is no historical record which indicates what kind of relationship Leonardo may have had with his mother or his stepmother, or which tells us what kind of people they were. Nor is it known at what age Leonardo was removed from his mother to be brought up by his stepmother and father; although it is recorded that he was part of that household by the time he was 5 years old.

Freud analyses a childhood recollection recorded by Leonardo in which he claimed that, while in his cradle, a large bird opened his mouth with its tail and struck him many times with its tail against his lips. Freud reasonably supposes that this is so unlikely to have happened in reality that it is probably a later phantasy of Leonardo's which he transposed to early childhood. As might be expected, Freud interprets the phantasy as being an expression of passive homosexuality; the bird's tail substituting for the penis, and the wish to take the penis in the mouth being ultimately derived from the experience of suckling, which Freud calls 'the first source of pleasure in our life'.

But why is the mother represented by a bird? Freud, assuming that the bird is a vulture, expounds the connection between mothers and vultures in Egyptian mythology. He claims that Leonardo chose this bird to represent his mother because vultures were supposed to be of the female sex only, and a vulture would therefore be a particularly appropriate image of the mother in the case of a child who lacked a father.

Unfortunately, Freud's interpretation is based upon a mistranslation. The bird was not a vulture, but a kite. Whereas vultures can be shown to have mythological connections with the mother, kites cannot. Moreover, although he admits that we have no actual record of when Leonardo was taken into his father's household, Freud goes on to affirm that the phantasy indicates that he must have spent his earliest years with his 'poor forsaken, real mother, so that he had time to feel the absence of his father'.

One cannot blame the art historians for dismissing Freud's interpretation as totally unjustified; but, as so often with Freud, there is wheat to be found among the chaff. Freud comments at length upon the famous picture *Virgin and Child with St Anne*. St Anne is represented as being scarcely older than her daughter, the Virgin Mary. Freud supposes that the subject of

mother, grandmother and child, which is rarely chosen by
painters, may have occurred to Leonardo because his father's
household included his paternal grandmother as well as his
stepmother. He goes on to suggest that the similarity in age
between the two women in the picture may be a reflection of
the fact that Leonardo in effect had two mothers: his real
mother and his stepmother.

This speculation seems both more interesting and more
legitimate. The subjects which an artist portrays, and the ways
in which he chooses to present them, are often determined by
his patrons and by the conventions of his time. But they are
also bound to reflect something of his own personality and personal history, although he himself may be unaware of any such
connection. Whether the subjects chosen are anything to do
with repressed infantile sexual phantasies is more dubious.

Freud estimated Dostoevsky's literary standing as 'not far
behind Shakespeare', and considered *The Brothers Karamazov*
'the most magnificent novel ever written'. He justifiably
claims that Dostoevsky's depiction of so many violent,
egotistical and murderous characters points to similar tendencies within the novelist himself, and refers to his possible
confession of a sexual assault upon a young girl. Dostoevsky's
friend and biographer Strakhov refers to this in a letter to
Tolstoy, and there is also a story that Dostoevsky confessed it
to Turgenev. The subject appears in Dostoevsky's writings
more than once. Freud also draws attention to the sado-
masochistic traits which Dostoevsky undoubtedly displayed,
and to his compulsive gambling. Freud's interpretation of
Dostoevsky's psychopathology rests chiefly upon the supposition that Dr Dostoevsky, the novelist's father, was 'especially
violent'. He assumes that Dostoevsky's disposition was rooted
in an unresolved conflict between masculine (sadistic) revolt
and feminine (masochistic) submission in relation to his
father, and that the severity of Dostoevsky's self-punitive conscience was derived from his father's punitiveness. Freud
wrote:

Thus the formula for Dostoevsky is as follows: a person
with a specially strong innate bisexual disposition, who can

defend himself with special intensity against dependence on a specially severe father (*SE*, XXI.185).

In reality, although Dr Dostoevsky was strict in insisting that his children devoted themselves to study from an early age, he was a particularly conscientious father who gave an unusual amount of his time to his children's education, who never employed physical punishment himself, and who sent his children to private schools in order to avoid having them beaten although he could scarcely afford the expense.

As Joseph Frank demonstrates in his definitive biography of Dostoevsky, Freud read a footnote in a biography published in 1883 which hinted at 'a very peculiar piece of evidence about the illness of Feodor Mihailovich which relates to his earliest youth and connects it with a tragic event in their family life'. Although there is nothing about either punishment or father in this passage, Freud recalls what he read in a letter to Stefan Zweig as:

Somewhere in a biography of D. I was shown a passage which traced back the later affliction of the man to the boy's having been punished by the father under very serious circumstances.

This is an instance of Freud unwittingly distorting his recollection in order to support the view of Dostoevsky's psychopathology which he had already constructed; a wish-fulfilling phantasy determining faulty recall in the way described in *The Psycho-Pathology of Everyday Life*. The illness of 'later affliction' referred to is Dostoevsky's epilepsy. On this 'evidence', Freud concludes that Dostoevsky's fits were almost certainly not true epilepsy, but were caused by emotional conflict rather than by brain damage. He also assumed that Dostoevsky had 'attacks' in childhood which foreshadowed his later epilepsy and which were characterized by fears of death and sudden states of lethargy. Joseph Frank conclusively demonstrates that neither symptom occurred during Dostoevsky's childhood, but dated from the years 1846 to 1847, when Dostoevsky would have been 25 years old.

Dostoevsky's father was murdered by his serfs when
Dostoevsky was a student of 18. Freud interprets Dostoevsky's
epilepsy, whether 'true' epilepsy or not, as a masochistic desire
for self-punishment, and states that it began on hearing of the
death of his father. In fact, all the evidence, with the exception
of one unsupported 'family tradition' recorded by his daughter,
suggests that Dostoevsky's first epileptic attack occurred in
1850, when he was in a prison camp in Siberia. The medical
reports strongly suggest that he suffered from typical 'grand
mal' convulsions (that is, 'true' epilepsy); and this is further
borne out by the fact that his son Aleksey died of epilepsy at
the age of 3, since there is evidence of a hereditary factor
in epilepsy.

Enough of Joseph Frank's detailed indictment of Freud's
guesswork has been quoted to demonstrate that, once Freud
had come to a conclusion, it was so difficult for him to modify
it that he was not above selecting only that 'evidence' which
supported his suppositions. One cannot help being reminded of
his failure to discover the true nature of Judge Schreber's
father. It must be recorded that Joseph Frank has no particular
animus against Freud. Although sceptical about Freud's interpretation of Dostoevsky's character, he had assumed that
Freud had based his interpretation upon accurate data. It was
only when he studied the events of Dostoevsky's early life in
detail that he found Freud to be unreliable at the purely factual
level.

Freud's paper 'The Moses of Michelangelo' is in a different
category. There are no speculations about Michelangelo's early
childhood, and no interpretations of his psychopathology.
Instead there is a learned and detailed review of what art
historians have written about this particular statue, combined
with Freud's own deductions about the meaning of the pose
which the artist has chosen. Anyone reading this essay will be
impressed with the acuteness of Freud's scrutiny, his attention
to detail, and the modesty of his claims. Whether or not
modern art historians agree with Freud's interpretation of the
statue as

a concrete expression of the highest mental achievement that is possible in a man, that of struggling successfully against an inward passion for the sake of a cause to which he has devoted himself (*SE*, XIII.233)

hardly matters. The essay reflects both Freud's learning and his considerable powers of observation. It is ironic that his best paper on art and artists should be one in which psycho-analytic theory scarcely figures.

As indicated at the beginning of this chapter, Freud considered that art and literature were produced by sublimation of unsatisfied libido. Although Freud considered that sublimation was necessarily employed by normal people living under the constraints imposed by civilization, the implication of Freud's view must be that, if libido was fully discharged, art and literature would not be necessary. It also follows that, since artists devote so much of their time to activities which are the product of sublimation, they must be closer to being neurotic than the average person. This, indeed, was Freud's view.

An artist is once more in rudiments an introvert, not far removed from neurosis. He is oppressed by excessively powerful instinctual needs. He desires to win honour, power, wealth, fame and the love of women; but he lacks the means for achieving these satisfactions. Consequently, like any other unsatisfied man, he turns away from reality and transfers all his interest, and his libido too, to the wishful constructions of his life of phantasy, whence the path might lead to neurosis (*SE*, XVI.376).

Freud thought that phantasy was derived from play. In his view, both play and phantasy involved turning away from, or denying, reality, and were therefore activities which ought to be outgrown.

The growing child, when he stops playing, gives up nothing but the link with real objects; instead of *playing*, he now *phantasies*. He builds castles in the air and creates what are called *day-dreams* (*SE*, IX.145).

The creative writer does the same as the child at play. He creates a world of phantasy which he takes very seriously – that is which he invests with large amounts of emotion – while separating it sharply from reality (*SE*, IX.144).

We may lay it down that a happy person never phantasies, only an unsatisfied one. The motive forces of phantasies are unsatisfied wishes, and every single phantasy is the fulfilment of a wish, a correction of an unsatisfying reality.

(*SE*, IX.146)

Neurotics turn away from reality because they find it unbearable – either the whole or parts of it (*SE*, XII.218).

So play, dreams, and phantasies are linked together as childish, escapist, wish-fulfilling techniques of compensating for an unsatisfying reality.

In Chapter 5 we referred to Freud's distinction between the two varieties of mental functioning which he called 'primary process' and 'secondary process'. The former is governed by wish-fulfilment and the pleasure principle; the latter by conscious planning and the reality principle.

With the introduction of the reality principle one species of thought-activity was split off; it was kept free from reality-testing, and remained subordinated to the pleasure principle alone. This activity is *phantasying*, which begins already in children's play, and later, continued as *day-dreaming*, abandons dependence upon real objects (*SE*, XII.222).

Freud did admit, though only grudgingly, that artists were not merely neurotics who used their gifts to evade reality.

Art brings about a reconciliation between the two principles in a new way. An artist is originally a man who turns away from reality because he cannot come to terms with the renunciation of instinctual satisfaction which it at first demands, and who allows his erotic and ambitious wishes full play in the life of phantasy. He finds a way back to reality, however, from this world of phantasy by making use of special gifts to mould his phantasies into truths of a new kind, which are valued by men as precious reflections of reality (*SE*, XII.224).

This strange conception of art and artist implies that, although the artist may just escape falling into a neurosis, his art is still an indirect way of obtaining instinctual satisfactions which, if he were better adapted to reality, he would either enjoy or else renounce. In other words, art is primarily escapist. In an ideal world in which everyone had matured sufficiently to replace the pleasure principle by the reality principle, there would be no need for art.

This conclusion, coming as it does from a brilliant writer who was deeply appreciative of both literature and the visual arts, will strike most readers as extremely odd. If Freud had lived long enough to become familiar with modern biological thinking, he might have revised his concepts.

For example, ethologists generally agree that play in young animals is not escapist, but adaptive. That is, play facilitates exploration and also, by repetition of movement sequences, encourages the development of muscular skills. Rough-and-tumble play between young animals and young humans is probably an important way of learning the controlled employment of aggression and may also facilitate later sexual fulfilment.

If play is adaptive in the biological sense, may it not be the case that phantasy is also adaptive? There are such things as 'idle' day-dreams which fit Freud's escapist category; but not all phantasies are of this kind. Einstein defined thinking as 'a free play with concepts' and specifically emphasized the need for creative thinking to be free of the constraints imposed by real objects. He could never have conceived the special theory of relativity if he had not employed phantasy, although, of course, the theory had later to be checked by experiment. Freud, as we noted, thought that *The Brothers Karamazov* was the greatest novel ever written. Although the novel originates from Dostoevsky's phantasy, it also contains portraits based upon real people, and, like every great novel, enhances and deepens our understanding of reality rather than providing an escape from it.

In Chapter 4, we found that Freud's theory that dreams were almost invariably hallucinatory fulfilments of repressed wishes would not hold water, and suggested that some dreams were a way of dealing with trauma, whilst others were concerned with processing information. These latter two functions are not escapist, but ways of coming to terms with reality.

Play, phantasy, and the dream, the three activities which Freud linked as escapist wish-fulfilment, can equally well be regarded as adaptive; more especially, as ways of selecting from, and making new combinations of, our inner and outer experience. Freud considered that the motives of the artist and the motives of the scientist could be sharply distinguished. The drive behind the artist's creative activity was unsatisfied libido manifesting itself in escapist phantasy. The drive behind the scientist's activity was to master the external world. What artists do and what scientists do is certainly very different; but, as we have already suggested, both are concerned with creating order, with making sense out of the world and our experience of it, with discovering or fashioning unity from diversity.

Many of the most creative psycho-analysts of recent years, including Rycroft, Winnicott, Bowlby, Marion Milner and Ehrenzweig reject Freud's concept of 'primary process' as archaic, childish, and maladaptive. Phantasy can be escapist, but, when manifest as creative imagination, is a vital aspect of man's adaptation to the world. Goya was surely right when he prefaced his *Caprichos* with this epigraph:

Phantasy abandoned by reason produces impossible monsters; united with reason, it is the mother of the arts and the origin of their marvels.

83

9 Culture and religion

The application of psycho-analytic theory to anthropology and religion has, on the whole, been disappointing. But Freud's views on these subjects, though not usually accepted by either anthropologists or theologians, are important in demonstrating the way in which psycho-analysis progressed from being a treatment of neurotic illness to being a system of thought which purported to explain almost every human endeavour.

As already indicated, Freud was a highly civilized man himself, but nevertheless regarded civilization as oppressive, since, in his view, it imposed more restraints upon instinctual fulfilment than most human beings could tolerate without developing at least some neurotic symptoms. It is therefore not surprising that Freud was an eager student of primitive and early man; of man as he might have been before civilization had instigated the iron grip of repression. Unfortunately, Freud was writing in the era of 'armchair' anthropology, characterized by extensive theorizing unsupported by evidence from field-work. It was still possible to refer to those belonging to pre-literate cultures as 'savages', and, quite unjustifiably, to equate 'primitive' with 'neurotic' or 'infantile' as Freud did. Today we realize that many so-called primitives may be well adapted to their environment in complex ways; but, before the First World War, Victorian ideas of progress dictated that there had been a clear advance from a 'savage' beginning to the giddy pinnacle of European civilization in the twentieth century. The revelation of the concentration camps and the experience of two world wars have put an end to that kind of complacency.

Totem and Taboo, which consists of four parts originally appearing separately, was first published as a single volume in 1913. Freud's principal sources for his anthropological speculations were Darwin's *The Descent of Man*, Sir James Frazer's *The Golden Bough*, and the theories of Robertson Smith and

J. J. Atkinson. These sources are now partly or wholly discredited.

A totem is a symbolic emblem of a particular social group within a tribe. It may be an animal or, less commonly, a plant or natural phenomenon like rain. A totem is an object of reverence or worship, and is protected by taboos which generally forbid killing it, eating it, or even touching it. On special occasions, however, there may be a ritualized killing and sacramental eating of the totem animal. Allegiance to a particular totem defines social relationships inasmuch as sexual relations between members of the same totem are usually forbidden.

Freud interpreted the totem as representing the father because he knew of three cases in which boys with Oedipal conflicts had phantasies about, or phobias of, animals in which the animal seemed to be a substitute for the father. Freud's own case 'Little Hans' had a fear of being bitten by a horse which Freud believed to have resulted from the repression and subsequent projection of the child's hostility towards his father.

Freud, following Darwin, supposed that primitive man lived in small groups or 'hordes' dominated by a single, powerful male, who not only kept all the females for himself, but also expelled his younger male rivals, thus preventing incest and encouraging the formation of sexual ties outside the original group. Freud went on to suggest that:

> One day the brothers who had been driven out came together, killed and devoured their father and so made an end of the patriarchal horde. . . . The totem meal, which is perhaps man's earliest festival, would thus be a repetition of this memorable and criminal deed, which was the beginning of so many things – of social organization, of moral restrictions and of religion (*SE*, XIII.141–2).

Freud then asserted that the sons who had slaughtered their father became afflicted with such guilt that:

> They revoked their deed by forbidding the killing of the totem, the substitute for their father; and they renounced its fruits by

resigning their claim to the women who had now been set free. They thus created out of their filial sense of guilt the two fundamental taboos of totemism, which for that very reason inevitably corresponded to the two repressed wishes of the Oedipus complex. Whoever contravened those taboos became guilty of the only two crimes with which primitive society concerned itself (*SE*, XIII.143).

The ritual totemic meal could be interpreted as a 'return of the repressed'; a temporary symbolic expression of the original impulses of hatred towards the father which guilt usually kept unconscious.

Freud thought that this primal slaughter of the father was a real event which had left 'ineradicable traces in the history of humanity'. In other words, he believed in the discredited Lamarckian hypothesis of the inheritance of acquired characteristics. In spite of his considerable knowledge of Darwin, whose evolutionary theory had displaced Lamarck's idea in the minds of virtually every biologist, Freud obstinately maintained until his death that acquired characteristics could be inherited, and that the origins of religion and morality could indeed be traced back to an actual event.

Freud seems to have been ambivalent about *Totem and Taboo*. On the one hand, he regarded it as a major achievement; on the other, he once said, 'Oh, don't take that seriously—I made that up on a rainy Sunday afternoon.' In reality, there are a number of untenable elements in Freud's theory, in addition to his adherence to Lamarck.

First, there is no evidence from anthropology or from studies of subhuman primates that a 'primal horde' dominated by a single male ever existed. Darwin derived his notion from hearsay reports about the organization of gorilla troops which have since been shown to be false.

Second, totemic meals are rare, and found only in a small minority of tribes professing totemism.

Third, Freud neglects any discussion of the possible importance of the mother in totemic religion; an omission characteristic of psycho-analytic theory, which, until late in its evolution, habitually emphasized the father's role at the expense of that of the mother. This emphasis probably originated from the fact that Freud himself had more problems in his relation to his father than he did in relation to his mother.

Fourth, in at least one of the cases upon which Freud based his theory of the totem representing the father, a quite different interpretation is possible. 'Little Hans', the 5-year-old son of Freud's friend Max Graf, was seen only once by Freud, who treated the child through his father. John Bowlby, re-examining the case, has demonstrated that, like other childhood phobias, Little Hans's phobia is likely to have been caused by fears that his mother would disappear. It has been established that the mother used alarming threats in disciplin-ing Hans, including the threat that she would leave and not come back if Hans were naughty.

In the light of modern anthropology, Darwinian theory, and Bowlby's work on 'attachment', it is easy to be wise after the event and accuse Freud of neglecting evidence to some of which he could not at the time have had access. Nevertheless, *Totem and Taboo* does belong to the wilder shores of specula-tion, and bears witness to Freud's tendency to generalization from an insufficient basis of fact when he thought that he could thereby find support for psycho-analytic theory. Thomas Mann, in an essay published in 1929, chose *Totem and Taboo* as the work of Freud which had made the strongest impression upon him. This seems bizarre until one realizes that Mann's evaluation is not based upon anthropology, but is entirely literary. Mann wrote that *Totem and Taboo*

is without doubt the one of Freud's productions which has the greatest artistic merit; both in conception and literary form, it is a literary masterpiece allied to, and comparable with, the greatest examples of literary essays.

Some of the same criticisms which have been levelled at *Totem and Taboo* also apply to *Moses and Monotheism*, which was Freud's last completed book, not finished until he was over 80. Freud controversially supposed that Moses, leader and creator of the Jewish people, was originally an Egyptian, as the etymology of his name suggests. The biblical story of Moses records that, in order to avoid the persecution of the Pharaoh, Moses' parents concealed him by the river in an ark of bulrushes, from which he was rescued by the Pharaoh's daughter. Since the princess brought up Moses as her own son, Freud makes the not unreasonable deduction that Moses was in fact her son, and therefore not Jewish in origin. He goes on to suggest that Moses had accepted the revolution of thought instigated by the Pharaoh Akhenaten, who had substituted monotheism for the worship of a multiplicity of gods. When Akhenaten died, a reaction set in threatening monotheistic beliefs. Moses therefore threw in his lot with the oppressed minority of Jews, reinforced their identity by insisting both on monotheism and the practice of circumcision, and finally instituted the Exodus, leading the Jews out of Egypt to discover the promised land. Although the Bible states that Moses died at the age of 120, Freud preferred to believe that Moses was murdered by his people, relying for evidence on a suggestion made by Ernst Sellin, which, when first announced, had been immediately rejected by all other Jewish scholars. Freud eagerly adopted Sellin's hypothesis because it supported his own speculation about parricide and the origins of religion. Freud guessed that the murder of Moses reinforced the inherited sense of guilt dating from the primal parricide described above, and caused a lasting unconscious sense of guilt in the Jewish people.

> It is plausible to conjecture that remorse for the murder of Moses provided the stimulus for the wishful phantasy of the Messiah, who was to return and lead his people to redemption and the promised world-dominion (*SE*, XXIII.89).

Moses and Monotheism has been rejected by most critics as one of the least convincing of Freud's writings. As in *Totem and Taboo*, Lamarckian inheritance of acquired characteristics is an integral part of the argument, and there are many historical objections to the book which it would be otiose to catalogue.

It was noted in Chapter 1 that Freud never practised the

Jewish religion. Although he acknowledged that religion might sometimes play a part in suppressing neurotic symptoms, he firmly maintained that religious faith was a wish-fulfilling illusion. In Freud's view, the gods have a threefold task.

> They must exorcize the terrors of nature, they must reconcile men to the cruelty of Fate, particularly as it is shown in death, and they must compensate them for the sufferings which a civilized life in common has imposed on them.
>
> (*SE*, XXI.18)

Freud believed that religion originated in man's feelings of helplessness. As an adult, man is confronted by all manner of dangers, from earthquakes to disease, which threaten him and which he cannot control. As a small child, he was even more helpless, but recognized that his father, however formidable, at least protected him from common dangers.

> The derivation of religious needs from the infant's helplessness and the longing for the father seems to me incontrovertible, especially since the feeling is not simply prolonged from childhood days, but is permanently sustained by fear of the superior power of Fate. I cannot think of any need in childhood as strong as the need for a father's protection (*SE*, XXI.72).

In an earlier paper, Freud had laid more emphasis upon the dangers threatening the individual from within. He noted the similarity between religious practices and obsessional rituals. In his view, obsessional rituals were ways of protecting the ego from the emergence of phantasies, thoughts, or sexual impulses which the individual had repressed; and, at the same time, a displaced and partial expression of those impulses. For example, a patient suffered from the common compulsion to wash his hands frequently; in this case, an expression of guilt about masturbation. In addition, he was compelled to wash each finger separately, thereby making an obscene gesture signifying coitus. Freud considered that religion, as part of civilization, was based on the suppression, the renunciation, of certain instinctual impulses. These impulses, however, are not, as in the neuroses, exclusively components of the sexual instinct; they are self-seeking, socially harmful instincts, though, even so, they are usually not without a sexual component.

(*SE*, IX.125)

Because pious people, in their confessional prayers, acknowledge themselves to be guilty sinners, they need to perform ritual observances as a defence against temptation and as a way of controlling or warding off the instinctive forces which are always threatening to break through. Freud went so far as to affirm that religion might be regarded 'as a universal obsessional neurosis'.

Religion, therefore, promises protection against unruly impulses from within, by means of ritual observance; and some protection against dangers from without by acquiescing in the restrictive demands of civilization upon the individual's selfish impulses. This renunciation makes possible some degree of solidarity with one's fellow men, and thereby diminishes the sense of helplessness.

In addition, religion promises an after-life. This not only diminishes man's terror in the face of death, but also implies that the dead person will be rewarded with heavenly pleasures to compensate for the earthly pleasures he has had to forego in the interests of civilization.

At the beginning of this chapter, it was noted that Freud regarded civilization as unduly oppressive and provocative of neurosis. His resentment went much further than this; so far, indeed, that one is justified in supposing that his own extreme, obsessional control over his own impulses was burdensome to him. Freud of course recognized that civilization was necessary if man as a species was to survive, but he nevertheless refers to the 'injuries' which civilization inflicts upon the individual. The following quotation is clearly ironically intended, but also reveals what Freud thought of the 'natural' man when unrestrained.

We have spoken of the hostility to civilization which is

produced by the pressure that civilization exercises, the renunciations of instinct which it demands. If one imagines its prohibitions lifted – if, then, one may take any woman one pleases as a sexual object, if one may without hesitation kill one's rival for her love or anyone else who stands in one's way, if, too, one can carry off any of the other man's belongings without asking leave – how splendid, what a string of satisfactions one's life would be! (*SE*, XXI.15).

This sombre picture derives from the fact that psychoanalytic theory is an 'instinct' theory. That is, it is primarily concerned with how the isolated individual finds or fails to find ways of discharging his instinctive impulses. The impression gained from reading Freud is that relationships with other human beings are of value only in so far as they facilitate instinctual satisfaction. There is no conception of friendship or other types of relationship as being valuable in themselves. All are considered 'aim-inhibited' substitutes for sexual relations. No wonder Freud repudiated the Christian commandment 'Thou shalt love thy neighbour as thyself', which he referred to as a precept lacking any point because 'its fulfilment cannot be recommended as reasonable'. As we shall see, modern psychoanalytic theory is much more concerned than was Freud with the quality and type of relationships which the individual makes from birth onwards.

Freud's concept of religion is open to criticism on a number of grounds. First, it is exclusively paternally based. Although Vienna was predominantly a Catholic city, the importance of the Virgin Mary or of any other female goddess is entirely passed over, an omission which was also noted in the discussion of *Totem and Taboo*.

Second, Freud makes no mention of religions like early Buddhism, which appears not to require belief in a god or gods, but which nevertheless prescribes a way of life which many have found profoundly fulfilling.

Third, Freud, as he himself admits, is incapable of understanding ecstatic and mystical experiences, which, for many people, are the origin of 'religious' feelings. When Freud sent a copy of his book dismissing religion, *The Future of an Illusion*, to his friend Romain Rolland, the latter complained that Freud had not comprehended the true source of religious sentiments. Freud wrote:

> This, he says, consists in a peculiar feeling, which he himself is never without, which he finds confirmed by many others, and which he may suppose is present in millions of people. It is a feeling which he would like to call a sensation of 'eternity', a feeling of something limitlcss, unbounded – as it were, 'oceanic' (*SE*, XXI.64).

Freud rightly characterizes this as

> a feeling of an indissoluble bond, of being one with the external world as a whole (*SE*, XXI.65).

Freud compares this feeling with the height of being in love, in which the lover feels totally at one with his beloved. Freud interprets this as an extreme regression to a very early state; that of the infant at the breast before he has learned to distinguish himself from the mother or the external world. Both being in love and the oceanic feeling are therefore illusions. Indeed, Freud referred to the state of being in love as a kind of madness, as 'the normal prototype of the psychoses'.

Freud partially agrees with Rolland when he admits that the oceanic feeling and the sense of being at one with the universe may become connected with religious sentiments at a later stage, and describes it as

> a first attempt at a religious consolation, as though it were another way of disclaiming the danger which the ego recognizes as threatening it from the external world.
>
> (*SE*, XXI.72)

Although everyone is subject to self-deception and to wish-fulfilling delusions, those who, unlike Freud, have experienced the oceanic feeling, will find themselves dissatisfied with his explanation. The accounts of ecstatic experiences furnished by a variety of people from religious mystics to explorers like

Admiral Byrd suggest that such experiences are the profoundest moments of their existence, and sometimes bring about a permanent alteration in the way in which they perceive themselves and the world. Such experiences do not need to be explained in religious terms, but neither can they be dismissed as totally illusory. Defensive wish-fulfilments usually seem partially inauthentic even to those indulging in them; but the oceanic experience is felt as deeply and inescapably authentic. This is not the context in which to venture an explanation of the oceanic experience. It is enough to state that, if Freud had ever experienced anything of the kind himself, he might have been forced to consider some other interpretation.

Freud ends *The Future of an Illusion* with a device which he constantly employed when discussing topics which he considered particularly controversial: an adversarial debate between himself and an imaginary opponent. Freud proposes that, at some remote date in the future, the intellect will finally assert its primacy and religious belief will thereby be abandoned.

> We may insist as often as we like that man's intellect is powerless in comparison with its instinctual life, and we may be right in this. Nevertheless, there is something peculiar about this weakness. The voice of the intellect is a soft one, but it does not rest till it has gained a hearing. Finally, after a countless succession of rebuffs, it succeeds.
>
> (*SE*, XXI.53)

Freud equates the intellect with science, although, as indicated earlier, it is impossible to endorse Freud's own view that psycho-analysis is, or could become, strictly scientific. The famous last sentence of Freud's book is:

> No, our science is no illusion. But an illusion it would be to suppose that what science cannot give us we can get elsewhere (*SE*, XXI.56).

It is, perhaps, worth noting that when Freud refers to his imaginary adversary's God as 'your God', the God of conventional religious belief, he opposes what he calls ironically 'our God', Logos, the voice of Reason. Freud's use of this verbal device reveals more about himself than he admitted. Exclusive belief in Reason or Science can be as irrational as belief in God. Certainly, Freud's belief in psycho-analysis went far beyond any evidence of its truth which could possibly be called scientific.

10 Freud as therapist

The Technique of Psycho-Analysis

In Chapter 4, three aspects of psycho-analytic technique were briefly described: free association, the interpretation of dreams, and the evaluation of transference and counter-transference. Freud wrote a number of papers on the technique of psycho-analytic treatment. A summary of what he had to say must be included in even a short book on Freud, for his procedure has influenced nearly every subsequent type of psychotherapy practised in the West. The principles of treatment which Freud enunciated were quite unlike those followed by conventional physicians in the practice of medicine, and must have seemed revolutionary in the period before the First World War when they were formulated. Modern psycho-analysts seldom adhere to all Freud's recommendations; but the general way in which psycho-analysis and other forms of psychotherapy are conducted is still based on Freud's procedure, and remains one of his most enduring legacies.

As early as 1904, Freud laid down certain criteria for the selection of patients as being suitable for psycho-analysis. He required that patients should possess 'a reasonable degree of education and a fairly reliable character'. He refused to take on patients who were psychotic; that is, who were suffering from schizophrenia or from the most severe type of melancholia (depressive illness). As noted earlier, patients suffering from mania or hypomania seldom consult psycho-analysts. Although some psycho-analysts have disregarded Freud's advice in this respect, and have attempted to analyse schizophrenics, the results have been disappointing.

Freud realized that psychotic varieties of mental illness might present as neuroses and not be immediately recognizable as something far more serious. On these grounds, he wisely recommended a trial period of analysis lasting for one or two weeks. He was also cautious in warning against the use of psycho-analysis in cases of *anorexia nervosa* or other dangerous conditions in which immediate removal of symptoms was required.

Freud laid it down that patients 'near or above the age of fifty' were not suitable for psycho-analysis on two grounds. First, he feared that the mass of material which had accumulated during the patient's lifetime would be so great that the treatment might go on indefinitely. This caveat is no longer accepted by modern psycho-analysts, who often treat older patients with success. Freud's other reason for excluding the middle-aged and elderly is more interesting. He says that 'old people are no longer educable', whilst persons under the age of adolescence 'are often exceedingly amenable to influence'. Freud usually claimed that psycho-analysis was a treatment in which direct influence and suggestion played little part. In this passage, he is revealing that suggestion plays a greater role in psycho-analysis than he generally admitted.

In Chapter 4, two reasons were given for requiring the patient to lie prone upon a couch while the psycho-analyst sat out of sight behind him. The first was that this encouraged the flow of free association; the second, Freud's admission that he shrank from being stared at for eight or more hours a day. A third reason was that Freud thought it desirable that the patient should not be aware of the psycho-analyst's changing facial expressions. All three reasons have a certain validity, and most Freudian analysts continue to employ the couch. Analysts belonging to other schools feel that the use of the couch is artificial, and prefer a face-to-face, more equal-seeming encounter, with patient and analyst sitting opposite each other.

Freud recommended that the psycho-analyst take no notes on the grounds that this might interfere with his maintaining an attitude of 'evenly-suspended attention' in which he refused to prejudge which of the patient's utterances were important. Freud pointed out that the significance of what the analyst hears in any particular session may only be established at a later date. The analyst must turn his own unconscious like a receptive organ towards the transmitting unconscious of the patient. He must adjust himself to the patient as a telephone receiver is adjusted to the transmitting microphone (*SE*, XII.113–14).

Any practising psychotherapist will recognize that this is sound advice. One of the commonest mistakes which psychotherapists make is premature interpretation: jumping to wrong conclusions on insufficient evidence.

Convention supposes that psycho-analysts are inhumanly detached; concerned only with the interpretation of the material furnished by the patient, and unmoved by the latter's distress. It has already been noted that Freud, when conducting an analysis, was 'curiously impersonal'. He wrote:

> I cannot advise my colleagues too urgently to model themselves during psycho-analytic treatment on the surgeon, who puts aside all his feelings, even his human sympathy, and concentrates his mental forces on the single aim of performing the operation as skilfully as possible. . . . The justification for requiring this emotional coldness in the analyst is that it creates the most advantageous conditions for both parties: for the doctor a desirable protection for his own emotional life and for the patient the largest amount of help that we can give him to-day (*SE*, XII.115).

A certain degree of detachment is undoubtedly required of the analyst. If the analyst identifies himself too closely with the patient, he will abandon objectivity and be unable to see in what way the patient himself is responsible for his own difficulties. On the other hand, if he remains as detached as Freud recommends, there is a danger that he will not be able to understand his patient as a person. Research has established that analysts need to be capable of genuine concern and that warm acceptance on the part of the analyst facilitates personality change. Psycho-analysis and other types of psychotherapy derived from it cannot really be regarded in the same light as surgery, partly because we are no longer as certain as was Freud that we can disinter the origin of every neurotic

97

symptom as a discrete entity. Modern analysts are more concerned with the patient's personality as a whole, and with the kind of relationships which he has made throughout his life, than with repressed infantile sexual phantasy. This concern demands a different attitude from that recommended by Freud. Although the analyst must preserve objectivity towards the patient's behaviour, which he may or may not approve of, he must also convey what Carl Rogers has aptly called 'unconditional positive regard'; that is, he must genuinely value the patient as a person.

In Chapter 4, Freud's acceptance of Jung's requirement that the analyst should himself be analysed was noted. Freud goes on to recommend that the analyst should not succumb to the temptation of talking about his own personality and problems, as would be natural in social life, when 'one confidence deserves another'. Freud recommended that:

> The doctor should be opaque to his patients and, like a mirror, should show them nothing but what is shown to him.
> (*SE*, XII.118)

Although not every psychotherapist would agree, I think Freud was entirely right in this requirement. Talking about oneself is a self-indulgence which should be shunned by the analyst who, during the analytic hour, must regard himself solely as the agent of the patient. As Freud points out, self-revelation on the part of the analyst also leads to insuperable difficulties in interpreting the transference.

Freud warns against didacticism: against recommending reading matter to the patient, and against trying to direct the liberated patient into new paths which the analyst thinks he should follow. Although some psychotherapists use books and papers as a way of introducing prospective patients to what is in store for them, Freud was once again perceptive in questioning such methods. Reading about psycho-analysis is apt to provoke intellectual argument at the expense of personal experience; whilst handing out unsolicited advice is patronizing, and therefore denigrating to the patient as an autonomous individual.

Freud advised that most analytic patients should be seen every day except on Sundays and public holidays, although he did say that 'slight cases' or cases 'well advanced' in treatment could be seen less often. He felt that even the interposition of Sunday often had an obscuring effect upon analytic work. The majority of modern psycho-analysts see their patients less often. This is partly because the habit of working on Saturdays has largely disappeared, and partly because only a minority of patients can afford the high fees charged by psycho-analysts if patients have to come on five or six days per week. It is obviously to the analyst's advantage to see more patients less frequently, for he can thereby ask higher fees per session. Freud would not have approved of this modification of his technique.

Freud himself could be generous to those in need, but was decidedly realistic about money. His principle was to allot one particular hour of each working day to each analytic patient and to demand payment for that hour, whether or not the patient made use of it. At first sight, this seems harsh; but Freud defended it on the grounds that, unless required to pay, patients would all too often manifest resistance by failing to appear, and would find manifold excuses for not coming, usually just at the time when some new analytic discovery was imminent.

Freud ostensibly ruled out taking on patients with whom he had any other kind of relationship outside the analytic hour.

> Special difficulties arise when the analyst and his new patient or their families are on terms of friendship or have social ties with one another. The psycho-analyst who is asked to undertake the treatment of the wife or child of a friend must be prepared for it to cost him that friendship, no matter what the outcome of the treatment may be: nevertheless he must make the sacrifice if he cannot find a trustworthy substitute (*SE*, XII.125).

Most psycho-analysts recognize this principle as valid, more especially since analysis of transference became so central a concern of psycho-analytic treatment. But Freud himself often failed to observe his own rules. For example, Freud analysed his own daughter Anna over a period of several years, a flagrant violation of psycho-analytic principles which most psycho-analysts would condemn. It is significant that Anna Freud was the only one of Freud's children to become a psycho-analyst, and that she manifested her continuing devotion to her father by remaining unmarried. During Freud's terminal illness, it was Anna, rather than his wife Martha, who became his nurse.

Freud often failed to obey his own injunctions by talking a good deal himself, sometimes chatting about his family. Hilda Doolittle, the poetess who was a friend of Ezra Pound and at one time married to Richard Aldington, records that, in old age, Freud beat his fist on the head of the couch on which she was lying and said:

> The trouble is—I am an old man—*you do not think it worth your while to love me*.

But those who criticize Freud for breaking the rules of psycho-analysis sometimes appear to forget that it was he who invented them.

Freud's own cases

Freud's case histories have become famous, both as illustrating his own way of conducting psycho-analysis and also as works of literature. A detailed search through Freud's collected works reveals that he mentioned 133 cases in passing, but that there are only six extended accounts of individual patients. These include the case of Judge Schreber, whom Freud never saw, and 'Little Hans', whose father acted as an intermediary. This leaves four cases personally analysed by Freud: 'Dora', who was treated for eleven weeks in 1900; the 'Rat Man', treated for eleven months from October 1907 onwards; and an unnamed female homosexual of 18, whose treatment was discontinued by Freud after 'a short time'. The fourth case is the famous 'Wolf Man', followed up for over sixty years, who died only in 1979.

The case-study of the patient called 'Dora' is judiciously entitled 'Fragment of an Analysis of a Case of Hysteria'. Dora was an 18-year-old girl, the daughter of an unhappily married couple, who were close friends of another unhappily married couple, referred to by Freud as Herr and Frau K. Frau K. was the mistress of Dora's father. Dora had what would now be called a 'crush' on Frau K. Herr K. had made sexual advances to Dora when she was 14. When she was 18, he renewed his advances and proposed marriage after obtaining a divorce. Dora violently repudiated him. According to Dora's father, it was this incident which provoked Dora's hysterical symptoms of recurrent loss of voice, nervous cough, and fainting spells, together with depression, social withdrawal, and a threat of suicide.

The case of Dora is important because, as Ernest Jones records, it served for years as a model for students of psycho-analysis. As Freud intended, it demonstrates the significance of dreams in psycho-analytic treatment, and bears witness to Freud's ingenuity in interpreting them. It also reveals a good deal which Freud did not intend. At an early point in treat-ment, Freud made up his mind that Dora, for years, had been in love with Herr K.; a conclusion which was emphatically denied by Dora until the penultimate session of her brief treat-ment. Freud treated her repeated denials as confirming, rather than negating, his interpretations.

The 'No' uttered by a patient after a repressed thought has been presented to his conscious perception for the first time does no more than register the existence of a repression and its severity; it acts, as it were, as a gauge of the repression's strength. If this 'No', instead of being regarded as the expres-sion of an impartial judgement (of which, indeed, the patient is incapable), is ignored, and if work is continued, the first evidence soon begins to appear that in such a case 'No' signifies the desired 'Yes' (*SE*, VII.58–9).

Yet, Dora persisted in denying being in love with Herr K. (who, after all, was much older than she was) until she had already decided to terminate her treatment. As others have remarked, Freud overwhelmed her with interpretations until, after that penultimate session, he was able to write:

And Dora disputed the fact no longer (*SE*, VII.104).

Any reader who studies the case of Dora without prejudice will conclude that, once Freud had made up his mind about a point, he would not take 'No' for an answer, and that he used all his ingenuity and his considerable powers of persuasion to compel his patient to admit that he was right. As already noted, Freud did the same in his writings, especially in those in which he tries to anticipate every objection which an imaginary adversary might raise.

'The Psychogenesis of a Case of Homosexuality in a Woman' underlines the point, now universally recognized by psychoanalysts, that adolescents who are pushed into treatment by their parents seldom do well. Freud recognized this, and also says that this 18-year-old patient

> was not in any way ill (she did not suffer from anything in herself, nor did she complain of her condition).
>
> (*SE*, XVIII.150)

However, six months previously she had made a suicide attempt. Freud had also recognized that the conversion of a homosexual preference into a heterosexual orientation was 'never an easy matter'. Freud warned the parents that their wish to see this change take place in their daughter was unlikely to be fulfilled. Within a short time, it became obvious that the analysis could not succeed. The girl repudiated Freud's interpretations, and, according to his account, manifested a negative transference, based upon her hatred of her father and of men in general. Freud broke off the treatment and recommended that the girl seek help from a woman doctor. His reconstruction of the girl's early sexual development, of what drove her to repudiate men and fall in love with mother-substitutes, and of the events and feelings leading up to her suicidal attempt are of considerable interest. But why, in the face of so many contra-indications to psycho-analysis of which Freud was well aware, did he accept her as a patient? The answer is to be found in the first sentence of the paper.

> Homosexuality in women, which is certainly not less common than in men, although much less glaring, has not only

been ignored by the law, but has also been neglected by psycho-analytic research (*SE*, XVIII.147).

It is clear that Freud took her into treatment in order to remedy this neglect. He must have realized that trying to analyse someone who was not ill and not asking for help was a futile exercise from the patient's point of view, though not from his own. Freud would have agreed that his intellectual curiosity always took precedence over any wish he may have had to act as a therapist. He may well have believed that, because few lesbians presented themselves for treatment, 'using' the patient for research was justified.

The 'Rat Man' is an entirely different proposition. This is one of Freud's most interesting and successful cases. The 'Rat Man' was a lawyer aged 29, who first came to see Freud on 1 October 1907. He complained of obsessional thoughts; that is, of unwanted ideas and phantasies which came into his mind spontaneously, of which he could not rid himself. (Those unfamiliar with such thoughts may recall the common experience of a tune 'running in the head' which cannot be expelled.) The thoughts which assailed Ernst Lanzer (for that was his name) were indeed horrifying. Many consisted of fears that something dreadful would happen to people he was fond of; to his father, or to a lady whom he admired. Freud was astonished to discover that his obsessional fears about his father persisted in spite of the father's actual death some years previously.

But the worst obsessional preoccupation concerned an Eastern punishment of which he had been told while serving in the army. This consisted of tying a pot containing rats to the buttocks of a criminal with the intention that they should bore their way into the man via the anus. Lanzer confessed that the idea had occurred to him that this punishment was being inflicted upon the lady already referred to, and he felt compelled to carry out certain obsessional rituals to ward off this danger.

Freud's long, but necessarily incomplete, account of this case comprises the second half of Volume X of the *Standard*

Edition. It displays Freud at his most brilliant and most convincing. Freud's analysis of obsessional doubts and ambivalence as being ultimately traceable to a conflict between love and hate is persuasive. Freud evidently had a particular empathy with obsessional neurotics, based upon his own obsessional personality. He succeeded in ridding the 'Rat Man' of his tormenting, horrifying thought, and was able to write:

> the treatment, which lasted for about a year, led to the complete restoration of the patient's personality, and to the removal of his inhibitions (*SE*, X.155).

Sceptics may point out that we have no long-term follow-up of Ernst Lanzer. Obsessional neurotics who have been plagued, as he was, with compulsive thoughts and rituals from early childhood seldom lose all their symptoms for ever, and remain vulnerable to relapse at times of stress. As we shall see, this was true of the next case, the 'Wolf Man', who provides us with a long-term follow-up unmatched in the annals of psycho-analysis.

Freud gave his account of the 'Wolf Man' the title 'From the History of an Infantile Neurosis'. The 'Wolf Man' was a wealthy Russian brought up on a large estate. He first consulted Freud in February 1910 and was treated by him until July 1914. Freud notes that at that time he regarded him as cured. The patient records in his memoirs that when he visited Freud in the spring of 1919, after the First World War was over, he was thoroughly satisfied with his own mental and emotional condition and had no thought of seeking further psycho-analysis. However, Freud, on hearing his account of himself, thought differently, and advised a further period of treatment. Freud saw the patient again from November 1919 until February 1920. He reported that

> a piece of the transference which had not hitherto been overcome was successfully dealt with (*SE*, XVII.122).

The 'Wolf Man' suffered from recurrent attacks of depression and from various obsessional symptoms, which, as in the case of the 'Rat Man', manifested themselves in varying degrees of intensity from early childhood onwards. His nickname originates from a fear of wolves dating from his fourth year, and, more particularly, from a nightmare dreamed at about the same period, in which he was terrified by seeing six or seven white wolves sitting on the branches of a walnut tree which stood outside his bedroom window. Freud wrote that he became convinced that behind this dream were concealed the causes of the patient's infantile neurosis. In this context it is impossible to detail the steps which led to Freud's interpretation. Indeed, perhaps wisely, he himself omits many of them from his account. What he concluded 'from the chaos of the dreamer's unconscious memory traces' was that, at the age of 1½, while lying in his cot, he must have witnessed three acts of *coitus a tergo* between his parents. Freud, since the very early days of psycho-analysis, had been convinced that witnessing the 'primal scene' of parental intercourse had a traumatic effect upon young children. This bears out the fact that most of his patients were upper class. In the cramped houses of the poor, such scenes must have been witnessed by young children several times per week; yet Freud more than once hinted that the labouring classes were less liable to neurosis.

Freud was so convinced of the truth of his interpretation that he confidently wrote that his patient's sexual life had been 'splintered up' by this early experience. Yet the 'Wolf Man' himself failed to recollect the incident. Since Freud had forbidden him to be critical, he may have appeared to accept Freud's reconstruction at the time, but he certainly did not do so later. In an interview conducted when he was 87 he revealed:

I never thought much of dream interpretation, you know. In my story, what was explained by dreams? Freud traces everything back to the primal scene which he derives from the dream. But that scene does not occur in the dream. When he interprets the white wolves as nightshirts or something like that, for example, linen sheets or clothes, that's somehow far-fetched, I think. That scene in the dream where

105

the windows open and so on and the wolves are sitting there, and his interpretation, I don't know, these things are miles apart. It's terribly far-fetched.

His account of his analysis with Freud repeatedly emphasizes how impressed he was with Freud's personality, and how he found in him 'a new father'. Freud had

a great deal of personal understanding for me, as he often told me during the treatment, which naturally strengthened my attachment to him.

The 'Wolf Man' reveals that Freud discussed Dostoevsky with him, talked about his son's skiing accident, and did not hesitate to give him direct advice when he thought it appropriate. At the end of the first period of treatment, Freud himself suggested that the 'Wolf Man' give him a present 'so that the feeling of gratitude wouldn't become too strong'. The 'Wolf Man' obliged by adding an Egyptian statuette to Freud's collection. There can be little doubt that the 'Wolf Man's' considerable improvement at this stage in his life was nothing to do with Freud's interpretations of his supposed infantile sexual experiences, and everything to do with the fact that he regarded Freud as an understanding father-figure upon whom he could rely.

When the 'Wolf Man' returned after the war for his second period of analysis, he had lost all his money. Freud treated him free, personally helped him financially, and raised money for him from other sources for a number of years. In 1926 he had another period of analysis with Dr Ruth Mack Brunswick. From then on, he was intermittently treated by Dr Brunswick and by at least three other psycho-analysts. Psychiatrists will recognize a typical history of a chronic obsessional neurotic. He finally died on 7 May 1979, at the age of 92. The series of interviews with him recorded by Karin Obholzer almost to the day of his death disclose that, in his late eighties, he still had problems with his relationships with women, was still subject to bouts of depression, and was still tormented by obsessional thoughts and doubts. Freud's most famous patient is not quite the advertisement for psycho-analysis which Freud might have hoped for after his first encounter with him.

Even when one takes into account the difficulty of presenting psycho-analytic cases without infringing confidentiality, the number of cases treated at any length and discussed in detail by Freud is almost incredibly small. Moreover, only one of the cases displays convincing evidence of substantial improvement. Fisher and Greenberg conclude that:

> Freud never presented any data, in statistical or case study form, that demonstrated that his treatment was of benefit to a significant number of the patients he himself saw.

Why was this? Some might argue that Freud could not produce such data because his treatment did not produce many good results. My own view is that Freud was far more interested in ideas than he was in patients. What he wanted was time and opportunity to present his ideas in so persuasive a way that the whole world would recognize and accept his revolutionary way of looking at human beings. It did not matter whether the cases he chose to present demonstrated the efficacy of psycho-analysis as a treatment. What was important was that the cases selected should support his theories about human nature.

11 Psycho-analysis today

Although Freud himself was primarily concerned with research and psycho-analytic theory rather than with therapy, the reader will wish to know how psycho-analysis stands today, and whether it is considered an effective treatment for neurotic disorders. In spite of the immense amount of research devoted to these questions, they remain extremely difficult to answer. There are a variety of reasons why this should be so.

First, research has demonstrated that psycho-analysts differ so markedly from each other in their treatment aims and expectations, and in how they behave to their patients, that it is not possible to state, even within the Freudian fold, that a defined form of psychotherapy which can be labelled 'psycho-analysis' actually exists. Most studies purporting to examine the outcome of psycho-analysis do not take these variants sufficiently into account. What does seem relatively firmly established is that psycho-analysis, practised in the way which Freud originally laid down, using free association, the couch, and five or six sessions per week, is not more effective in relieving neurotic distress than are less intensive types of analytically orientated psychotherapy. In the 1950s, Eysenck and others tried to demonstrate that psycho-analysis was totally ineffective. This attack had the good effect of stimulating a great deal of research. While it cannot be said that psycho-analysis as practised by Freud is more effective than other forms of psychotherapy derived from it, the consensus is that a person suffering from neurotic problems is certainly more likely to recover if she seeks help from an experienced psychotherapist than if she merely waits for her troubles to pass.

Second, what constitutes cure is very difficult to define. Psycho-analysis, as Freud originally developed it, was primarily concerned with ridding patients of hysterical and obsessional symptoms. In their enthusiasm, the early psycho-analysts and their patients when much further than this in hoping that psycho-analysis would bring about profound changes in personality and character structure. There was much concern with whether 'X' or 'Y' was 'completely analysed', as if this were an achievable result. Freud himself professed no such extravagant aims. Today, most psycho-analysts are less certain than was Freud about defining the 'cause' of a neurosis. When psycho-analysis is effective, and it certainly can be so, it is probable that it works by enabling the patient to make effective use of his psychopathology rather than by abolishing it. Patients presenting themselves for psycho-analysis feel overwhelmed, unable to cope with their problems. Greater understanding of their own strengths and limitations can often be extremely helpful, even if their personality is not fundamentally modified.

In another book I quoted a case of my own which aptly illustrates the difficulty of evaluating the results of any form of psychotherapy. I received a letter from a man whom I had treated rather briefly in a National Health Service setting twenty-five years previously. He wanted me to see his daughter. In his letter he wrote: 'I can quite truthfully say that six months of your patient listening to my woes made a most important contribution to my life style. Although my transvestism was not cured my approach to life and to other people was re-orientated and for that I am most grateful. It is part of my life that I have *never* forgotten.'

Here is an example of a case which might be rated as a dismal failure, since his main symptom, his transvestism, was not abolished. Yet, reading his letter so long after his period of treatment, one is bound to recognize that something important did take place which is directly attributable to that treatment. What seems to have happened is that the limited amount of psychotherapy which I was able to offer made the patient more capable of accepting himself, of coping with his psychopathology rather than letting himself be overwhelmed by it. Such results are more common than is usually admitted; but how they can be scientifically evaluated is an unsolved problem.

In Chapter 1, some aspects of the obsessional personality were outlined. Such personalities are easy to recognize. Although obsessional symptoms can be relieved, as they were in the case of the 'Rat Man', the basic traits which constitute the obsessional personality are not abolished by psycho-analysis. From the 1930s until the 1950s, psycho-analysis was oversold, especially in the United States. More was expected of it than Freud ever claimed it could achieve. Radical change in personality was confidently expected by both patients and psycho-analysts; and the duration of psycho-analytic treatment became more and more extended. I well remember an elderly British psycho-analyst, who appears in the photograph of the Oxford Psycho-Analytic Congress of 1929, telling me about a young man whom he had had in analysis for a number of years. Dr W. was convinced that his patient must have been the victim of a homosexual assault when he was a very small child. If only he could so pierce his defences that he could recall this incident, Dr W. was sure that his patient would recover. Yet any evidence that such an assault had actually occurred was entirely lacking.

That generation of psycho-analysts has passed away. Their modern counterparts are more sceptical. In fact, the case of the 'Wolf Man' aptly prefigures one of the major changes which have come about in psycho-analytic thinking since the death of Freud on 23 September 1939. Freud clearly believed that the patient's apparent cure after his first period of analysis was the result of making conscious his presumed infantile observation of the primal scene. But the 'Wolf Man' thought otherwise. He repudiates Freud's reconstruction of his psychopathology, but constantly reiterates his admiration for Freud.

If you look at everything critically, there isn't much in psycho-analysis that will stand up. Yet it helped me. He was a genius.

The 'Wolf Man' goes on to recall that his father had died before he entered upon treatment with Freud; that his relationship with his father had been poor because has father had preferred his sister; and that it was because of his father's death that he developed a transference to Freud which was so intense that he describes himself as 'worshipping' him.

In other words, the 'Wolf Man' attributes his improvement wholly to his relationship with Freud; to his having discovered a new 'father' who was more tolerant and accepting than his own; one who was prepared to listen to his intimate and sometimes shocking revelations for four years without criticism, revulsion or repudiation of him as a person.

A brief account of transference was given in Chapter 4. Since the 1950s, psycho-analysts have been moving away from Freud's instinct theories to what is unhappily called 'object-relations' theory; that is, towards attributing neurotic problems to early difficulties in interpersonal relationships rather than to blocked instinctual development. Freud originally used the term 'object' as signifying that towards which libido is directed for the purpose of obtaining sexual release. Objects are usually persons; but the term may refer to parts of persons, like the breast, or to substitutes for persons, like fetishes or animals. What has happened is a change of emphasis. Freud was primarily concerned with disinterring repressed infantile sexual phantasies which, he was convinced, were causally implicated in the arrest of the neurotic's libidinal development. Because his sexuality had remained in an infantile state, the neurotic was unable to achieve adult sexual satisfaction, which Freud regarded as the *sine qua non* of mental health. Freud of course realized that deprivation or disturbance in the individual's early relationships with parents were implicated in his arrested development; but his emphasis was upon treating the isolated individual by undoing repression and discovering phantasies or traumatic events dating from earliest childhood, as he professed to do in the case of the 'Wolf Man'. Freud defined the therapeutic aim of psycho-analysis as follows:

Its intention is, indeed, to strengthen the ego, to make it more independent of the super-ego, to widen its field of perception and enlarge its organization, so that it can appropriate fresh portions of the id. Where id was, there ego

111

shall be. It is a work of culture – not unlike the draining of the Zuider Zee (*SE*, XXII.80).

In this statement, there is not a word about improving the patient's interpersonal relationships.

The object-relations school of psycho-analysis is concerned with studying the kind of relationships made by the individual from infancy onward. It particularly emphasizes, as Freud originally did not, the importance of the child's tie with its mother. All psycho-analysts inherit from Freud the conviction that fulfilling sexual relationships are a major component of human health and happiness. But they assume that the ability to achieve satisfying sexual relationships depends upon the prior establishment of secure, loving ties with parents or other care-takers. With Freud, sex comes first, attachment afterwards. With John Bowlby, now established as the most important of the object-relations theorists, secure attachment comes first, sex afterwards.

The consequence of this change in emphasis is that modern psycho-analysts are particularly concerned with analysing transference. The patient who, in early childhood, has been misunderstood, rejected, or ill-treated, will tend to go through life expecting similar treatment from those he encounters. How can he possibly make a satisfactory sexual relationship if, at some level of which he is probably unconscious, he treats every woman as if he was expecting her to criticize or reject him? Moreover, he will exhibit similar attitudes towards the psycho-analyst. The way we were treated in early childhood is bound to condition our expectations of how others will treat us later. The task of the psycho-analyst is to point out such repetitions, and, by continually drawing the patient's attention to the false assumptions which he is making about the analyst, provide a corrective emotional experience, gradually transforming the relationship between them into one in which the patient feels accepted and understood. In severe cases, it may be that the patient never reaches this happy stage; or it may be that he is able to learn to trust the analyst, but is not able to transfer this trust to anyone else. In more favourable instances, the patient will transfer his new-found security to other people in the external world, and, because he is now able to confide in others, become capable of finding love and happiness.

This brief and simplified exposition may seem to be a diversion from the subject of Freud himself. It is not so, because it makes it possible to understand a vital part of Freud's legacy. Anyone who is ignorant of psycho-analysis and who reads the abbreviated account of Freud's description of his cases given in the last chapter might be forgiven for dismissing much of the psycho-analytic theory as nonsense. Apart from the 'Rat Man', the patients show either transient improvement or none at all. Some of Freud's reconstructions are bound to seem far-fetched. Moreover, many people today number among their acquaintances people whom they know to have been 'in analysis' for long periods, but who appear not to have lost all or any of their symptoms. Why do these people persist in pursuing an expensive treatment which appears to do little for them? Why do many psycho-analysts continue to include among their case load a number of patients who do not necessarily lose their symptoms? It is easy to be cynical; to suggest that, provided a patient wants to continue treatment and is prepared to go on paying for it, there is no reason for the psycho-analyst to discharge him. But most psycho-analysts are not short of patients; and it is much more rewarding to treat someone who shows convincing signs of improvement by losing symptoms than it is to continue with a patient who does not.

The situation is further complicated by the fact that the patients who seek psycho-analysis today are rather different from those who consulted Freud. Whereas Freud's patients sought help for clear-cut hysterical or obsessional symptoms, today's patients often consult the analyst for what Szasz has called 'problems in living'; difficulties in inter-personal relationships, or a generalized dissatisfaction with life. This has led to some dispute in psycho-analytic circles. Is the object of psycho-analysis reduction or abolition of neurotic symptoms, or is it the acquisition of self knowledge? Both are laudable aims, and both may be partially realized in the course of psycho-analysis. But is this all that patients are seeking?

113

What many people underestimate is the revolutionary nature of Freud's procedure, and the effect which this has, irrespective of either insight or the cure of symptoms. Psycho-analysis provides a unique experience which cannot be matched by any other situation in life. What other social circumstance supplies a dedicated listener who, for hour after hour, year after year, will provide a tolerant, understanding, accepting presence; a steadfast friend or substitute parent who never rejects, is never angry, and never punishes? Many psycho-analytic patients embark on treatment because they feel that no one has previously understood them or accepted them; or believe that they dare not reveal their true feelings to anyone because, if they do so, they will be rejected. Psycho-analysis may, at times, be a painful ordeal; but, even if the symptoms do not all disappear, the experience is often so rewarding that psycho-analysts complain that their principal difficulty is in terminating the analysis, not in persuading patients to persist. Freud encountered this difficulty with the 'Wolf Man' during the first period of his treatment, and eventually had to set a date on which the analysis must end.

Freud's technique, which demanded an attitude on the part of the analyst quite unlike that which conventionally obtained between doctor and patient, was, and is, much more important than his theories about infantile sexuality. We have seen that his theory of dreams, on which he so prided himself, cannot withstand critical scrutiny. Freud repeatedly misconceived what was important and what was questionable in his discoveries. His reconstruction of the 'Wolf Man's' infantile sexuality was unconfirmed guesswork. His acceptance of him as a person, his patience, his continuing care over a long period, were underestimated by Freud, yet vital.

In Chapter 4, it was suggested that Freud was reluctant to acknowledge that he became emotionally important to his patients because he wished to be regarded as a skilled technician, an impersonal investigator, a detached scientist. His way of dealing with transference was to treat it wholly as repetition: as a projection upon himself of characteristics which had belonged to the patient's parents and were nothing to do with him in reality. There are two objections to regarding transference only in this light. First, as suggested in Chapter 4, some patients exhibit positive feelings towards the analyst which they have never had before; feelings which they were unable to have towards their parents because the latter were indifferent, hostile or rejecting. Second, Freud was under-estimating the significance of what the long-term nature of his technique actually provided in the here-and-now. He thought that psycho-analysis was bound to be prolonged because of the time required to penetrate the secrets of the patient's infancy. But distressed, alienated people need and value someone whom they perceive as being perceptive, accepting, kind, and continuously concerned with them over a long period, whether or not this acceptance results in the relief of symptoms or in an increase in self-knowledge. In cases in which anything positive is achieved, this is the minimum which can be expected. It is an achievement which should not be underestimated. At best, psycho-analysis and the various forms of individual psychotherapy derived from it can provide insight, relief of distressing symptoms, and an increased capacity for making fruitful interpersonal relationships.

Modern psycho-analysts have recognized the difficulty of defining the exact nature of psycho-analysis. However, an attempt has been made to do so in terms of five basic assumptions. The first is that psycho-analysis is a general psychology which applies to normal human beings as well as to neurotics. Since we all have some neurotic symptoms, the difference between neurotic and normal is one of degree, not of kind.

Secondly, psycho-analysts accept Freud's construct of a 'mental apparatus' which receives stimuli from the external world and which also interacts with the internal physiological systems of the subject's body. Psycho-analysis differs from the kind of psychology employed by experimental psychologists in laboratories in that it is primarily concerned with the individual's subjective experience, and only secondarily with his overt behaviour.

Thirdly, psycho-analysis is concerned with adaptation; with

how the subject (or ego) deals with the stimuli impinging upon him both from without and from within. Psycho-analysts do not necessarily accept Freud's Nirvana principle; that is, they think of the organism as striving to reach equilibrium, but this may be a steady state in which conflicting stimuli are balanced one against the other rather than total discharge. Thus, conflict within the mind, conflict between competing stimuli like sex and hunger, or conflict between different parts of the mind like ego and super-ego, are essential aspects of psycho-analytic thinking. So is the notion of the ego using 'defence mechanisms' like repression, projection, denial, and sublimation as ways of coping with the pressures upon it. Psycho-analysis still has rather little to say about 'stimulus hunger': the need to search for stimuli when deprived of them.

Fourthly, psycho-analysts, when considering mental activity, follow Freud in subscribing to determinism. That is, they consider that mental events are subject to the laws of cause and effect. Quite where this leaves the question of free will is unclear. It is certainly possible to argue that neurotic symptoms, like phobias or obsessions, are strictly determined. But their abolition must surely result in the patient having greater freedom to make choices, and choosing is a voluntary act demanding will and intention. While recognizing that everyone has been subjected to genetic and environmental pressures which have restricted power of choice in some respects—for example, sexual orientation—social life would be impossible if we did not assume that we and other people are generally capable of making voluntary decisions and choices. Thomas Szasz, admittedly an unorthodox psycho-analyst, has defined the aim of psycho-analysis as being 'to increase the patient's knowledge of himself and others and hence his freedom of choice in the conduct of his life'.

Fifthly, psycho-analysis assumes that some aspects of mental life are inaccessible to consciousness. Although such mental contents may partially betray themselves in dreams, neurotic symptoms, slips of the tongue, and states of mind encountered in mental illness, most can only be brought into consciousness by the special techniques of recovery and interpretation which are an integral part of the psycho-analytic process. This, perhaps is as far as anyone can go today in trying to define what beliefs and theories are held in common by those calling themselves psycho-analysts.

12 The appeal of psycho-analysis

Freud has graduated from being a 'Modern Master' to being a 'Past Master'. It is now possible to discuss both his achievements and his limitations objectively, without being accused either of swallowing psycho-analysis whole as an uncritical disciple, or else of rejecting it because of personal resistance or lack of insight. Freud has not led us into the promised land, as his staunchest adherents hoped that he would. But Freud's ideas have exerted so powerful an influence that, as Ernest Gellner puts it, psycho-analysis has become 'the dominant idiom for the discussion of the human personality and of human relations'. How and why has this come about?

Freud certainly had many original ideas; but even the most inventive minds are indebted to their predecessors. The thinkers who are credited with causing revolutions in thought are those who appear at times when ideas have been around long enough for a new synthesis to be both possible and generally acceptable. Freud is still sometimes credited with having invented the unconscious; but, as L. L. Whyte demonstrated in *The Unconscious Before Freud*, 'the idea of unconscious mental processes was, in many of its aspects, conceivable around 1700, topical around 1800, and became effective around 1900'. Freud did not invent the idea of the unconscious, but he applied it clinically and made it operational.

L. L. Whyte lists a large number of philosophers, physicians, and others who accepted and promulgated the idea that unconscious processes played an important part in the mental life of man. Those who were most directly influential in shaping Freud's thought include the German physician C. G. Carus (1789–1869), who was a friend of Freud's favourite author Goethe. Carus wrote an influential book, *Psyche*, published in 1846, which began:

The key to the knowledge of the nature of the soul's conscious life lies in the realm of the unconscious. This explains the difficulty, if not the impossibility, of getting a real comprehension of the soul's secret.

Freud's library contained works by Carus, although the latter's name does not appear in the index to Freud's collected works.

Eduard von Hartmann (1842–1906), the author of *Philosophy of the Unconscious*, published in 1869, was another writer whom Freud consulted, Freud acknowledges similarities in their thinking in a footnote added in 1914 to *The Interpretation of Dreams* (*SE*, V.528).

In *An Autobiographical Study*, Freud particularly acknowledges his debt to G. T. Fechner (1801–87), a German psychologist whose ideas influenced Freud's conception that a main function of the mental apparatus was to restore tranquillity by discharging tensions caused by disturbing stimuli. Fechner's ideas are also referred to in *Beyond the Pleasure Principle* (*SE*, XVIII.8–9).

Freud's lack of interest in philosophy was mentioned in Chapter 1 of this book. In an essay entitled 'The Resistances to Psycho-Analysis', first published in 1925, Freud affirmed:

The philosophers' idea of what is mental was not that of psycho-analysis. The overwhelming majority of philosophers regard as mental only the phenomena of consciousness. For them the world of consciousness coincides with the sphere of what is mental (*SE*, XIX.216).

This curious and inaccurate statement hardly matches what he wrote in the same year in *An Autobiographical Study*:

Even when I have moved away from observation, I have carefully avoided any contact with philosophy proper. This avoidance has been greatly facilitated by constitutional incapacity. . . . The large extent to which psycho-analysis coincides with the philosophy of Schopenhauer—not only did he assert the dominance of the emotions and the supreme importance of sexuality but he was even aware of the mechanism of repression—is not to be traced to my acquaintance with his

119

teaching. I read Schopenhauer very late in my life. Nietzsche, another philosopher whose guesses and intuitions often agree in the most astonishing way with the laborious findings of psychoanalysis, was for a long time avoided by me on that very account; I was less concerned with the question of priority than with keeping my mind unembarrassed (*SE*, XX.59–60).

A number of writers, including Thomas Mann, Philip Rieff, and Henri Ellenberger, have claimed that Freud must have been more influenced by Schopenhauer and Nietzsche than he acknowledged or perhaps realized. Mann claimed that psychoanalytic concepts were Schopenhauer's ideas translated from metaphysics into psychology. Rieff points out that Freud's attack on religion, *The Future of an Illusion*, is closely similar to Schopenhauer's *Dialogue on Religion*. It was at the suggestion of the maverick analyst Groddeck that Freud adopted the term 'id', which Nietzsche had originally invented. Nietzsche's duality of Dionysian and Apollinian closely resembles Freud's duality of primary process and secondary process. The ideas of Schopenhauer and Nietzsche were widely discussed in intellectual circles. Indeed Freud, while a university student, belonged for five years to a Reading Society of the German Students of Vienna, described by Sulloway as 'a radical pan-German organization in which the views of Schopenhauer, Wagner, and Nietzsche were avidly discussed'.

Every writer concerned with ideas has had the mortifying experience of discovering that what he considered to be an original idea of his own is to be found in the works of another author whom he had forgotten having read. If Freud sometimes claimed priority to which he was not entitled, he is exemplifying his own theories of the wish-fulfilling tendencies of the unconscious rather than engaging in deliberate deception.

Freud is often linked with Darwin and Marx as being one of the three original thinkers who have most altered man's view of himself in the twentieth century. The appetite for books about Freud and his theories still seems to be insatiable, and, even fifty years after his death, bears witness to the pervasiveness of his influence. At the beginning of the twentieth century, when Freud's main theories about the mind were being formulated, Darwin's ideas on evolution and the descent of man had recently won acceptance. Darwin, by demonstrating that man was not a special creation, but simply the most highly evolved primate, had paved the way for a psychology which was not based upon the philosophy of mind, or upon perception, or upon conditioned reflexes, or upon man's spiritual qualities, but one which was rooted in his kinship with animals. The time was ripe for a psychology based upon 'instinct'; that is, upon the basic biological forces or 'drives' motivating the behaviour of both man and animals, of which sex is certainly one of the most important.

Darwin had even concluded that language, a distinctive form of social interaction peculiar to man, had originated from expressive cries emitted during courtship, gradually evolving into words capable of defining more and more complex emotions. As Frank Sulloway has pointed out in his study *Freud, Biologist of the Mind*, it was Darwin who 'singled out the biological importance of the instincts for survival and for reproduction, laid before the medical community a dynamic and dualist paradigm of instinct that seemed to encompass the whole of organic behaviour'.

Darwin had shaken man's self-esteem by demonstrating his kinship with other animals. Freud shattered it still further by asserting that man was far less a master in his own mental house than he had supposed. The voice of the intellect might be persistent as well as soft, but men were far more governed by emotion and irrationality than they commonly realized; and Freud affirmed that even man's loftiest achievements in the arts and philosophy were sublimations of primitive instinct.

Darwin's portrayal of man was 'reductive', in that he not only dispelled the notion of man as a special creation in God's image, but also tended to reduce highly complex behaviour to simple biological origins. Freud was attempting to do exactly the same thing; and one reason why psycho-analysis spread so widely was that it appeared to be in line with the new biology. Freud's debt to Darwin was certainly considerable, as he himself admitted.

Freud also belonged to the era in which physicists were beginning to discern the structure of matter. The electron was discovered in the 1890s. Soon, a multiplicity of subatomic particles made their appearance. It is hardly fanciful to say that, at the beginning of the century, scientific understanding was equated with reducing structures, including that of the mind, to their elementary constituents. This may explain why some of the deficiencies of psycho-analytic theory were overlooked or dismissed. As indicated earlier, Freud's attempt to explain art and religion in terms of sublimated infantile sexuality and escapist phantasy is profoundly unsatisfactory. Freud's purely reductive stance omits any consideration of synthesis, of the need to make new wholes out of apparently disparate entities, of Gestalt psychology, or of what Koestler later called 'bisociation'. Freud also omitted to study cognitive development, or to define social development in any other terms than those of psychosexual development within the nuclear family. He only felt that he was on solid ground when he had succeeded in reducing the mental to the physical, 'the indispensable organic foundation' upon which he insisted.

This uncompromising reductionism has a considerable emotional appeal. Any system of thought which is called 'scientific' and which promises a new understanding of human nature by getting down to a few basic essentials, is likely to appeal to those people who pride themselves on being hard-headed realists, undeceived by talk of altruism, self-sacrifice, disinterested love, or clap-trap about morality. Freud was expert at reducing all human striving to the lowest common denominator. It is not inappropriate to point out that this technique is also characteristic of Jewish humour. Those who subscribe to psycho-analysis as an all-embracing system of explaining human behaviour not only tend to pride themselves on being aggressively realistic and upon possessing esoteric knowledge denied to others, but also commonly use this knowledge in a manner reminiscent of the 'one-upmanship' techniques catalogued by Stephen Potter. 'I understand everything better than you do; you are neurotic, but I really know.' Carried to extremes, this results in the 'character assassination' referred to earlier in connection with Freud and Bullitt's biography of Woodrow Wilson.

Psycho-analysis has often been referred to as a religion, partly because of the intensity of the disputes within the movement which so often led to rebels leaving it and setting up rival schools, or splinter groups, in a manner reminiscent of religious sects. Freud always denied that psycho-analysis provided a *Weltanschauung* of its own, and devoted the last of his *New Introductory Lectures on Psycho-Analysis* to claiming that psycho-analysis did not depart from the criteria of science, and therefore looked at the world through scientific eyes. Yet, virtually everyone except a few fundamentalist Freudians agrees that psycho-analysis is very far from being a science, since its theories are not open to refutation and cannot be used for prediction. But psycho-analysis has certainly provided a belief system. In his last introductory lecture, Freud wrote that Marxism

> has acquired the energy and the self-contained and exclusive character of a *Weltanschauung*, but at the same time an uncanny likeness to what it is fighting against. . . . Any critical examination of Marxist theory is forbidden, doubts of its correctness are punished in the same way as heresy was punished by the Catholic Church (*SE*, XXII.180).

Exactly the same was true of psycho-analysis in its early days, although its heretics, Adler, Stekel, Jung, Rank, and many others, were not subjected to torture or execution, but only to character assassination by being labelled neurotic or psychotic. Some of the language used to describe such heretics is almost unbelievably intemperate. Today, there is a truce between the previously warring factions of the British Psycho-Analytical Society; but it is an armed truce, and, in private, psycho-analysts belonging to one of the three groups into which the Society is divided are apt to make scathing remarks about other psycho-analysts who are not of their persuasion. The delusion that one group rather than another is the guardian of psycho-analytic 'truth' is still regrettably evident.

As indicated earlier, Freud was inclined to derive intellectual curiosity and a passion for knowledge from infantile sexual researches, rather than accepting that man might possess a propensity for exploratory behaviour analogous to that shown by many other species. Perhaps this interpretation derived from his own childhood memory of penetrating his parents' bedroom out of curiosity, and of being ordered out by an angry father. Freud himself certainly possessed a huge appetite for knowledge, and a powerful drive to make sense out of the bewildering maze of mental phenomena. Freud attacked philosophy on the grounds that, unlike science, it attempted to present a picture of the universe which was too coherent, too lacking in gaps. Moreover, he affirmed, philosophy was of interest only to a few intellectuals, and was scarcely intelligible to anyone else. Yet Freud himself did not confine himself to an explanation of neurotic symptoms. As we have seen, from the earliest days of psycho-analysis onwards, he strove to create a coherent system of ideas which would not only explain all forms of mental illness, but also religion, art, literature, humour, the descent of man, and man's social organizations. The appeal of psycho-analysis, the fact that it became a movement rather than remaining as a type of medical treatment for neurosis, surely derives from its claim to explain so much. Psycho-analysis lacks many of the features usually associated with religion, but, in a secular age, in which those who could not subscribe to the old faiths often felt rootless and insecure, psycho-analysis offered an explanatory system which was eagerly embraced as a substitute.

It also offered membership of an esoteric brotherhood which consisted of those who had been analysed, if not by Freud himself, by one of his disciples, or by one of the disciples of his disciples. A great deal of psycho-analytic wisdom seems to have depended upon oral transmission rather than upon writings. Psycho-analysis, at least in its earlier days, seemed to proffer a secular form of salvation. Moreover, if patients did not get better, or if trainees did not whole-heartedly embrace all the principles which Freud had laid down, psycho-analysts were often able to convince them that it was their fault, not the fault of the system. This is typical of all esoteric systems of belief, from the Plymouth Brethen to the Moonies.

The widespread adoption of psycho-analysis was fostered by Freud's marvellously persuasive style of writing. Even when the ideas he is advancing do not stand up to scrutiny, it is still a pleasure to read him, even in translation. I cannot think of any other psycho-analytic writer who is his equal, although I can think of many who appear to be wilfully obscure. Jacques Lacan, the revolutionary French psycho-analyst who attempted to link psycho-analysis with linguistics, is the prime example. But when an author combines elegance of style, persuasiveness, and an absolute conviction of his own rightness, it is hard to resist him. Freud is often praised by Freudians for his apparent flexibility; for his willingness to alter his theories as psycho-analysis grew and developed. But the history of the psycho-analytic movement bears witness to Freud's intolerance of opposition. Although he himself might alter or develop his theories, virtually no one else was allowed to do so, with the possible exception of members of his supposedly loyal Committee, a small inner circle which included Karl Abraham and Ernest Jones. In his certainty of his own rightness, Freud resembled one of his severest critics, the philosopher of science, Karl Popper. It is interesting that Popper uses the same adversarial technique as did Freud to undermine his opponents.

Freud's confidence that his basic ideas were correct added considerably to his power to attract a large following, although it is out of keeping with a truly scientific stance. The majority of human beings are only too ready to follow a leader who professes complete conviction, since such a course relieves them from the anxiety inseparable from uncertainty, and from the effort of thinking for themselves. It is not difficult to point to recent political examples of leaders exhibiting single-minded confidence of a comparable kind, however narrowly based. As Norman Cohn demonstrated in *The Pursuit of the Millennium*, utter conviction lends charisma even to figures much less original and impressive than Freud.

Freudian theory made Western man suspicious of conduct previously regarded as virtuous, often with unfortunate consequences. In 1900 the person who displayed altruism and self-sacrifice would simply have been regarded as 'good'. Since Freud, people are inclined to suspect unselfishness as masochistic self-punishment, and altruism as concealing a wish to patronize. Unselfishness and generosity are still virtues; but Freud has made it easier for those who do not wish to cultivate these virtues to justify their avoidance of them. Celibacy used to be admired. Now it is invariably interpreted as concealing perversion or as an ignominious flight from sex, rather than as self-control or evidence of spiritual excellence. The Victorians were more, not less, tolerant of homosexual feelings, if not of homosexual practices, than we are. Tennyson's *In Memoriam*, his long lament over the death of his beloved friend Arthur Hallam, could not be published today except by a poet who had 'come out'; that is, who was openly and avowedly homosexual. Those who are certainly predominantly heterosexual, as was Tennyson, seem to be allowed less latitude than formerly in expressing passionate friendship involving their own sex. As Freud asserted that everyone is bisexual at some level, this seems odd. However, psychoanalysis has, on the whole, increased both understanding and tolerance for those who do not follow conventional sexual patterns. Sex may not be quite the prime mover which Freud thought it to be; but we do owe him a considerable debt for having lifted the covers of Victorian prudery and made sex into a subject which can be openly and seriously discussed.

Freudian theory has also increased tolerance in other respects. Because of Freud's insistence that the seeds of neurosis are sown in early childhood, we pay more attention to our children's emotional needs, and are, perhaps, more inclined to try and understand them rather than to punish them when they behave antisocially. The same is true of our attitudes to criminals. Although we are still almost totally ineffective at dealing with habitual criminals, there is a greater realization that savage punishments neither deter nor reform, and a greater inclination to perceive that antisocial conduct may reflect alienation from society or feelings of despair rather than innate wickedness.

Although psycho-analysis has not proved more effective than other forms of psychotherapy in the treatment of neurosis, Freud's technique of listening to distressed people over long periods has had a strikingly beneficial effect upon all forms of psychotherapy derived from psycho-analysis. As indicated earlier, even those who do not lose all their symptoms usually gain increased self-understanding and a sense of being accepted as persons which they may never have previously experienced. Freud's passion for investigation and his lack of therapeutic enthusiasm led, ironically, to his most important legacy. Anyone can give 'good advice' to people in distress. It was Freud who taught us how to listen.

Freud's excursions into fields outside the consulting room seem for the most part ill-judged. It requires a very dedicated Freudian to accept Freud's ideas about religion, anthropology, or art. It may even be that the status of psycho-analysis would be higher if Freud had not used his theories to try and explain so much in addition to neurosis, perversion, and psychosis. But perhaps it was unavoidable, given that he was determined to construct a psychology which applied as much to the normal person as it did to the neurotic. It is worth repeating Breuer's judgement, which was quoted in Chapter 1:

> Freud is a man given to absolute and exclusive formulations: this is a psychical need which, in my opinion, leads to excessive generalization.

What one can say with conviction is that, even if every idea which Freud put forward could be proven wrong, we should still be greatly in his debt. Although psycho-analysis is not a science in the same category as the 'hard' sciences of physics and chemistry, the history of ideas demonstrates that, in so far as our understanding of ourselves and the world can be said to increase, it progresses in the way that Popper claims for science; that is, by refutation of existing hypotheses. Freud was enormously inventive and ingenious. He did cause a revolution in the way we think. He produced a considerable number of hypotheses which, even when wrong, deserve serious con- sideration and detailed refutation. Eysenck dismisses psycho-analysis as unworthy of attention because it is unscientific. Medawar called it a 'stupendous intellectual confidence trick'. But psycho-analysis has had such an inescapable influence upon our thinking that it must resonate with something deep within us. At the very least, psycho-analysis deserves informed critical examination rather than simple dismissal. Perhaps the 'Wolf Man' was right when he said:

> Freud was a genius, there's no denying it. All those ideas that he combined in a system. . . . Even though much isn't true, it was a splendid achievement.

Further reading

Freud, Sigmund, *The Standard Edition of the Complete Psychological Works of Sigmund Freud*, translated from the German under the general editorship of James Strachey, in collaboration with Anna Freud, assisted by Alix Strachey and Alan Tyson, 24 vols. (London, 1953–74). Referred to throughout this book as *SE* followed by vol. no. and page: e.g. (*SE*, V.96).

Clark, Ronald W., *Freud: The Man and the Cause* (London, 1980). One of the three major biographies published in English. Workmanlike, thorough, readable.

Farrell, B. A., *The Standing of Psycho-Analysis* (Oxford, 1981). An appraisal of psycho-analysis by a philosopher who does not let his knowledge of, and sympathy with, the subject impair his critical stance.

Fisher, Seymour, and Greenberg, Roger P., *The Scientific Credibility of Freud's Theories and Therapy* (New York, 1977). A comprehensive review of all the important objective research into psycho-analytic theory and treatment undertaken before 1977. An indispensable work of reference.

Gay, Peter, *Freud: A Life for Our Time* (London, 1988). The most recent biography of Freud by a distinguished cultural historian. Gay is also a graduate of the Western New England Institute of Psychoanalysis and thus understands the subject from the inside.

Gellner, Ernest, *The Psychoanalytic Movement* (London, 1985). A malicious, sometimes unfair, but invariably funny attack upon psycho-analysis which seeks to explain the social needs and climate which fostered the acceptance of psycho-analysis and turned it from a medical treatment into a movement.

Horden, Peregrine, ed., *Freud and the Humanities* (London, 1985). A collection of papers originally given as the Chichele Lectures during 1984 under the auspices of All Souls College,

Oxford. The contributors include the art historian Ernst Gombrich, the Regius Professor of Greek at Oxford, Hugh Lloyd-Jones, and the late Richard Ellmann, biographer of James Joyce and Oscar Wilde.

Jones, Ernest, *Sigmund Freud: Life and Work*, 3 vols. (London, 1953–7). A classical biography by Freud's closest English adherent. Although Jones is too uncritical a disciple, and although subsequent biographies have uncovered more facts, this still remains indispensable.

Kline, Paul, *Fact and Fantasy in Freudian Theory* (London, 1972). Another valuable account of objective research into Freud's theories which supplements Fisher and Greenberg's book in a number of areas.

Masson, Jeffrey M., tr. and ed., *The Complete Letters of Sigmund Freud to Wilhelm Fliess, 1887–1904* (Cambridge, Mass. and London, 1985). These letters are the most important source book for understanding the development of psycho-analysis in its early stages. This is the first complete edition in English, since many of the letters (which were never intended for publication) were previously withheld or heavily censored by the guardians of the Freud archives.

McGuire, William, ed., *The Freud/Jung Letters* (London, 1974). A scrupulously edited, fascinating collection of letters which tell the sad story of how two original thinkers discovered each other, became deeply involved, both intellectually and emotionally, and then became gradually estranged, finally parting in bitterness.

Rieff, Philip, *Freud: The Mind of the Moralist* (London, 1960). An extremely intelligent American appraisal of Freud, with especial emphasis on Freud's place in the history of ideas. Rieff calls psycho-analysis 'the last great formulation of nineteenth-century secularism'.

Roazen, Paul, *Freud and His Followers* (New York, 1975). Between 1964 and 1967, Roazen succeeded in interviewing over seventy people who had known Freud personally. Roazen has a nose for scandal and an unrivalled knowledge of many of those who were closest to Freud, as well as being a scholarly chronicler of the psycho-analytic movement. There is a good deal of material here which cannot be found elsewhere, presented in highly readable form.

Rycroft, Charles, *A Critical Dictionary of Psychoanalysis* (London, 1968). Anyone puzzled by psycho-analytic terminology, as most of us sometimes are, will find Rycroft's book an invaluable source of accurate definitions which elegantly explain even the most obscure concepts.

Sulloway, Frank J., *Freud: Biologist of the Mind* (New York, 1979). A long, detailed, and important account of the biological origins of Freud's theories. Sulloway places Freud in the context of the history of ideas in unique fashion, and demolishes the myth that Freud was an isolated, heroic figure whose ideas were universally repudiated. Every modern Freudian scholar acknowledges a debt to Sulloway.

Whyte, Lancelot Law, *The Unconscious Before Freud* (London, 1962). Essential reading for anyone interested in the history of ideas. Whyte demonstrates that Freud's theories were the culmination of a cultural process extending over several centuries, and that many of his 'discoveries' had been anticipated by previous thinkers.

Wollheim, Richard, *Sigmund Freud* (London, 1971). Freud as a 'Modern Master'. A valuable exposition of Freud's theories of the mind by a distinguished philosopher. But Professor Wollheim is too convinced a Freudian to be entirely objective. Perhaps this is why there is little discussion of Freud's incursions into art, and an uncritical acceptance of Freud as a therapist.

Index

Abraham, Karl, 22, 57, 125
abreaction, 13
Adler, Alfred, 8, 123
aggression, 16, 43, 49–55, 58, 69–71
amnesia, infantile, 27, 67
anaclitic, 56–7
'Anna O.', see Pappenheim, Bertha
anthropology, 9, 84–7, 127
anxiety, 34–5
art, 6, 9, 72–82, 121–2, 127
Atkinson, J. J., 85
auto-erotism, 21, 43

Bowlby, John, 83, 87, 112
Breuer, Josef, 3–4, 8, 11–12, 127
Brown, Roger, 15
Brücke, Ernst, 2, 16
Brunswick, Ruth Mack, 106
Bullitt, William C., 73, 123
Byrd, Admiral, 93

Carus, C. G., 118–19
castration, castration complex, 24–5, 28
catharsis, 12
Charcot, Jean-Martin, 2, 11, 59
civilization, 52–3, 69, 84, 89–91
Cohn, Norman, 125
conflict, 12
counter-transference, 41, 95

Darwin, Charles, 84–7, 120–1
day-dream, 73, 80–2
death, 51–3, 90
defence, mechanisms of, 12, 116
depression, 43, 55, 57–9, 95, 104, 106
Doolittle, Hilda, 100
'Dora', 100–2
Dostoevsky, Feodor, M., 77–9, 106
dreams, 6, 19, 30–7, 67, 73, 75, 83, 95, 101, 105–6, 114, 116; anxiety, 34; 'convenience', 34; latent content, 33–4; manifest content, 33–4; traumatic, 34, 83
'dream-work', 33–4

ego, 43–54, 56–9, 111; bodily, 47
ego-ideal, 48–9, 59
ego-libido, 43
Ehrenzweig, Anton, 83
Einstein, Albert, 82
Ellenberger, Henri, 120
emotions, 11–16, 47
Eros, 52–3
Eysenck, Hans, 127

father: as seducer, 16–17; as authority, 24–7; primal murder of, 85–6
Fechner, G. T., 119
Fisher, Seymour, 27, 63, 107
Flechsig, Professor P. E., 61–2
Fliess, Wilhelm, 4, 8, 18, 23, 31, 68
form, aesthetic, 6, 71–2, 75
Frank, Joseph, 78–9
Frazer, Sir James, 84
'free association', 30, 38, 45, 73, 95–6
Freiberg, 1
Freud: Amalie (mother), 1; Anna (sister), 2; Anna (daughter) 3, 99–100; Jacob (father) 1, 17; Martha (wife), 2–3, 100; Mathilde (daughter), 3
FREUD, SIGMUND: as dualist, 44, 52; as linguist, 1, 2; as medical student, 2; as research zoologist, 2; birth, 1; cancer, 5; cardiac arrhythmia, 5; certainty, 8, 33, 102, 125; collecting habits, 6; death of, 1, 110; dedication to work, 4; determinism of, 2, 9; engagement, 2; Goethe prize, 6; impersonality, 7, 38, 40, 97, 114; indif-

ference to music, 6, 74; intolerance of dissent, 7, 125; Jewish allegiance, 1, 122; literary style, 6, 8–9, 125; marriage, 3; money, attitude to, 4, 99, 106; obsessional traits, 3–6, 9; personality, 3–6, 104; puzzlement about women, 24; reading, 2; scientific claims, 9, 15, 93–4; self-analysis, 23, 41; sex life, 3; smoking, 5; superstitions, 4–5; tendency to generalization, 8, 17, 33, 67, 127
Writings cited:
An Autobiographical Study, 119; 'Beyond the Pleasure Principle', 50, 119; *Delusions and Dreams in Jensen's 'Gradiva'*, 74; 'Dostoevsky and Parricide', 74; 'From the History of an Infantile Neurosis', 104; 'Fragment of an Analysis of a Case of Hysteria', 100; *Inhibitions, Symptoms and Anxiety*, 35; 'Instincts and their Vicissitudes', 49; *Jokes and their Relation to the Unconscious*, 68; *Leonardo da Vinci and a memory of his Childhood*, 74–7; 'Mourning and Melancholia', 55; *Moses and Monotheism*, 87–8; *New Introductory Lectures on Psycho-Analysis*, 123; 'On Narcissism: An Introduction', 44, 48, 56; 'Project for a Scientific Psychology', 16; *Studies on Hysteria* (with Josef Breuer), 3, 12, 17; *The Future of an Illusion*, 92–4, 120; *The Interpretation of Dreams*, 5, 31, 119; 'The Moses of Michelangelo', 6, 74–5, 79–80; 'The Psychogenesis of a Case of Homosexuality in a Woman', 102; *The Psychopathology of Everyday Life*, 65–72; 'The Resistances to Psycho-Analysis', 119; 'The Unconscious', 37; *Thomas Woodrow Wilson* (with William C. Bullitt), 73–4; *Totem and Taboo*, 84–7, 91

'Freudian slip', 65–8, 116

Gellner, Ernest, 118
Goethe, Johann Wolfgang, 2, 6, 118
Goya, Francisco, 83
Greenberg, Roger P., 27, 63, 107
Groddeck, Georg, 120
Groos, Carl, 71

Hallam, Arthur
'Hans', *see* 'Little Hans'
Hartmann, Eduard von, 119
hate, 44, 49
heaven, 53
homosexuality, 21, 27, 61–4, 75–6, 102–3, 110, 126
hypnosis, 11–12, 30, 38
hysteria, 2, 11–12, 15–17, 23, 32, 45, 101, 108; conversion hysteria, 8, 13

id, 46–9, 120
instincts, 48, 50–3, 69–70, 74–5, 121; death, 51–4, 74; destructive, 49, 54; duality of, 52; ego-instincts, 45; self-preservative, 44; sexual, 44–5, 74; instinctual impulse, 13, 19, 72
'Irma', 31

jokes, 68–72
Jones, Ernest, 4–5, 44, 101, 125
Jung, C. G., 4–5, 7–8, 16, 26, 41, 53, 60, 65, 67, 98, 123

Kant, Immanuel, 9
'Katharina', 17
Koestler, Arthur, 122
Krafft-Ebing, Richard von, 64

Lacan, Jacques, 125
Lamarck, Jean-Baptiste, 86, 88
latency, period of, 27–8
literature, 6, 9, 73–4, 77, 80, 82
'Little Hans' (Herbert Graf), 85, 100
Lusitania, 66

mania, manic-depressive, 43, 58–60, 69, 95

Index

Mann, Thomas, 87, 120
Marx, Karl, 120, 123
Masson, Jeffrey M., 18
Mauretania, see *Lusitania*
Medawar, Sir Peter, 10, 128
melancholia, 55–9, 95
Michelangelo, 6, 79
Mill, John Stuart, 9
Milner, Marion, 83
Moses, 87–8
mother, 21, 23–4, 26, 28, 76–7, 86–7, 112
mourning, 55–7

narcissism, 43–4, 48, 56, 58
neurosis, 2, 8, 11–18, 13, 21, 30, 65, 80, 82, 127; actual, 14; negative of perversion, 22; obsessional, 3–5; organic foundation of, 16, 20, 33, 122; traumatic, 13
Nietzsche, Friedrich, 120
Nirvana principle, 14, 16, 52, 116

Obholzer, Karin, 106
object-libido, 43, 55–8
object-relations, 111–12
objects, transitional, 36
obsessional: neurosis, 3–4, 13, 45, 90, 108; rituals, 67, 89; superstitions, 4–5; thoughts, 103–4, 106; traits of personality, 3–6, 9, 44, 90, 110
'oceanic feeling', 92–3
Oedipus complex, 23–8, 55, 85–6
orgasm, 16, 35

Pappenheim, Bertha ('Anna O.'), 11
paranoia, 24, 60–4
parsimony, 4, 23
Pavlov, Ivan Petrovich, 49
penis, penis envy, 20, 24–6, 76
perversion, sexual (deviation) 8, 21–2, 43, 64, 74, 127; exhibitionism, 21; fetishism, 21, 28; sado-masochism, 21, 28, 54, 71, 77; voyeurism, 21
Pfister, Oskar
phantasy, 16–19, 30, 39–40, 75–8, 80–3, 98

play, 27, 51, 71, 80–3
pleasure principle, 46–7, 50–1, 81–2
Popper, Karl, 9, 125, 127
'primal scene', 105, 110
primary process, 37, 46, 81
psycho-analysis, 3, 6, 8, 9, 10, 16–17, 32, 108–17; aim of, 111–12; and art, 73; and biography, 73; as 'character assassination', 74, 122–3; as esoteric belief system, 124–5; as exploration of phantasy, 18–19; as general theory of mind, 9, 32, 65, 84, 115, 122, 127; as hermeneutic system, 10; as history, 41–2; as theory of neurosis, 12, 115–16; as treatment, 30, 38, 95–107, 127; as unique situation, 40, 114; as *Weltanschauung*, 9, 123–4; basic assumptions of, 115–17; outcome of, 108–9
psychosis, 58–64, 92, 95, 127

Quincey, Thomas de, 68

Rank, Otto, 8, 123
'Rat Man' (Ernst Lanzer), 100, 103–5, 113
reaction-formation, 23
reality principle, 50, 81–2
religion, 9, 84–94, 120, 122–3, 127
repression, 12–13, 19, 27, 32, 34, 37–8, 45, 67, 69, 74, 84, 101, 116
resistance, 45, 118–19
Rieff, Philip, 120
Rogers, Carl, 98
Rolland, Romain, 92
Rycroft, Charles, 22, 36, 67–8, 83

Sade, Marquis de, 23
Schatzman, Morton, 63
schizophrenia, 43, 60, 95
Schopenhauer, Arthur, 119–20
Schreber, Daniel Gottlob Moritz, 62
Schreber, Daniel Paul, 60–4, 100
science, 9, 42, 53, 83, 93–4, 122, 127–8

secondary process, 37, 46, 81
seduction, sexual, 16–18, 20
Sellin, Ernest, 88
sex, sexual development, emotions, impulses, instincts, 14–22, 28–9, 43, 73, 89–90; bisexuality, 22, 77, 126; infantile sexuality, 15, 17–29, 32–35, 60, 64, 74, 77, 98, 144; as instigating dreams, 32–3; stages of: anal, 20, 22–3; genital, 20; oral, 20, 22, 57; phallic, 20, 22, 24; premature sexual experience, 15–16
Shakespeare, William, 2, 6, 77
Signorelli, Luca, 66
Smith, Robertson, 84
Stekel, Wilhelm, 8, 123
stimulus hunger, 14, 116
Strakhov, Nicolay N., 77
sublimation, 72, 74–5, 80, 116, 122
Sulloway, Frank J., 121
super-ego, 26, 46, 48–9, 54, 58, 111
Swinburne, Algernon, 52
symbolism, 33, 35–7
Szasz, Thomas, 113, 115

Tennyson, Alfred Lord, 126
Timpanaro, Sebastiano, 67

Tolstoy, Leo N. 77
totem, totemism, 85–7
transference, 37–42, 95, 98, 111–12, 114–15
'transitional objects', 36
trauma, 13, 15, 19, 34, 50, 83; traumatic dreams, 34, 50, 83; traumatic neurosis, 13, 50
Turgenev, Ivan S., 77

unconscious, 11, 27, 33, 37, 41, 45–6, 73, 97, 118–20

Vienna, 1–3, 53, 64
Vinci, Leonardo da, 28, 75–7

Wagner, Richard, 120
Whyte, Lancelot Law, 118
Wilson, Woodrow, 73–4
Winnicott, Donald W., 36, 83
wish-fulfilment, 32–5, 78, 81, 83, 92–3, 120
Wittgenstein, Ludwig, 9
'Wolf Man' (Sergei Pankejeff), 100, 104–6, 110–11, 114, 128
Woolf, Virginia, 73

Zweig, Stefan, 78

JUNG

by

A NTHONY S TEVENS

To Chuck and Sue Schwartz

Preface

To give a comprehensive account of Jung and his Psychology (commonly referred to as *analytical psychology* to distinguish it from Freud's *psychoanalysis* and from *experimental psychology*, the pure science of the academics) in a slim volume of 128 pages is a tall order. Jung was both a polymath and prolific writer: in addition to psychology, psychiatry, and medicine, he had an encyclopaedic knowledge of mythology, religion, philosophy, gnosticism, and alchemy, knew English, French, Latin, and Greek, as well as his native German, and was at home in the literature of each. Although he carried this massive erudition with a cheerful lack of pomposity, it is evident in everything he wrote; and since he was not good at organizing his material, *The Collected Works of C. G. Jung* in twenty large volumes afford a daunting prospect to the uninitiated reader.

Jung recognized his failings as a communicator ('Nobody reads my books', he said, and 'I have such a hell of a trouble to make people see what I mean'), but this awareness did not prompt him to revise his work in the same systematic way as Freud. Consequently, much time and labour are required to understand Jung from his original papers and books, and while there can be no escape from the effort involved if one wishes to stake one's claim to a portion of Jung's rich legacy, the task can be made less arduous by a concise introduction of the type this small book is meant to provide.

Acknowledgements

I should like to express my thanks to Routledge and the Princeton University Press for permission to quote from *The Collected Works of C. G. Jung*; to Random House, Inc. for permission to quote from *Memories, Dreams, Reflections* by C. G. Jung, recorded and edited by Aniela Jaffé; and to Routledge for permission to reproduce the diagram on p. 34 from *On Jung*.

I must also thank my secretary, Norma Luscombe, for word processing the original manuscript with infinite care and goodwill, and Mary Worthingon for her skilful editing of the final product.

Contents

1 The man and his psychology   1

2 Archetypes and the collective unconscious   32

3 The stages of life   44

4 Psychological types   66

5 Dreams   81

6 Therapy   96

7 Jung's alleged anti-Semitism   113

8 The summing-up   123

   Further reading   129

   Index   133

1   The man and his psychology

Jung was a man of paradox. In one sense he was an individualist, a great eccentric. In another he was the living embodiment of the universal man. He strove to realize in his own life his full human potential; but he was determined, at the same time, to live in an uncompromisingly unique way. If this meant upsetting people, as was often the case, he did not, on the whole, seem to mind. 'To be normal', he said, 'is the ideal aim of the unsuccessful.'

Although considering himself a rational scientist, he was willing to give his attention to matters conventionally regarded as irrational or esoteric, and he was not unduly perturbed on those occasions when such interests put him beyond the scientific pale. In his view, to adopt an exclusively rational attitude to human psychology was not only inadequate but, in the light of history, preposterous. He had to keep faith with the truth as he saw it, and it was not his fault if this led him into realms of theory and experience which were deeply at variance with the prejudices and preoccupations of his time. 'I feel it is the duty of one who goes his own way to inform society of what he finds on his voyage of discovery,' he wrote.

Not the criticism of individual contemporaries will decide the truth or falsity of these discoveries, but future generations. There are things that are not yet true today, perhaps we dare not find them true, but tomorrow they may be. So every man whose fate it is to go his individual way must proceed with hopefulness and watchfulness, ever conscious of his loneliness and its dangers.   (*CW* VII, para. 201)

This sense of being drawn by destiny to swim against the prevailing tide makes him a richly intriguing character. And it means that any book on Jungian psychology has to take full account of the life and personality of its founder, for, more than any other psychologist, Jung's understanding of humanity grew directly out of his understanding of himself.

Throughout his long life, Jung remained a deeply introverted man, more interested in the inner world of dreams and images than

1

in the outer world of people and events. From childhood he possessed a genius for introspection which enabled him to attend closely to experiences proceeding on or below the threshold of consciousness—experiences of which the great majority of us remain almost completely unaware. This gift was derived, at least in part, from the peculiar circumstances of his birth and upbringing.

Background

Born in the hamlet of Kesswil on the Swiss shore of Lake Constance on 26 July 1875, Jung was the only son of the village pastor, the Reverend Paul Achilles Jung and Emilie Jung, née Preiswerk. His grandfather, Carl Gustav Jung (1794–1864), after whom he was christened, was a much respected physician, who became Rector of Basel University and Grand Master of the Swiss Lodge of Freemasons. He was rumoured to be the illegitimate son of Goethe. Though he bore a strong physical resemblance to the great poet, this is probably a legend and not fact.

Jung's mother was the youngest daughter of Samuel Preiswerk (1799–1871), a well-known but eccentric theologian, who devoted his life to studying Hebrew in the belief that it was the language spoken in heaven. He was an early advocate of Zionism, had visions, and held conversations with the dead. Right up to the time of her marriage, Emilie was obliged to sit behind him as he composed his sermons in order to stop the devil peering over his shoulder. Most male members of the large Preiswerk family were clergymen, who shared Samuel's preoccupation with the occult. This Jung–Preiswerk mixture of medicine, theology, and spiritualism was to have its influence on Carl's intellectual development.

The family moved twice during Jung's childhood, first to Laufen, near the Falls of the Rhine, when he was six months old, and then to Klein-Hüningen, just outside Basel, when he was four. Neither of the large vicarages which they inhabited provided a happy environment for a growing child. In his autobiography, *Memories, Dreams, Reflections*, Jung describes the home atmosphere as 'unbreathable': he says he was oppressed with a pervasive sense of death, melancholy, and unease, and with 'dim intimations of trouble' between his parents. He tells us that they did not share the same bedroom and that he, Carl, slept with his father. When he was 3, his mother had a breakdown for which she had to spend several months in hospital, and this enforced separation at a critical stage in his development seems to have affected Jung for the rest of his life. This is not an unlikely consequence, for, as has been well established by John Bowlby and his followers, the despair displayed by young children on loss of their mother is a normal response to frustration of their absolute need for her presence. Should this disaster occur, children usually manage to survive, it is true, but at the cost of developing a defensive attitude of emotional detachment, and by becoming self-absorbed and self-reliant to an unusual degree. Typically, they are left with lasting doubts about their capacity to elicit care and affection. They also tend to become odd and aloof in manner, which does not endear them to others. Although Carl was cared for by an aunt and a maid while his mother was away, he recalled being 'deeply troubled' by her absence: he suffered from nervous eczema and had terrifying dreams. 'From then on,' he says, 'I always felt mistrustful when the word "love" was spoken. The feeling I associated with "woman" was for a long time that of innate unreliability' (*MDR* 23).

Jung's father was a kind, tolerant man, but his son experienced him as powerless, and emotionally immature. Quite early in his ministry, Paul Jung seems to have lost his faith, but, lacking any alternative source of income, felt compelled to persevere with his parish duties. The strain of keeping up the appearance of piety while lacking all religious conviction helped to turn him into a querulous hypochondriac whom it was difficult for his wife and son to love or respect.

An only child until his sister Gertrud was born in 1884, Carl was unhappy at school, feeling alienated both from his companions and from his inner self: his rather schizoid (i.e. withdrawn, aloof, and self-absorbed) manner made him unpopular, and the school environment was one in which he just could not flourish. A sense of personal singularity was aggravated by traumatic incidents, as when a master accused him of plagiarizing an essay which he had composed with immense care. When he protested his innocence, his schoolmates sided with the master. Such experiences made him feel 'branded' and utterly alone. For a long period he dropped out altogether, having developed a proneness to fainting attacks after a blow on the head when knocked over by another boy. (As he lay on the ground, much longer than necessary, he thought to himself, 'Now you won't have to go to school any more.') He spent as much time as he could on his own. 'I remained alone with my thoughts. On the whole I liked that best. I played alone, day-dreamed or strolled in the woods alone, and had a secret world of my own' (*MDR* 58).

This secret world compensated for his isolation. The fantasies and rituals common to childhood assumed a heightened intensity for him, and they influenced the rest of his life. For example, his adult delight in studying alone in a tower he built for himself at Bollingen on the upper lake of Zürich was anticipated by a childhood ritual in which he kept a carved manikin in a pencil box hidden away on a beam in the vicarage attic. From time to time, he visited the manikin and presented him with scrolls written in a secret language to provide him with a library in the fastness of his attic retreat. This gave Carl a feeling of 'newly won security' which sustained him through his father's irritable moods, his mother's depressive invalidism, and his 'alienation' at school. 'No one could discover my secret and destroy it. I felt safe, and the tormenting sense of being at odds with myself was gone' (*MDR* 34).

Another childhood ritual prepared him for his later insights into the importance of *projection* in psychology. It was an imaginative game which he played as he sat on a large stone in the garden. He would intone, 'I am sitting on top of this stone and it is under-neath.' Immediately, the stone would reply, 'I am lying here on this slope and he is sitting on top of me.' Then he would ask himself, 'Am I the one who is sitting on the stone, or am I the stone on which *he* is sitting?' This left him with 'a feeling of curious and fascinating darkness', but he knew that his secret relationship with the stone held some unfathomable significance (*MDR* 33). In this game we can trace the origins of Jung's mature insight into the mysteries of alchemy—that the alchemists had *projected* the contents of their own psyches into the materials on which they worked in their laboratories.

Jung's adult delight in solitude, his alchemical studies, and his research into the dynamics of psychic transformation were also foreshadowed in an adolescent fantasy which entertained him as he walked each day from the vicarage at Klein-Hüningen to the school he attended in Basel. It was a vision of an ideal world in which everything would be better than it was. There would be no school and life could be arranged exactly as he wished. On a rock rising out of a lake sat a well-fortified castle with a tall keep, a watchtower, surrounded by a small medieval city, ruled by a council of elders. The castle was Carl's home. Here he lived as Justice of the Peace, emerging only occasionally 'to hold court'. In the harbour lay his personal two-masted schooner, armed with an array of small cannon.

The crux of the fantasy was the keep: it contained a wonderful secret of which Carl was the sole possessor. Inside the tower, extending from the battlements down to the vaulted cellar, was a copper column as thick as a man's arm: at the top were fine branches or filaments extending into the air. These extracted a 'spiritual essence' from the atmosphere which the copper column drew down into the cellar, where there was a laboratory in which he transformed the airy substance into gold. 'This was certainly no mere conjuring trick, but a venerable and vitally important secret of nature which had come to me I know not how and which I had to conceal not only from the council of elders but, in a sense, also from myself' (*MDR* 87).

The need to create a citadel in which to hide from the world is characteristic of people with a schizoid disposition. Young Carl's castle was defensively fortified and only tenuously connected to the mainland by a narrow isthmus cut through by a broad canal, with a drawbridge over it. Later, he began building model castles, surrounded by fortified emplacements, and he spent hours studying the virtually impregnable fortifications of Vauban.

Within the security of his inner citadel, Carl experienced himself as made up of two separate personalities, which he referred to as 'No. 1' and 'No. 2' respectively. No. 1 was the son of his parents who went to school and coped with life as well as he could, while No. 2 was much older, remote from the world of human society, but close to nature and animals, to dreams, and to God. He conceived No. 2 as 'having no definable character at all—born, living, dead, everything in one, a total vision of life' (*MDR* 92). As a psychiatrist he came to understand that these two personalities were not unique to himself but present in everyone. However, he

5

acknowledged that he was apparently more aware of them than most, particularly of No. 2. 'In my life No. 2 has been of prime importance, and I have always tried to make room for anything that wanted to come from within' (*MDR* 55). Much later he was to rename these two personalities the ego and the Self and to maintain that the play and counter-play between them constitutes the central dynamic of personality development.

He believed that his No. 2 personality conferred on him a privilege denied to his unfortunate father, namely, direct access to the mind of God. This was confirmed for him by the revelatory nature of his dreams, which contained images (such as that of an underground phallic deity which occurred when he was only 3) which he knew must derive from a source beyond himself, and by a powerful vision, which he struggled unsuccessfully to resist, of the Almighty seated on a golden throne defecating on the roof of Basel Cathedral (which signified to him, not unreasonably, that God had scant respect for His Church). Such revelations made him intolerant of his father's spiritual perplexity and gave rise to heated discussions between them. Whenever Carl tackled him with religious questions the pastor became irritable and defensive: 'You always want to *think*,' he complained. 'One ought not to think, but *believe*.' The boy reflected inwardly, 'No, one must experience and *know*!' But aloud he said, 'Give me this belief.' Whereupon his father merely shrugged and turned away.

Matters came to a head with Carl's confirmation, for which his father prepared him. He reached the pinnacle of religious initiation and was appalled to find that he experienced nothing whatsoever. An unbridgeable gulf opened between him and his father, for whom he felt 'a most vehement pity'. 'All at once I understood the tragedy of his profession and his life . . . I saw how hopelessly he was entrapped by the Church and its theological teaching . . . I now found myself cut off by the Church and from my father's and everybody else's faith' (*MDR* 64–5).

Whereas other boys in similar circumstances might have turned to their peers for support, Carl Jung, possessing no friends, turned inwards to embrace his 'No. 2', the Self. Throughout his adolescence he experienced the Self as God-like and the strength of his commitment to this internal 'other' took precedence over all outer relationships. He did not feel himself to be among people, but alone with God.

Inevitably, this confirmed him not in the Church but in his isolation: 'Other people all seemed to have totally different concerns. I felt completely alone with my certainties. More than ever I wanted someone to talk to, but nowhere did I find a point of contact... Why has no one had similar experiences to mine? I wondered... Why should I be the only one?' (*MDR* 71).

He cured himself of his fainting attacks when one day he overheard his father telling an acquaintance about his grave anxiety for his son's future. He returned to school and applied himself to his studies. Lacking all communication with like minds, he turned to literature, philosophy, and the history of religion. Heraclitus was to prove a lifelong favourite, as were Goethe and Meister Eckhart. He was much excited by Schopenhauer's *The World as Will and Idea*, which, together with Kant's *Critique of Pure Reason*, brought him such illumination that, he says, it revolutionized his attitude to the world and to life. In Goethe's *Faust* he found a legendary equivalent of his own No. 2 personality and this not only heightened his feeling of inner security but gave him, rather belatedly, a 'sense of belonging to the human community' (*MDR* 93).

Student years

Jung enrolled as a student at Basel University in 1895. It is characteristic of him that his decision to study natural science and medicine was determined not so much by his reading as by his dreams. Student life seems to have had a liberating effect on him, as did the premature death of his father at the age of 54, when Jung was only 21. ('He died in time for you,' his mother commented darkly.) 'I now began to display a tremendous appetite on all fronts. I knew what I wanted and went after it. I also became noticeably more accessible and communicative' (*MDR* 93).

One idea that Jung borrowed from Heraclitus was to be of crucial importance to him: the notion that all entities possess an inherent tendency to turn into their opposite. This tendency Heraclitus called *enantiodromia* (lit. 'running counter to'). Jung believed it to be characteristic of all dynamic systems, and saw the human family as a prime example: as children grow up, they display a propensity to compensate in their own lives for the failings of their parents. This tendency was particularly apparent in Jung himself, and his life may be understood in many ways as an effort to make good his father's deficiencies.

Whereas Paul Jung was spiritually timid, intellectually incurious, and inclined to accept dogma, showed signs of emotional immaturity, and ducked the major issues of his life, Carl, by contrast, was to display spiritual courage and intellectual rigour, resisted dogma wherever he encountered it, spent his life refining techniques for the development of the personality, and was disposed to confront all important issues head on, even when this meant courting unpopularity or disapproval.

The same compensatory propensity turned him into a lifelong gnostic (Greek, *gnostikos*, one who knows)—one dedicated to knowing the reality of the psyche through direct experience and personal revelation. It was this quest for gnosis which led him to grant fundamental importance to his dreams, fantasies, and visions, to attempt to understand them through the study of literature, philosophy, and religion, and, ultimately, to adopt psychiatry as a career.

A crucial dream came shortly after he commenced his studies at Basel. He dreamt that it was night-time and he was making painful headway through dense fog against a mighty wind, his hands cupped round a tiny light, which threatened to go out at any moment. Feeling there was something behind him, he glanced backwards and saw that he was being followed by a gigantic black figure. He was terrified, but knew he would be all right as long as he could keep his little light flickering through the murky night and the wind. 'When I awoke,' he says, 'I realized at once that the figure was a "spectre of the Brocken", my own shadow on the swirling mists, brought into being by the little light I was carrying. I knew, too, that this little light was my consciousness, the only light I have. My own understanding is the sole treasure I possess, and the greatest' (*MDR* 93).

His dedication to scholarship, which was to remain with him all his life, became apparent in his student years, with the result that he qualified in the shortest possible time. Emerging from his social isolation, he joined the Basel branch of the Swiss student Zofingia Society, and began to discover his capacity to influence people through the force and originality of his ideas. Significantly, the title of the first paper he presented before the Society was 'On the Limits of the Exact Sciences' in which he attacked scientists for their inflexible materialism. In a later talk, he proposed that the soul, though immaterial and existing outside space and time, should nevertheless prove susceptible to empirical investigation through research into the phenomena of hypnotism, somnambulism, and mediumistic communication. His presentations drew large audiences and provoked lively discussion.

Determined to put his ideas to the test, he began while still a student to attend and record the seances of a young medium who was also a cousin, Hélène Preiswerk. His meticulously detailed observations collected over a period of two years subsequently formed the basis of his doctoral dissertation 'On the Psychology and Pathology of So-Called Occult Phenomena' presented at Basel University in 1902.

His approach to this subject was influenced by an earlier study by Theodore Flournoy (1854–1920) of a medium called Catherine Muller (better known under her pseudonym, Helen Smith), who, in the trance state, gave details of her previous lives. Flournoy concluded that her utterances were 'romances of the subliminal imagination', and that they were evidence of the myth-making powers of the unconscious mind.

Two aspects of his cousin's performances particularly impressed Jung. One was how real her 'spirits' seemed to her: 'I see them before me,' she told him, 'I can touch them, I speak to them about everything I wish as naturally as I'm talking to you. They must be real' (*CW* I, para. 43). The other was the way in which a quite different, more dignified personality emerged when Hélène was in a trance. Her 'control' spirit, who said her name was 'Ivenes', spoke in perfect High German instead of Hélène's customary Basel dialect. Jung concluded that 'Ivenes' was the mature, adult personality that was developing in Hélène's unconscious. The seances provided a means through which this development could proceed.

The importance of this study for Jung was greater than the doctorate it earned him. In it we can detect the origins of two ideas which were to become central to the practice of analytical psychology: (1) that part-personalities or 'complexes' existing in the unconscious psyche can 'personate' in trances, dreams, and hallucinations, and (2) that the real work of personality development proceeds at the unconscious level.

These ideas, in turn, gave rise to (1) a therapeutic technique (*active imagination*) and (2) a teleological concept (*individuation*): the notion that the goal of personal development is *wholeness*, i.e. to become as complete a human being as personal circumstances allow. We shall return to these issues later on.

Jung's decision to be a psychiatrist came towards the end of his medical studies when he dipped into Krafft-Ebing's *Textbook of Psychiatry*. The Preface alone had such an impact on him that his heart began to pound and he had to stand up to draw a deep breath. What excited him was Krafft-Ebing's description of the psychoses (major mental illnesses such as schizophrenia and severe manic-depression in which sufferers are deprived of their reason) as 'diseases of the personality' and his statement that books about psychiatry must, of necessity, be stamped with a subjective character.

Jung tells us that 'in a flash of illumination' he saw psychiatry as the only possible profession: 'Here alone the two currents of my interest could flow together and in a united stream dig their own bed. Here was the empirical field common to biological and spiritual facts, which I had everywhere sought and nowhere found. Here at last was the place where the collision of nature and spirit became a reality' (*MDR* 111).

Years of apprenticeship

When Jung informed his tutors and fellow students that he proposed to specialize in psychiatry, they were shocked, for they felt he would be wasting his talents: psychiatry was the least respected speciality in medicine and they believed Jung could have a promising future as a physician. 'My old wound, the feeling of being an outsider, and of alienating others, began to ache again' (*MDR* 111). However, having obtained his medical degree with distinction at the end of 1900, he had the good fortune to be taken on to the staff of the Burghölzli Psychiatric Hospital in Zürich as an assistant to Eugen Bleuler (1857–1939), one of the outstanding psychiatrists of his time, and destined to enter history as the

10

originator of the term schizophrenia. The Burghölzli enjoyed an excellent reputation as the Psychiatric Clinic of Zürich University and Jung regarded the years he spent there as an invaluable apprenticeship. Bleuler was quick to recognize Jung's brilliance and did much to advance his career, promoting him to be his deputy, making him head of the out-patient department, and arranging his appointment as lecturer in psychiatry and psychotherapy at Zürich University. More important still, Bleuler set him to work on Galton's word-association test. This research was to earn Jung considerable fame in the world of psychology as well as the friendship of Sigmund Freud.

The word-association test, with which all students of psychology are familiar, was devised by Sir Francis Galton (1822-1911) and developed by Wilhelm Wundt (1832-1920). The procedure is simple. The experimenter reads out to the subject a series of words from a carefully prepared list, pausing after each word to allow the subject to respond with the first word that comes to mind. The response word is recorded together with the time, in seconds, taken to elicit the response. When all the words have been presented, the procedure is repeated, the subject being asked to respond with the same words as on the previous occasion.

One researcher who worked on the test before Jung, Theodor Ziehen, had already demonstrated that a prolonged reaction time occurred when a stimulus word was associated in the subject's mind with some disagreeable or disturbing idea. When all words resulting in delayed responses in a given subject were gathered together it was sometimes possible to detect in them a cluster of related ideas—what Ziehen called 'an emotionally charged complex of representations'. This finding particularly intrigued Jung because his work on Hélène Preiswerk's trances had already alerted him to the existence of part-personalities made up of dissociated unconscious components similar to those described as 'subconscious fixed ideas' by the French psychologist, Pierre Janet (1859-1947), under whom Jung studied briefly in Paris, on leave from the Burghölzli, in 1902. These Jung identified with Ziehen's 'complexes', and when he read Freud's *The Interpretation of Dreams* (1900) he recognized them again in the 'repressed wishes' and 'traumatic memories' which Freud held to be responsible for neurotic symptoms and for the content of dreams.

Jung says that dominating his research interests was one burning question: what actually takes place inside the mentally ill? Unlike the majority of psychiatrists before or since, he gave serious attention to what his schizophrenic patients actually said and did, and was able to demonstrate that their delusions, hallucinations, and gestures were not simply 'mad' but full of psychological meaning. For example, he discovered that one old lady, who had spent the fifty years of her incarceration in the Burghölzli making stitching movements as if she was sewing shoes, had been jilted by her lover just before she became ill: as Jung was able to discover, he was a cobbler.

Although Jung believed psychotic phenomena were associated with the presence of a biochemical toxin circulating in the patient's bloodstream, he nevertheless argued that schizophrenia could be understood in psychoanalytic terms as 'an introversion of libido'—the libido being withdrawn from the outer world of reality and invested in the inner world of myth-creation, fantasy, and dreams. The schizophrenic, he maintained, was a dreamer in a world awake. He published his observations in *The Psychology of Dementia Præcox* in 1907, which added to his already considerable reputation as a research psychiatrist.

Friendship with Freud

Realizing that his experimental findings provided objective support for Freud's theory of *repression*, Jung sent him a copy of his book *Studies in Word-Association* on its publication in 1906. Freud's enthusiastic response encouraged Jung to go to Vienna to meet him in March 1907. They got on so well that they talked without interruption for thirteen hours. There is no doubt that they were intellectually infatuated with one another and the friendship which blossomed between them, largely sustained by correspondence, lasted for nearly six years.

Like Bleuler, Freud was impressed by Jung's energy, enthusiasm, and commitment. He became powerfully attached to him, recognizing him as 'the ablest helper to have joined me thus far' and seeing him as his probable successor as leader of the psychoanalytic movement. Although Freud was only 50 when they met, he was something of a hypochondriac, and had a superstitious fear that he had only twelve years longer to live. Securing 'the succession' was thus a high priority for him, and, on the face of it, Jung was an excellent choice for the role. He had a first-rate mind, was a successful psychiatrist working at one of Europe's most respected hospitals, and, perhaps most important of all, he was not Viennese and he was not a Jew. Freud was acutely aware of the danger that anti-Semitism, associated with public disgust at his ideas on infantile sexuality, could result in the widespread rejection, or even suppression, of psychoanalysis, and he hoped that the adherence of a Swiss Christian of Jung's stature could help rescue his movement from this fate.

In addition, Jung was able to make significant contributions to psychoanalytic theory and practice. Not only did his word-association experiments provide hard empirical evidence for the existence and power of unconscious complexes, but his work with schizophrenics carried psychoanalytic concepts into areas beyond Freud's reach. (Freud trained as a neurologist and had little psychiatric experience, having worked only briefly as a *locum tenens* in a mental hospital.) Moreover, Jung infected Freud with his enthusiasm for the study of mythology and comparative religion, though with potentially disastrous consequences, for the conclusions that both men drew from these studies were explosively at variance with one another.

On Jung's side, the desire for Freud's friendship was as much personal as professional. In the older, more experienced man, he found a mentor—a distinguished colleague who represented the intellectually courageous father that his own father, the doubting theologian, was not. Both men understood this. 'Let me enjoy your friendship not as one between equals but as that of father and son,' wrote Jung soon after their first meeting. Freud responded at a later date by formally anointing Jung as his 'Son and Heir', his 'Crown Prince'. In fact, Freud needed a 'son' no less than Jung needed a 'father', but the kind of son Freud wanted was one who would be willing to defer unconditionally to his authority and to perpetuate, without modification, the doctrines and principles of his rule. For his part, Jung needed a father-figure through whose influence he could overcome his adolescent misgivings and discover his own masculine authority. Although Jung basked in Freud's approval and was flattered to be deemed a worthy successor to him, he knew

13

that he could not endorse Freud's ideas in their entirety. Nor could he sacrifice his intellectual integrity to a set of dogmas in the way that his father had done. He nevertheless acquiesced in Freud's wish that he should serve as the first president of the International Psychoanalytic Association when it was set up in 1910, and as chief editor of the first psychoanalytic journal, the *Jahrbuch*.

As time passed, Jung's differences with Freud became harder to conceal. Two of Freud's basic assumptions were unacceptable to him: (1) that human motivation is exclusively sexual and (2) that the unconscious mind is entirely personal and peculiar to the individual. Jung found these and other aspects of Freud's thinking reductionist and too narrow. Instead of conceiving psychic energy (or *libido* as Freud called it) as wholly sexual, Jung preferred to think of it as a more generalized 'life force', of which sexuality was but one mode of expression. Moreover, beneath the personal unconscious of repressed wishes and traumatic memories, posited by Freud, Jung believed there lay a deeper and more important layer that he was to call the *collective unconscious*, which contained *in potentia* the entire psychic heritage of mankind. The existence of this ancient basis of the mind had first been hinted to him as a child when he realized that there were things in his dreams that came from somewhere beyond himself. Its existence was confirmed when he studied the delusions and hallucinations of schizophrenic patients and found them to contain symbols and images which also occurred in myths and fairy-tales all over the world. He concluded that there must exist a dynamic psychic substratum, common to all humanity, on the basis of which each individual builds his or her private experience of life.

Whenever he attempted to express these ideas to Freud, however, they were attributed either to youthful inexperience or to *resistance*. 'Don't deviate too far from me when you are really so close to me, for if you do, we may one day be played off against one another,' Freud admonished him, adding: 'My inclination is to treat those colleagues who offer resistance exactly as we would treat patients in the same situation.' Jung was irked by such condescension, and it was inevitable, given the character of the two men, that a row would eventually break out between them. It was heralded in 1911 by the publication of the first part of Jung's

Transformations and Symbols of the Libido ('It is a risky business for an egg to be cleverer than the hen,' Jung wrote to Freud. 'Still what is in the egg must find the courage to creep out') and finally erupted in 1912 with publication of part two (in a letter to Freud Jung quoted Zarathustra: 'One repays a teacher badly if one remains only a pupil'). In this work, and in a series of lectures given in New York in September 1912, Jung spelt out the heretical view that libido was a much wider concept than Freud allowed and that it could appear in 'crystallized' form in the universal symbols or 'primordial images' apparent in the myths of humanity. Jung drew special attention to the myth of the hero, interpreting the recurrent theme of his fight with a dragon-monster as the struggle of the adolescent ego for deliverance from the mother. This led him to interpretations of the Oedipus complex and the incest taboo which were very different from those proposed by Freud. In Jung's view, a child became attached to his mother not because she was the object of incestuous passion, as Freud maintained, but because she was the provider of love and care—a view which anticipated the theoretical revolution wrought some forty years later by the British analyst and psychiatrist John Bowlby. Furthermore, Jung maintained that the incest taboo was primary: it existed a priori, and was not derived from the father's prohibition of the boy's lust for his mother, as Freud insisted. Oedipal longings, when they occurred, were the consequence of incest prohibition rather than its cause. Jung also argued that the Oedipus complex was not the universal phenomenon that Freud declared it to be.

In redefining libido as undifferentiated psychic energy Jung looked beyond psychology to parallels in physics, in particular to the theory of the transformation of energy as proposed by Robert Mayer. All psychological phenomena, like all physical phenomena, Jung argued, are *manifestations of energy* and this gives symbols their dynamic transformative power. We shall give further consideration to this propensity in Chapter 5.

Publication of these views provoked a major rift with Freud which resulted in the formal termination of their relationship early in 1913. Jung resigned his presidency of the Association, his editorship of the *Jahrbuch*, and his lectureship at the University of Zürich, and withdrew from the psychoanalytic movement. Once again, he was entirely on his own.

15

The manner in which their friendship ended was typical of them both. To Jung, the purpose of life was to realize one's own potential, to follow one's own perception of the truth, and to become a whole person in one's own right. This was the goal of *individuation*, as he later called it. If he was to keep faith with himself, he *had* to go his own way: it would have been impossible for him to spend his life playing second fiddle in a two-man band. As for Freud, belief in the correctness of his own theories was absolute, and this made him so intolerant of dissent that he usually ended up provoking it. He was a strange amalgam of autocrat and masochist: as he once admitted to Jung, his emotional life demanded the existence of an intimate friend and a hated enemy, and, not infrequently, he encountered both in the same person. This pattern was apparent in his childhood relationship with his nephew John (who happened to be his own age), and in the friendship which supported him through his period of 'splendid isolation' (1894–9, when he was conducting his self-analysis and establishing the principles of psychoanalysis) with Wilhelm Fliess. Freud's friendship with Jung, the quarrel, and Jung's subsequent loss to psychoanalysis constituted but one of a number of such painful episodes. A similar fate overtook Freud's relationship with Breuer, Adler, Stekel, Meynert, Silberer, Tausk, and Wilhelm Reich. Reich developed a psychosis, from which he recovered only temporarily, while Silberer and Tausk eventually committed suicide. For Jung the consequences were almost as dire, for he fell into a protracted 'state of disorientation', at times verging on psychosis, which lasted four or five years. Although profoundly disturbing, this proved to be a period of intense creativity which Jung referred to as his 'confrontation with the unconscious', and it was triggered as much by upheavals in his domestic life as by the loss of his friendship with Freud.

Married life

In 1903 Jung had married Emma Rauschenbach (1882–1955), the daughter of a rich industrialist. Between 1904 and 1914 they had five children: four daughters and a son. At first they lived in a flat in the Burghölzli. Then in 1908 they moved into a handsome house which they designed and built beside the lake at Küsnacht, and there they remained for the rest of their lives.

Emma Jung was an attractive, elegant woman, who, with her husband's encouragement, was destined to become a gifted analyst, lecturer, and author. She was an admirable wife and mother, and there can be no doubt that Jung loved her all his life. However, as he confessed to Freud, he recognized 'polygamous components' in himself, asserting that 'The pre-requisite of a good marriage, it seems to me, is the licence to be unfaithful' (*The Freud/Jung Letters*, 289; 30 January 1910).

Jung maintained that essentially two kinds of women are important for a man: on the one hand, he needs a wife to create his home, and to bear and rear his children; on the other, a *femme inspiratrice*, a spiritual companion, to share his fantasies and inspire his greatest works. This assertion probably resulted from a split in his own *anima* (the female complex in his unconscious) and the most likely explanation of this split derives from the period in his fourth year when, separated from his mother, he was looked after by a young maid from his father's parish. The latter made an indelible impression, and he still remembered her in his eighties:

She had black hair and an olive complexion, and was quite different from my mother. I can see her, even now, her hairline, her throat, with its darkly pigmented skin, and her ear. All this seemed to me very strange yet strangely familiar . . . This type of girl later became a component of my anima. The feeling of strangeness which she conveyed, and yet of having known her always, was a characteristic of that figure which later came to symbolize for me the whole essence of womanhood. (*MDR* 23)

This temporary nursemaid was the first embodiment of a maternal adjunct, the *femme inspiratrice*, the consolation of his lonely inner journeying. Although well content with Emma as a wife, his anima continued to demand the additional presence of a loving companion and confidante with whom to share his latest dreams and ideas. On at least two occasions this enticing figure was to present herself to him in the guise of a patient, briefly in the case of Sabina Spielrein (the first patient he treated successfully with Freud's methods) and, more lastingly, in Antonia Wolff, who became a lifelong intimate and colleague. In addition, Jung

17

gathered round himself a number of female devotees (irreverently known to Zürich wits as the *Jungfrauen*), who came to Zürich to analyse and study with him and could seldom bring themselves to leave. It was as if the early separation from his mother had taught him that he could never trust the love of one woman and must always seek safety in numbers.

Understandably, Emma was not happy with this state of affairs, though with time, and out of necessity, she came to endure it. Jung's affair with Toni Wolff began sometime in 1910, and it caused a scandal when he insisted on bringing her, together with Emma, to the Weimar Conference of the International Psychoanalytic Association in 1911. There were bitter rows in which Jung resisted Emma's demands that he give up his extra-marital relationship, insisting that Toni was far too important for him to do without her. Since there could be no question of a divorce, Emma must adjust to the situation and accept Toni as an indispensable part of his life. Emma appears to have given way to him as much out of fear for his sanity as a determination to preserve her marriage. Certainly it was a traumatic time for both of them, and it may well have been a precipitating cause of the prolonged psychic disturbance which began to afflict Jung towards the end of 1913.

Confrontation with the unconscious

This started with a horrifying vision that recurred during the autumn of 1913 in which he saw the whole of Northern Europe flooded by a sea of blood. This was followed by dreams in which all Europe had been frozen by an Arctic wave and in which he shot and killed the Teutonic hero Siegfried as he rode past in a chariot. 'An incessant stream of fantasies had been released . . . I was living in a constant state of tension; often I felt as if gigantic blocks of stone were tumbling down upon me. One thunderstorm followed another' (*MDR* 170–1).

At times the disturbance was so severe as to bring him to the edge of madness. He played in his garden like a child, heard voices in his head, walked about holding conversations with imaginary figures, and, during one episode, believed his house to be crowded with the spirits of the dead. Yet it is a measure of his unusual qualities that he regarded this disaster *as if is were an experiment being performed on him*: a psychiatrist was having a breakdown thus providing a golden opportunity for research. He could study the whole experience at first hand and then use it to help his patients.

This idea—that I was committing myself to a dangerous enterprise not for myself alone, but also for the sake of my patients—helped me over several critical phases . . . It is, of course, ironical that I, a psychiatrist, should at almost every step in my experiment have run into the same psychic material which is the stuff of psychosis and is found in the insane. This is the fund of unconscious images which fatally confuse the mental patient. But it is also the matrix of a mythopoeic imagination which has vanished from our rational age. (*MDR* 172, 181)

The dream of killing Siegfried suggested to him that the conscious ideals embodied in this heroic figure with whom his No. 1 personality had identified itself, were no longer appropriate and had to be sacrificed, 'for there are higher things than the ego's will, and to these one must bow' (*MDR* 174). He turned inwards to encounter his No. 2 personality and gave free rein to the powerful energies he found there.

In order to seize hold of the fantasies, I frequently imagined a steep descent. I even made several attempts to get to the very bottom. The first time I reached, as it were, a depth of about a thousand feet; the next time I found myself at the edge of a cosmic abyss. It was like a voyage to the moon, or a descent into empty space. First came the image of a crater, and I had the feeling that I was in the land of the dead. The atmosphere was that of the other world. (*MDR* 174)

This method of seizing hold of the fantasies was much later used by him as a therapeutic technique in his analytic practice. He called it *active imagination*, and its discovery owed much to the example of his mediumistic cousin, Hélène Preiswerk. Going down the steep descent was akin to entering a state of trance during which unconscious personalities emerged with sufficient clarity for him to hold conversations with them. Essentially, what he had discovered was a knack—the knack of descending into the underworld, like Odysseus, Heracles, or Orpheus, while remaining fully conscious. Two of the figures he regularly encountered on these excursions were a beautiful young woman called Salome and

19

an old man with a white beard and the wings of a kingfisher called Philemon. Jung came to see these as the embodiment of two archetypes—the eternal feminine and the wise old man.

His conversations with these figures brought him the crucial insight that things happen in the psyche that are not produced by conscious intention: they possess a life of their own.

Philemon represented a force which was not myself. In my fantasies I held conversations with him, and he said things which I had not consciously thought. For I observed clearly that it was he who spoke, not I. He said I treated thoughts as if I generated them myself, but in his view thoughts were like animals in the forest, or people in a room, or birds in the air, and added, 'If you should see people in a room, you would not think that you had made those people, or that you were responsible for them.' It was he who taught me psychic objectivity, the reality of the psyche. (*MDR* 176)

By 'the reality of the psyche' Jung meant that he understood the psyche to be an a priori fact of nature, an objective phenomenon which is irreducible to any factor other than itself. 'Psychic existence is the only category of existence of which we have *immediate* knowledge, since nothing can be known unless it first appears as a psychic image' (*CW* XI, para. 769). Like 'Ivenes' for Hélène, Philemon inhered Jung's own potential for maturity. 'At times he seemed to me quite real, as if he were a living personality. I went up and down the garden with him, and to me he was what the Indians call a guru' (*MDR* 176). Far from being destructive psychotic phenomena, these conversations with Philemon helped Jung to discover a new security. Having lost his outer father-figures in the form of Bleuler and Freud and destroyed their heroic representative in the shape of Siegfried, he now found his own inner authority in Philemon. Moreover, Philemon was the first clear manifestation of the richly charismatic personality Jung was destined to become—the wise old man of Küsnacht.

That such experiences did not tip him over into a full-blown psychosis may well have been due to the attitude he adopted to them: he says that he took great care to record every detail of what occurred to him, first in what came to be known as the Black Book, consisting of six black-bound notebooks, the contents of which he later transferred to the Red Book, a folio volume bound in red leather, written in Gothic script, and embellished with illustrations.

One day while engaged in this work he heard a female voice say that what he was doing was not science but 'art'. He was intensely irritated by this and expostulated, 'No, it is not art! On the contrary, it is nature.' He resented the suggestion that he was engaged in an artistic activity because this would imply that his experiences were wilfully contrived and not the spontaneous eruptions from the unconscious that he took them to be. However, he reflected deeply on the existence of this inner woman who possessed the power to upset him, and concluded that she must be the personification of his soul. 'Later I came to see that this inner feminine figure plays a typical, or archetypal, role in the unconscious of a man, and I called her the "anima"' (*MDR* 179).

The whole crisis resolved itself during the months immediately following the Armistice in 1918 when Jung served as the commandant of a camp for British internees. The duties were not onerous and he spent his mornings working on a series of spontaneous drawings which seemed to express his psychic state at the time. He subsequently realized that these drawings resembled ancient mandalas. Mandalas have been found all over the world and are primordial images of wholeness or totality. Although circular, they commonly incorporate some representation of quaternity, such as a cross or a square. The centre usually contains a reference to a deity. Jung began to understand these as representations of the *Self*, the central nucleus of the personality, which he sometimes referred to as the 'archetype of archetypes'. He found that his mandala drawings enabled him to give objective form to the psychic transformations that he underwent from day to day. 'I had a distinct feeling that they were something central, and in time I acquired through them a living conception of the Self' (*MDR* 187).

Finally, there was a dream which had an extraordinary impact on him. He found himself in Liverpool (lit. 'pool of life'), a city whose quarters were arranged radially about a square. In the centre was a round pool with a small island in the middle. The island blazed with sunlight while everything round it was obscured by rain, fog, smoke, and dimly-lit darkness. On the island stood a single tree, a magnolia, in a shower of reddish blossoms. Although the tree stood in the sunlight, Jung felt that it was, at the same time, itself the source of light.

This seemed to sum up all he had been through, and to symbolize the point he had reached. 'When I parted from Freud, I knew that I was plunging into the unknown. Beyond Freud, after all, I knew nothing; but I had taken the step into darkness. When that happens, and then such a dream comes, one feels it as an act of grace' (*MDR* 190).

When they were over, he regarded the years of his 'experiment' as the most important of his life: 'in them everything essential was decided' (*MDR* 191). They determined the future course of his development and were to provide him with the basis of the psychotherapeutic discipline that bears his name. 'It all began then; the later details are only supplements and clarifications of the material that burst forth from the unconscious, and at first swamped me. It was the *prima materia* for a lifetime's work' (*MDR* 191).

Creative illness

There has been much discussion about what actually happened to Jung during this critical phase of his life. One of the most persuasive interpretations is that of Henri Ellenberger, who, in his encyclopaedic *The Discovery of the Unconscious* (1970), suggests that Jung underwent a form of 'creative illness' similar to that suffered by Freud at an identical period (i.e. between the ages of 38 and 43).

The illness is prone to strike after a time of intense intellectual activity and resembles a neurosis or, in severe cases, a psychosis. Still struggling with the issues that were a prelude to the condition, the sufferer grows convinced that he is beyond outside help, becomes socially isolated, and turns deeper into himself. The disturbance can last four or five years. When recovery sets in it occurs spontaneously, and is associated with euphoria and a transformation of the personality. The subject feels that he has gained insight into important truths and believes that he has a duty to share these with the world. Thus, Jung observed:

there were things in the images which concerned not only myself but many others also. It was then that I ceased to belong to myself alone, ceased to

have a right to do so. From then on my life belonged to the generality . . . It
was then that I dedicated myself to the service of the psyche. I loved it and
hated it, but it was my greatest wealth. (*MDR* 184)

Jung's experience was similar to that undergone by shamans and
religious mystics, as well as some artists, writers, and philosophers. Examples include van Gogh, Strindberg, Nietzsche,
Theodor Fechner (the founder of psychophysics), and the theos-
ophist, Rudolph Steiner. Jung himself compared it to Odysseus'
Nekyia (his visit to the Sojourn of the Dead) and it was prefigured
in the fantasies of Miss Miller (which formed the basis of his book
Transformations and Symbols of the Libido) as much as by the
trance performances of Hélène Preiswerk and Helen Smith. In Miss
Miller's case, Jung has detected first a 'renunciation of the world'
(associated with an introversion and regression of libido) followed
by an 'acceptance of the world' (associated with an extraversion of
libido and a more mature adaptation to outer reality). The theme of
the descent into the underworld and the return also occurs in the
epic of Gilgamesh, Virgil's *Aeneid*, and Dante's *Divine Comedy*.
But the most interesting parallel is, as we have already noted, the
neurotic breakdown suffered by Freud in the 1890s which he cured
with his own self-analysis, discovering in the process the basic
principles of psychoanalysis—the use of free association and dream
analysis, the role of sexuality in the aetiology of neurotic illnesses,
the stages of libidinal development in childhood, the fixation and
regression of libido, the repression of forbidden wishes, and so on.
  On their recovery, both men published major and original books:
Freud's *The Interpretation of Dreams* appeared in 1900 when he
was 45, and Jung's *Psychological Types* in 1921 when he was 46.
Thus it was that most of Freud's ideas were already developed and
had become fixed before he met Jung, whilst most of Jung's were
developed after he had found the courage to part company from
Freud and suffer the consequences of his loss. If the six years of
their friendship was a period of discovery and preparation for Jung,
for Freud it was a time of retrenchment, during which he became
increasingly intolerant of those who would revise his ideas, which
for him had become matters of indisputable fact.
  Gregory Bateson (*Steps to an Ecology of Mind*, 1973) was not
wrong when he described Jung's *Nekyia* as an *epistemological*

23

crisis, during which he threw off Freud's reductionist theories and established the groundwork for his own. With the energy of one emerging from a creative illness, he returned to the study of myth, philosophy, and religion to find objective parallels to what he had experienced. *Psychological Types* was the fruit of this labour. In this book he began to organize his ideas about the structure and function of the psyche and to examine the basis of his differences (and Adler's differences) with Freud. He argued that in the course of development people come to adopt habitual attitudes which determine their experience of life. From a wide-ranging review of cultural history he concluded that two fundamental psychological orientations are apparent, which he called *introverted* and *extraverted attitudes*. Introversion is characterized by an inward movement of interest away from the outer world to the inner world of the subject, extraversion by an outward movement of interest away from the subject to the outer realm of objective reality. Jung believed that his differences with Freud were due to his own introversion working in opposition to Freud's extraversion.

This explanation contains more than a grain of truth, but it did not give sufficient weight to other no less important factors. Both men were products of very different backgrounds. Freud, an urban Jew, doted on as a child by a young and beautiful mother, was educated in a progressive tradition that led him naturally into science; while Jung, a rural Protestant, insecurely bonded to a depressed, sometimes absent, mother, was steeped in theology and Romantic idealism. Consequently, it is not surprising that Freud should be a sceptical empiricist and that he should believe in the universal significance of the Oedipus complex, while Jung retained a commitment to the life of the spirit and held that the Oedipus complex had no universal validity.

Another important distinction between them was Freud's habitual tendency to look backwards, which gave him a reductive concern with origins, and Jung's tendency to look forwards, which gave him an adaptive concern with goals. This distinction is apparent in their respective approaches to art as well as to mental illness. Jung came to the nub of the matter when rehearsing his differences with Freud in an article he wrote in 1920: 'Philosophical criticism has helped me to see that every psychology—my own included—has the character of a subjective confession,' he wrote. 'Even when I am dealing with empirical data, I am necessarily speaking about myself' (*CW* IV, para. 774). The same was true of Freud.

Individuation: the realization of the Self

For the rest of his life Jung was preoccupied with the dynamics of personal transformation and growth. He was one of the few psychologists in the twentieth century to maintain that development extends beyond childhood and adolescence through mid-life and into old age. It was this lifelong developmental process that he called *individuation*, and he believed that it could be brought to its highest fruition if one worked with and *confronted* and unconscious in the manner he had discovered in the course of his *Nekyia*.

What did he mean by confronting the unconscious? He experienced the unconscious as a living, numinous presence, the constant companion of every waking (and sleeping) moment. For him, the secret of life's meaning lay in relating to this daemonic power in such a way as to *know* it. To this secret the first sentence of his autobiography alerts us like a fanfare of trumpets: 'My life is the story of the self-realization of the unconscious.' How can we enable the unconscious to realize itself? By granting it freedom of expression and then examining what it has expressed. Thus, self-realization requires the psyche to turn round on itself and *confront* what it produces. In conducting this experiment Jung again experienced himself as split in two—between the conscious *subject*, who experienced, recorded, and struggled to survive, and the unconscious *other*, manifesting in the personalities and powers that forced themselves on him, demanding his attention and respect. Two consequences followed: a heightening of consciousness, and recognition of the psyche as a real, objective entity.

As it turned out he was a good advertisement for his own theories. Many have testified to the change that came over him as he entered middle age. The rather aloof, prickly young man gradually gave place to the wise, genial figure of his late maturity. Though never losing his taste for seclusion, he developed a talent for getting on with people in all walks of life, and those who came to consult or visit him were impressed as much by his courtesy and humour as by his wisdom and the quality of his mind. It was the

25

degree of individuation achieved by him that drew people to Zürich from all over the world, that attracted millions when they saw him on television in old age, and which accounts for the interest that has grown in him since he died.

He never ceased to work with the unconscious or to pursue his research into the material he had collected during his 'confrontation'. In 1922 he purchased some land at Bollingen, beside the beautiful upper lake of Zürich, and here he built a simple tower, round which he was to construct additions at various times during the rest of his life, turning it into an architectural mandala. At the heart of this intimate complex of stone, he reserved a room which only he was allowed to enter and there he accomplished his most important work both on himself and on his Psychology. At the end of his life he wrote: 'At Bollingen I am in the midst of my true life, I am most deeply myself' (*MDR* 214). It was the fulfilment in actuality of his childhood fantasy of the castle keep with its secret laboratory.

One crucial event that occurred after his mid-life crisis was his 'discovery' of alchemy. This happened in 1927 when the sinologist Richard Wilhelm sent him a German translation of a Taoist alchemical treatise called *The Secret of the Golden Flower*, requesting that he should write a commentary on it. As he read it, Jung realized with mounting excitement that he had found a historical parallel to his own experience: here was the most extraordinary and unexpected confirmation of his insights into the meaning of the mandala, the circumambulation of the centre, and the phenomenology of the Self. 'That was the first event which broke through my isolation,' he wrote (*MDR* 189). He was struck by the extraordinary affinity he felt with this rich psychic material, coming as it did from a source so remote from himself, and it set in train the series of alchemical investigations which were to absorb much of the life that was left to him.

Two dreams prepared him for what was in store. In one he discovered a seventeenth-century library in a previously unknown annexe to his house; and in the other some gates clanged shut behind him, trapping him in the same century. Patiently he began to assemble one of the largest collections of alchemical texts in existence, and it became clear to him that the alchemists had used a secret language which they expressed in arcane symbols. At first he understood little of what they signified, but as he worked along philological lines, compiling an elaborate lexicon of key phrases and cross-references, 'the alchemical mode of expression gradually yielded up its meaning' (*MDR* 196).

In alchemy, Jung realized, he had found a precursor of his own Psychology. 'The experiences of the alchemists were, in a sense, my experiences, and their world my world. This was, of course, a momentous discovery: I had stumbled upon the historical counterpart of my psychology of the unconscious' (*MDR* 196). Hitherto, alchemy had been dismissed as no more than a crude anticipation of chemistry, but Jung believed that, in their efforts to turn base metals into gold, the alchemists were symbolically engaged in a process of psychic transformation. In other words, alchemy was a metaphor for individuation.

Just as nature abhors a vacuum, so, in matters where one knows nothing, imagination will rush in to fill the void. Confronted by a field of ignorance, we project into it our own psychic activity and fill it up with meaning. Psychological *projection tests* make use of this propensity by inviting subjects to report what they see in ink blots or ambiguous figures. Leonardo da Vinci advocated a similar technique for inspiring landscapes by staring at wet patches on a wall. Jung was the first to recognize such practices as a useful means for studying otherwise inaccessible contents of the psyche: they enable us to become aware of new meanings arising from the unconscious by seeing them mirrored in outer reality; and this provides the key to one of the most valuable functions of art therapy. The alchemists, Jung realized, were, without knowing it, making use of the same mechanism: alchemy was an elaborate discipline based entirely upon the psychological phenomenon of *projection*.

Accounts of the stages through which the transformations of the alchemical opus progressed particularly fascinated Jung for he saw in them direct parallels to the stages of analysis. In the relationship between the alchemist and his female assistant, the *soror mystica*, Jung also detected an early model of the transference and countertransference relationship which develops between the analyst and patient in the course of analytic treatment. The discovery that alchemical symbols occur spontaneously in dreams, even in those of a modern scientist, confirmed for him the validity of his insight that archetypal psychic factors determined alchemical symbolism, and he published a series of such dreams (provided by the physicist and Nobel Laureate, Wolfgang Pauli, 1900–58) in *Psychology and Alchemy* (*CW* XII).

These researches renewed his commitment to analysis, which he now conceived more as a means to produce personal growth than as a technique for treating mental disorder, and he increasingly devoted his energy to teaching others, whether as pupils or patients, the same methods he had perfected during his own confrontation with the unconscious and which he had excavated in all their bizarre ambiguity from an occult science of the seventeenth century.

Ageing and growth

What distinguishes the Jungian approach to developmental psychology from virtually all others is the idea that even in old age we are growing towards realization of our full potential. This certainly appears to have been true of Jung himself. If, like so many of his European contemporaries, he had died during the First World War, we should have heard very little of him. As it was, his reputation flourished as he *grew* into old age. Not only were his most influential books published in the latter part of his life but his intellectual horizons continued to widen, as can be judged from the variety of subjects to which he turned his attention—synchronicity and flying saucers, for example, as well as psychotherapy, alchemy, the *I Ching*, and religion. For Jung, ageing was not a process of inexorable decline but a time for the progressive refinement of what is essential. 'The decisive question for a man is: is he related to something infinite or not?' (*MDR* 300). This insight was at the root of his life and his Psychology. The infinite, the eternal, the imperishable were ever present and imminent for him as the bedrock of reality, all the more fascinating for being hidden ('occult'). 'Life has always seemed to me like a plant that lives on its rhizome,' he wrote. 'The part that appears above ground lasts only a single summer. Then it withers away— an ephemeral apparition . . . Yet I have never lost a sense of something that lives and endures underneath the eternal flux. What we see is the blossom that passes. The rhizome remains'

(*MDR* 18). The great secret is to embody something essential in our lives. Then, undefeated by age, we can proceed with dignity and meaning, and, as the end approaches, be ready 'to die with life'. For the goal of old age is not senility, but wisdom.

The productive vitality of Jung's late maturity was heralded by a second 'creative illness'. Early in 1944, when he was 68, he suffered emboli in his heart and lungs which nearly killed him. As he lay in hospital he had a near-death experience in which he saw the earth from a thousand miles out in space. He felt he was detaching himself from the world and was resentful when his physician brought him back to life. Nevertheless, he made a full recovery, and threw himself into his writing which, for the next seventeen years, took precedence over all other activities. The illness seems to have carried a stage further the transition from his No. 1 to his No. 2 personality. This was confirmed for him by two dreams. In the first he saw a yogi, in lotus posture, deep in meditation. Jung realized that the yogi possessed his own face, and awoke in alarm. 'Aha, so he is the one who is meditating me,' he thought. 'He has a dream, and I am it.' In a second dream, which came much later, he experienced himself as the *projection* of an unknown flying object shaped like an old-fashioned magic lantern. He understood these dreams as showing that the unconscious is the generator of the empirical personality and that the Self assumes human shape in order to enter three-dimensional reality.

At the age of 82 he wrote:

In the end, the only events of my life worth telling are those when the imperishable world erupted into this transitory one . . . All other memories of travels, people and my surroundings have paled beside these interior happenings . . . But my encounters with the 'other' reality, my bouts with the unconscious, are indelibly engraved on my memory. In that realm there has always been wealth in abundance, and everything else has lost importance by comparison.   (*MDR* 18)

The major themes that preoccupied Jung up to the end of his life were the mystery of opposites, their division, their union, and their transcendence, and the cosmic significance of human consciousness. He recorded his reflections in three difficult and challenging books: *Aion* (1951), *Answer to Job* (1952), and *Mysterium Coniunctionis* (1955–6). *Answer to Job*, the most accessible of these, brought him into conflict with theologians, for in it he denounced God for burdening humanity with responsibility for all the evil in the world while absolving Himself of all blame. This lack of self-awareness on the part of the Almighty, Jung argued, can only be corrected by human consciousness, and it explains why God found it necessary to incarnate Himself in man. 'That is the meaning of divine service, or the service that man can render to God, that light may emerge from the darkness, that the Creator may become conscious of His creation, and man conscious of himself' (*MDR* 312).

The germ of this insight came to him in 1925 on a visit to the Athai Plains in East Africa. With his travelling companions he stood on a hill looking down on the savannah stretching to the far horizon, gigantic herds of gazelle, antelope, gnu, zebra, and warthog grazing and moving forwards like slow rivers.

There was scarcely any sound save the melancholy cry of a bird of prey. This was the stillness of the eternal beginning, the world as it had always been, in the state of non-being; for until then no one had been present to know that it was this world. I walked away from my companions until I had put them out of sight, and savoured the feeling of being entirely alone. There I was now, the first human being to recognize that this was the world, but who did not know that in this moment he had first really created it.

There the cosmic meaning of consciousness became overwhelmingly clear to me. 'What nature leaves imperfect, the art perfects,' say the alchemists. Man, I, in an invisible act of creation put the stamp of perfection on the world by giving it objective existence ... Now I knew what it was, and knew even more: that man is indispensable for the completion of creation; that, in fact, he himself is the second creator of the world, who alone has given to the world its objective existence—without which, unheard, unseen, silently eating, giving birth, dying, heads nodding through hundreds of millions of years, it would have gone on in the profoundest night of non-being down to its unknown end. Human consciousness created objective existence and meaning, and man found his indispensable place in the great process of being. (*MDR* 240–1)

Thus Jung's psychology became also a cosmology, for he saw the journey of personal development towards fuller consciousness as occurring in the context of eternity. The psyche, existing *sui generis* as an objective part of nature, is subject to the same laws that govern the universe and is itself the supreme fulfilment of those laws: through the miracle of consciousness, the human psyche provides the mirror in which Nature sees herself reflected.

In old age he had many premonitions of approaching death and what impressed him was the lack of fuss the unconscious makes about it. Indeed, death seemed to him to be a goal in itself, something to be welcomed. Thus, in one dream he saw 'the other Bollingen' bathed in a glow of light, and a voice told him that it was complete and ready to receive him. Looking back on his life he reflected, 'In my case it must have been a passionate urge to understanding that brought about my birth. For that is the strongest element in my nature' (*MDR* 297). This need to understand and to *know* kept him creatively alive well into his eighty-sixth year, when he suffered two strokes within a week of one another and died peacefully on 6 June 1961 at Küsnacht.

2   Archetypes and the collective unconscious

In 1909 Jung and Freud were both invited to lecture at Clark University in Worcester, Massachusetts. They were away for seven weeks and they spent long periods every day talking and working on each other's dreams. Of all the dreams they analysed, two were to be critical for their friendship. The first was one of Freud's, which Jung did his best to interpret on the basis of only a few associations from Freud. When Jung pressed him for more, Freud looked rather suspiciously at him and declined: 'I cannot risk my authority,' he said. At that moment, commented Jung, he lost it altogether. 'That sentence burned itself into my memory; and in it the end of our relationship was already foreshadowed. Freud was placing personal authority above truth' (*MDR* 154).

The other dream was one of Jung's. He dreamt that he was on the top floor of an old house, well furnished and with fine paintings on the walls. He marvelled that this should be his house and thought 'Not bad!' But then it occurred to him that he had no idea what the lower floor was like, so he went down to see. There everything was much older. The furnishings were medieval and everything was rather dark. He thought, 'Now I really must explore the whole house.' He looked closely at the floor. It was made of stone slabs, and in one of these he discovered a ring. When he pulled it, the slab lifted, and he saw some narrow stone steps leading down into the depths. He went down and entered a low cave cut out of the rock. Bones and broken pottery were scattered about in the dust, the remains of a primitive culture, and he found two human skulls, obviously very old and half-disintegrated. Then he awoke.

All that interested Freud about this dream was the possible identity of the skulls. He wanted Jung to say who they belonged to, for it seemed evident to him that Jung must harbour a death-wish against their owners. Jung felt this was completely beside the point, but, as was habitual with him at that stage in the relationship, he kept his doubts to himself. To Jung, the house was an image of the psyche. The room on the upper floor represented his conscious personality. The ground floor stood for the first level of the unconscious, which he was to call the *personal* unconscious, while in the deepest level of all he reached the *collective* unconscious. There he discovered the world of the *primitive man within himself.* To him, the skulls had nothing to do with death-wishes. They belonged to our human ancestors, who helped shape the common psychic heritage of us all.

When he finally summoned up the courage to announce his hypothesis of a collective unconscious, it proved to be his most significant departure from Freud, and his most important single contribution to psychology. Although Freud did make some passing reference to there being 'archaic vestiges' in the psyche, he remained intractably resistant to the enormous implications of Jung's bold and revolutionary idea.

What Jung was proposing was no less than a fundamental concept on which the whole science of psychology could be built. Potentially, it is of comparable importance to quantum theory in physics. Just as the physicist investigates particles and waves, and the biologist genes, so Jung held it to be the business of the psychologist to investigate the collective unconscious and the functional units of which it is composed—the *archetypes*, as he eventually called them. Archetypes are 'identical psychic structures common to all' (*CW* V, para. 224), which together constitute 'the archaic heritage of humanity' (*CW* V, para. 259). Essentially, he conceived them to be innate neuropsychic centres possessing the capacity to initiate, control, and mediate the common behavioural characteristics and typical experiences of all human beings. Thus, on appropriate occasions, archetypes give rise to similar thoughts, images, mythologems, feelings, and ideas in people, irrespective of their class, creed, race, geographical location, or historical epoch. An individual's entire archetypal endowment makes up the collective unconscious, whose authority and power is vested in a central nucleus, responsible for integrating the whole personality, which Jung termed the Self.

Jung never disagreed with Freud's view that personal experience is of crucial significance for the development of each individual, but he denied that this development occurred in an unstructured personality. On the contrary, for Jung, the role of personal experi-

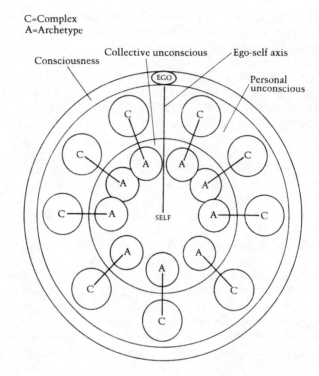

C=Complex
A=Archetype

FIG. 1. Schematic diagram of Jung's model of the psyche

ence was *to develop what is already there*—to activate the archetypal potential already present in the Self. Our psyches are not simply a product of experience, any more than our bodies are merely the product of what we eat.

A diagrammatic representation of Jung's model of the psyche (Fig. 1) will help to make this clear. The model should be visualized as a globe or a sphere, like a three-layered onion. At the centre, and permeating the entire system with its influence, is the Self. Within the inner of the three concentric circles, is the collective unconscious, composed of archetypes. The outer circle represents consciousness, with its focal ego orbiting the system rather like a planet orbiting the sun, or the moon orbiting the earth. Intermediate between the conscious and the collective unconscious, is the personal unconscious, made up of complexes, each of which is linked to an archetype: for complexes are *personifications* of archetypes; they are the means through which archetypes manifest themselves in the personal psyche.

To a limited extent Jung's archetypes resemble Plato's *ideas*. For Plato, 'ideas' were pure mental forms existing in the minds of the gods before human life began and were consequently above and beyond the ordinary world of phenomena. They were *collective* in the sense that they embodied the *general* characteristics of a thing, but they were also implicit in its *specific* manifestations. The human fingerprint, for example, is instantly recognizable for what it is on account of its unmistakable configuration of contours and whorls. Yet every fingerprint has a configuration unique to its owner, which is why those who turn their hands to burglary must remember to wear gloves if they wish to escape detection and arrest. Archetypes similarly combine the universal with the individual, the general with the unique, in that they are common to all humanity, yet nevertheless manifest themselves in every human being in a way peculiar to him or to her.

Where Jung's archetypes differ from Plato's ideas is in their dynamic, goal-seeking properties. Archetypes actively seek their actualization in the personality and the behaviour of the individual, as the life cycle unfolds in the context of the environment.

The actualization of archetypes

The most important archetype to be actualized in the personal psyche of a child is the mother archetype. Actualization (Jung also speaks of 'evocation', and 'constellation') of an archetype seems to proceed in accordance with the laws of association worked out by psychologists at the end of the nineteenth century. Two of these laws are particularly apposite: they are the law of *similarity* and the law of *contiguity*. Thus, the mother archetype is actualized in the child's psyche through the *contiguity* of a female caretaker whose behaviour and personal characteristics are sufficiently *similar* to the built-in structure of the maternal archetype for the child to perceive her and experience her as 'mother'. Then, as the attachment relationship develops, the archetype becomes active in the personal psyche of the child in the form of the mother *complex*. At the same time, through similarity and contiguity, the infant constellates the child archetype in the mother. Each partner of this dyad creates the perceptual field responsible for evoking the archetype in the other.

Throughout Jung's lifetime, most psychologists maintained that children were passive recipients of maternal care and that they became attached to their mothers because they were fed by them (the so-called 'cupboard love' theory). Jung maintained, on the contrary, that children actively participated in the formation of all their relationships with the world, insisting that it was 'a mistake to suppose [as did the majority of his contemporaries] that the psyche of the newborn child is a *tabula rasa* in the sense that there is absolutely nothing in it' (*CW* IX. i, para. 136). We bring with us an innate psychic structure enabling us to have the experiences typical of our kind.

Thus the whole nature of man presupposes woman, both physically and spiritually. His system is tuned into woman from the start, just as it is prepared for a quite definite world where there is water, light, air, salt, carbohydrate, etc. The form of the world into which he is born is already inborn in him as a virtual image. Likewise parents, wife, children, birth, and death are inborn in him as virtual images, as psychic aptitudes. These *a priori* categories have by nature a collective character; they are images of parents, wife, and children *in general*, and are not individual predestinations. We must therefore think of these images as lacking in solid content, hence as unconscious. They only acquire solidity, influence, and eventual consciousness in the encounter with empirical facts, which touch the unconscious aptitude and quicken it to life. They are, in a sense, the deposits of all our ancestral experiences, but they are not the experiences themselves. (*CW* VII, para. 300)

All those factors, therefore, that were essential to our near and remote ancestors will also be essential to us, for they are embedded in the inherited organic system. (*CW* VIII, para. 717)

Very similar ideas to Jung's have become current in the last forty years in the relatively new science of ethology (that branch of behavioural biology which studies animals in their natural habitats). Every animal species possesses a repertoire of behaviours. This behavioural repertoire is dependent on structures which evolution has built into the central nervous system of the species. Ethologists call these structures *innate releasing mechanisms*, or IRMs. Each IRM is primed to become active when an appropriate stimulus—called a *sign stimulus*—is encountered in the environment. When such a stimulus appears, the innate mechanism is released, and the animal responds with a characteristic *pattern of behaviour* which is adapted, through evolution, to the situation. Thus, a mallard duck becomes amorous at the sight of the handsome green head of a mallard drake, the green head being the *sign stimulus* which releases in the duck's central nervous system the *innate mechanism* responsible for the characteristic *patterns of behaviour* associated with courtship in the duck.

This is very much how Jung conceived of archetypes operating in human beings, and he was aware of the comparison. An archetype, he said, is not 'an inherited idea' but rather 'an inherited mode of functioning, corresponding to the inborn way in which the chick emerges from the egg, the bird builds its nest, a certain kind of wasp stings the motor ganglion of the caterpillar, and eels find their way to the Bermudas. In other words, it is a "pattern of behaviour". This aspect of the archetype,' concludes Jung, 'the purely biological one, is the proper concern of scientific psychology' (*CW* XVIII, para. 1228). In a sense, ethology and Jungian psychology can be viewed as two sides of the same coin: it is as if ethologists have been engaged in an extraverted exploration of the archetype and Jungians in an introverted examination of the IRM.

The currency of archetypal theory

Many other disciplines have produced concepts similar to the archetypal hypothesis, but usually without reference to Jung. For example, the primary concern of Claude Lévi-Strauss and the French school of structural anthropology is with the unconscious *infrastructures* which they hold responsible for all human customs and institutions; specialists in linguistics maintain that although grammars differ from one another, their basic forms—which Noam Chomsky calls their *deep structures*—are universal (i.e. at the deepest neuropsychic level, there exists a universal [or 'archetypal'] grammar on which all individual grammars are based); an entirely new discipline, sociobiology, has grown up on the theory that the patterns of behaviour typical of all social species, the human species included, are dependent on *genetically transmitted response strategies* designed to maximize the fitness of the organism to

37

survive in the environment in which it evolved; sociobiology also holds that the psycho-social development in individual members of a species is dependent on what are termed *epigenetic rules* (*epi* = upon, *genesis* = development; i.e. rules upon which development proceeds); more recently still, ethologically oriented psychiatrists have begun to study what they call *psychobiological response patterns* and *deeply homologous neural structures* which they hold responsible for the achievement of healthy or unhealthy patterns of adjustment in individual patients in response to variations in their social environment. All these concepts are compatible with the archetypal hypothesis which Jung had proposed decades earlier to virtually universal indifference.

This raises an important question. If Jung's theory of archetypes is so fundamental that it keeps being rediscovered by the practitioners of many other disciplines, why did it not receive the enthusiastic welcome it deserved when Jung proposed it? The explanation is, I think, twofold: namely, the time at which Jung stated the theory, and the way in which he published it.

In the first place, throughout Jung's mature lifetime, researchers working in university departments of psychology were in the grip of behaviourism, which discounted innate or genetic factors, preferring to view the individual as a *tabula rasa* whose development was almost entirely dependent on environmental factors. Jung's contrary view that the infant comes into the world with an intact blueprint for life which it then proceeds to implement through interaction with the environment, was so at variance with the prevailing *Zeitgeist* as to guarantee it a hostile reception.

Secondly, Jung did not state his theory in a clear, testable form, nor did he back it up with sufficiently persuasive evidence. His book *Transformations and Symbols of the Libido* in which he first put forward his idea of a collective unconscious giving rise to 'primordial images' (as he originally called archetypes) was so densely written and so packed with mythological exegesis as to make it virtually impenetrable to any but the most determined reader. Moreover, in arguing that 'primordial images' were derived from the past history of mankind, Jung exposed himself to the accusation that he, like Freud, subscribed to the discredited theory of the *inheritance of acquired characteristics*, originally proposed by Jean-Baptiste Lamarck (1744–1829), i.e. that ideas or images

occurring in members of one generation could be passed on genetically to the next and subsequent generations.

In fact, the collective unconscious is a respectable scientific
hypothesis and one does not have to adopt a Lamarckian view of
biology to entertain it. Indeed, as we have seen, it is entirely
compatible with the theoretical formulations of contemporary
ethologists, sociobiologists, and psychiatrists. Precisely in order to
acquit himself of the charge of Lamarckism Jung eventually made
a clear distinction between what he termed the *archetype-as-such*
(similar to Kant's *das Ding-an-sich*) and the archetypal images,
ideas, and behaviours that the archetype-as-such gives rise to. It is
the *predisposition* to have certain experiences that is archetypal
and inherited, not the experience itself. The French molecular
biologist and Nobel Laureate Jacques Monod reached an identical
conclusion: 'Everything comes from experience, yet not from actual experience, reiterated by each individual with each generation,
but instead from experience accumulated by the entire ancestry of
the species in the course of its evolution.'

Thus, the Jungian archetype is no more scientifically disreputable than the ethological IRM. Just as the behavioural repertoire of
each species is encoded in its central nervous system as innate
releasing mechanisms which are activated in the course of development by appropriate sign stimuli, so Jung conceived the programme for human life to be encoded in the collective unconscious
as a series of archetypal determinants which are actualized in
response to inner and outer events in the course of the life cycle.
There is nothing Lamarckian or unbiological in this conception.

Archetypes versus cultural transmission

Those who reject the archetypal hypothesis remain unimpressed
by the discovery of parallel themes in myths derived from different
parts of the world, maintaining that these can be explained just as
well by human migration and cultural diffusion as by an innate
predisposition. Jung sought to refute this interpretation by pointing
to the spontaneous occurrence of the same themes in the dreams,
hallucinations, and delusions of unsophisticated patients, who had
never previously encountered them in waking life: 'Typical
mythologems were observed among individuals to whom all

knowledge of this kind was absolutely out of the question,' he declared, concluding that 'we must be dealing with "autochthonous" revivals independent of all tradition, and, consequently, that "myth-forming" structural elements must be present in the unconscious psyche' (*CW* IX. i, para. 259). One example which Jung frequently quoted was that of a schizophrenic patient who told him that if he stared at the sun with half-closed eyes he would see that the sun had a phallus and that this organ was the origin of the wind. Years later Jung came across a Greek text describing an almost identical vision: 'And likewise the so-called tube, the origin of the ministering wind. For you will see hanging down from the disc of the sun something that looks like a tube . . .' (*CW* VIII, para. 318). The patient was a poorly educated man who could not, in any case, have seen the text, even if he could have understood it, since it was published after his admission to hospital, where no such literature was available.

Although this seems to have been Jung's favourite example to illustrate his thesis, it is not readily explicable as the result of archetypes operating in different individuals living in different places at different times in history. Much more persuasive examples could have been given, such as the one we have just used, namely, the behaviour of generations of mothers and children as they live out the mother–child archetypal programme. To explain Jung's example it is necessary to postulate three archetypal objects (sun, phallus, and wind), an archetypal principle (that of masculine generativity), and an archetypal association between them (the sun's phallus generating the wind). Although such an association is statistically improbable, it is not impossible, as Jung's example would seem to demonstrate. But he could have found a more persuasive example to support his theory.

Essentially, the theory can be stated as a psychological law: *whenever a phenomenon is found to be characteristic of all human communities, it is an expression of an archetype of the collective unconscious.* It is not possible to demonstrate that such universally apparent phenomena are exclusively due to archetypal determinants or entirely due to cultural diffusion, because in all probability both are involved. However, the likelihood is that there will be a strong *bias* for those phenomena which are archetypally determined to diffuse more readily and more lastingly than those that are not. Behavioural characteristics such as maternal bonding, dominance striving, sexual mating, and home building satisfy three critical biological criteria, namely, *universality, continuity,* and *evolutionary stability,* and as such are liable to be archetypally based, giving rise to typical psychological experiences as well as typical patterns of behaviour in all human communities wherever they exist.

The psychoid archetype and the *unus mundus*

The archetype possesses a fundamental duality: it is both a psychic structure and a neurological structure, both 'spirit' and 'matter', and Jung came to see it as the essential pre-condition of all psychophysical events: 'the archetypes are as it were the hidden foundations of the conscious mind, or, to use another comparison, the roots which the psyche has sunk not only in the earth in the narrower sense but in the world in general' (*CW* X, para. 53). He proposed that archetypal structures are not only fundamental to the existence and survival of all living organisms but that they are continuous with structures controlling the behaviour of inorganic matter as well. The archetype is not to be conceived, therefore, as merely a psychic entity but rather as 'the bridge to matter in general' (*CW* VIII, para. 420). This purely physical aspect of the archetype Jung sometimes referred to as the *psychoid* archetype, and it was an idea that greatly excited the physicist Wolfgang Pauli, who believed it made a major contribution to our ability to comprehend the principles on which the universe has been created.

Pauli's enthusiasm encouraged Jung to persevere in his attempts to penetrate that unitary reality which he, like the mystics of many religious traditions, believed to underlie all manifest phenomena. To describe this unitary dimension, Jung resurrected the ancient term *unus mundus,* or 'unitary world'—the eternal ground of all empirical being. He conceived archetypes to be the mediators of the *unus mundus,* responsible for organizing ideas and images in the psyche as well as for governing the fundamental principles of matter and energy in the physical world. Pauli argued that by conceiving archetypes in this way, Jung had discovered the 'missing link' between the physical events (which are the legitimate study of science) and the mind of the scientist who studies them.

In other words, the archetypes which order our perceptions and ideas are themselves the product of an objective order which transcends both the human mind and the external world. At this supreme point physical science, psychology, and theology all coalesce.

Synchronicity

With characteristic lack of caution, Jung extended these ideas into the realm of parapsychology, particularly the phenomenon of 'meaningful coincidence'—which he called *synchronicity*: 'A co-incidence in time of two or more causally unrelated events which have the same or similar meaning' (*CW* VIII, para. 849)—as when one dreams of the death of a distant friend the very same night that she dies. There can be no causal connection between the two events, yet we *experience* their conjunction as meaningful.

This 'acausal connecting principle', as Jung called it, is the basis of the ancient Chinese attitude to reality incorporated in the *I Ching* or *Book of Changes*—namely, that anything that happens is related to everything else that happens at the same time. Our Western world-view teaches that time is a purely abstract measure; but, if we are honest, it never *feels* as if it is. Indeed, the whole 'nostalgia industry' depends on our psychic awareness that time has a character all its own which colours events as they transpire. Jung intuitively felt this pointed to an acausal archetypal order at the root of all phenomena which is responsible for the meaningful-ness implicit in the coincidence of associated physical and mental events.

Certainly, synchronistic happenings are occasionally part of the experience of most of us, and there is something inherently un-satisfactory about the way in which they are customarily dis-missed in our culture as 'mere coincidence'. It is typical of Jung's approach that he was concerned with *all* experiences and that he took the irrational and apparently unconnected manifestations of human life as seriously as the rational and connected ones.

Implications

Whether or not one is persuaded by Jung's application of archetypal theory to the more esoteric areas of human experience, it is hard to deny that it is an idea with profound implications. If, as Jung believed, archetypes pre-condition all existence, then they must be manifest in the spiritual achievements of art, science, and religion as well as in the organization of organic and inorganic matter, and can provide a standpoint capable of transforming our understanding of all these phenomena. As far as psychology is concerned, the conception of the archetype as the common source of both behavioural and psychic events enables us to move beyond the intellectual quagmires of vitalism and epiphenomenalism which have so far hampered the progress of those seeking to explore the mysterious relationship between the body and the mind. Whatever else the archetypal hypothesis may achieve, it can at least provide a bridge between the science of mind and the science of behaviour.

3 The stages of life

The most profound influence of archetypes is in their regulation of the human life cycle. Jung maintained that as we mature we follow a natural sequence of steps which he describes in his essay 'The Stages of Life' (*CW* VIII, paras. 749–95). Each stage is mediated through a new set of archetypal imperatives which seek fulfilment in both our personality and our behaviour. Since the archetypes evolved to equip us for the hunter/gatherer existence in which our species has lived out 99 per cent of its existence, the archetypal programme equips us for a life which is not always in tune with the life of contemporary urban society. Essentially, the programme provides for being parented, exploring the environment, distinguishing familiar figures from strange, learning the language or dialect of one's community, acquiring a knowledge of its values, rules, and beliefs, playing in the peer group, meeting the challenges of puberty and adolescence, being initiated into the adult group, accomplishing courtship and marriage, and child-rearing, contributing to the economy through gathering and hunting, participating in religious rituals and ceremonials, assuming the responsibilities of advanced maturity, old age, and preparation for death. All these stages are apparent in all human communities known to anthropology and therefore obey the psychological law stated above on p. 40. As we have noted, the psychic nucleus responsible for co-ordinating this lifelong sequence Jung called the Self.

· In addition to the Self, Jung postulated archetypal components which play specific roles in the psychic development and social adjustment of everyone. These include the *ego*, *persona*, *shadow*, *anima*, and *animus*. Jung considered these to be archetypal structures which are built into the personal psyche in the form of complexes during the course of development. Each is a psychic organ operating in accordance with the biological principles of adaptation, homeostasis, and growth. Though we make use of them and experience them in ways unique to ourselves, they nevertheless perform the same functions in all human beings everywhere. 'Ultimately,' wrote Jung, 'every individual life is at the same time the eternal life of the species' (*CW* XI, para. 146). In other words, we come into the world bearing with us an archetypal endowment which enables us to adapt to reality in the same way as our remote ancestors. The sum total of this endowment is incorporated in the Self and it is out of this matrix that the other psychic structures develop, and they remain under its guiding influence for the rest of life. We shall consider these now.

The Self

This is both architect and builder of the dynamic structure which supports our psychic existence throughout life. A capital S is used to distinguish between the 'self' of everyday usage (which refers to the ego or persona) and Jung's 'Self' which transcends the ego and inheres the age-old capacities of the species. Its goal is wholeness, the complete realization of the blueprint for human existence within the context of the life of the individual. *Individuation* is the *raison d'être* of the Self. Though it has evident biological goals, the Self also seeks fulfilment in the spiritual achievements of art and religion and in the inner life of the soul. Hence we can experience it as a profound mystery, a secret resource, or a manifestation of the God within. For this reason, it has been identified with the notion of deity in numerous cultures and finds symbolic expression in such universal configurations as the mandala. As a consequence, the Self came in Jung's view to provide the means of personal adjustment not only to the social environment but also to God, the cosmos, and the life of the spirit.

The ego

The ego complex emerges out of the Self in the course of early childhood development, rather as the moon is thought to have separated from the earth when the latter was in its early molten state. It remains linked to the Self by what Jung's followers have called the *ego–Self axis*, and it is on this axis that the stability of the personality depends. The ego is itself the centre of consciousness and it is what we refer to when we use the terms 'I' or 'me'. It is responsible for our continuing sense of identity so that we still feel ourselves at 80 to be exactly the same person we were at 8. Jung never made a clear distinction between the terms 'ego' and 'consciousness', using them interchangeably and sometimes together as 'ego-consciousness'. As a result, he did not examine the more unconscious functions of the ego in defending consciousness against unwanted contents arising from the unconscious—those functions that Anna Freud described in her classic work *Mechanisms of Ego-Defence* (1946) (e.g. repression, denial, projection, rationalization, reaction-formation, to mention only the most familiar of them).

Although we experience the ego as the continuing centre of our existence it is, in fact, merely the Self's executive. 'For indeed our consciousness does not create itself—it wells up from unknown depths. In childhood it awakens gradually, and all through life it wakes each morning out of the depths of sleep from an unconscious condition. It is like a child that is born daily out of the primordial womb of the unconscious' (*CW* XI, para. 935). Again and again he stresses the dependency of ego-consciousness on the continuing vitality of the Self. 'The ego stands to the self as the moved to the mover, or as object to subject, because the determining factors which radiate out from the self surround the ego on all sides and are therefore supraordinate to it. The self, like the unconscious, is an *a priori* existent out of which the ego evolves' (*CW* XI, para. 391).

Put in terms of Jung's childhood experience the ego can be identified with his 'No. 1' personality and the Self with his 'No. 2'. In the first half of life it is essential to develop a strong and effective ego if one is to deal competently with the tasks of this stage— separating off from the parents, establishing oneself in a job or profession, marrying, providing a home for one's family, etc. Only in the second half of life does it become possible for the ego to recognize its subordinate status in relation to the Self—an indispensable stage in the progress of individuation. Then the ego begins to *confront* the Self and the Self the ego, and through the mediation of the *transcendent function* (which we will examine later) bring about the attainment of personality integration and higher consciousness.

The persona

Just as every building has a façade so every personality has a *persona* (literally a mask, as worn by actors in ancient Greece). Through the persona we codify ourselves in a form which we hope will prove acceptable to others. It has sometimes been referred to as the *social* archetype or the *conformity* archetype, for on it depends the success or failure of one's adaptation to society. There is always some element of pretence about the persona, for it is a kind of shop window in which we like to display our best wares; or one might think of it as a public relations expert employed by the ego to ensure that people will think well of us. 'One could say, with a little exaggeration, that the persona is that which in reality one is not, but which oneself as well as others think one is' (*CW* IX. i, para. 221).

The persona begins to form early in childhood out of a need to conform to the wishes and expectations of parents, peers, and teachers. Children quickly learn that certain attitudes and behaviours are acceptable and may be rewarded with approval while others are unacceptable and may result in punishment or the withdrawal of love. The tendency is to build acceptable traits into the persona and to keep unacceptable traits hidden or repressed. These socially undesirable aspects of the maturing personality are usually relegated to the personal unconscious, where they coalesce to form another complex, or part personality, that Jung called the shadow.

The shadow

Jung felt 'shadow' to be an appropriate term for this disowned subpersonality for there is inevitably something 'shady' about it, hidden away as it is in the dark lumber-room of the Freudian unconscious. Unwanted though it is, it persists as a powerful dynamic that we take with us wherever we go as a dark companion which dogs our steps—just like a shadow in fact. Much of the time we manage to ignore it, but it has an uncomfortable way of reminding us of its presence, particularly in our dreams.

In dreams the shadow tends to appear as a sinister or threatening

47

figure possessing the same sex as the dreamer, and is not infrequently a member of a different nation, colour, or race. There is usually something alien or hostile about it, which gives rise to powerful feelings of distrust, anger, or fear. This is why Jung felt justified in regarding the shadow as a *complex*—that is to say, a cluster of traits bound together by common affects—which, like all complexes, had an archetypal core, in this instance, the archetype of the Enemy, the Predator, or the Evil Stranger.

Of all archetypes the enemy is one of the most important and, potentially, the most deadly. Its influence becomes apparent during the first year of life. Just as the infant will show delight at being approached by its mother, so it will also show signs of wariness and withdrawal when approached by a stranger. By the second year, this xenophobic propensity has ripened into expressions of full-blown fear and hostility.

Both attachment and xenophobia are evidently the product of innate predispositions because they are apparent in all infants wherever they are born and under whatever circumstances they are brought up. Both are even apparent in children who have been blind and deaf from birth, who differentiate strangers from familiars by their smell. The biological significance of both patterns of behaviour is apparent from their manifestation by all social species: it is obviously a matter of survival to be able to distinguish between friend and foe from the earliest possible age.

The archetype of the enemy is actualized in the personal psyche as the shadow complex through growing up in a human social environment. There are two important sources of the complex: (1) cultural indoctrination, and (2) familial repression.

The cultural source includes all that one has been taught politically about out-groups considered to be hostile to one's in-group (i.e. nation, tribe, or band) and theologically about the concept of evil (in our culture, Satan, the Devil, Hell). Inevitably, the shadow comes to possess qualities opposite to those of the persona, the shadow compensating, as it were, for the superficial pretensions of the persona, the persona balancing the antisocial characteristics of the shadow. The coexistence of these two sharply contrasting personalities within the same individual is as apparent in literature as in life: Dorian Gray, the handsome, witty, man-about-town, keeps his portrait hidden where no one can see it, for it bears all the features of his vicious secret life; Dr Jekyll and Mr Hyde are the same man, by turns respectable physician and monstrous ogre; the popular TV personality with the compassionate manner and caring smile can be a hysterical termagant at home with her family.

To some extent we all resemble Dorian Gray in keeping our shadow out of sight, not as an act of will but as an act of submission to that inner authority which Freud called the *super-ego* and Jung called the *moral complex*. In the light of Bowlby's work, it seems that the impetus to develop this inner watch-dog is not, as Freud believed, a fear of being castrated by the father as a reprisal for entertaining incestuous desires, but rather a fear of being *abandoned* by the mother for being unacceptable. The dread prospect of being rejected on account of some 'bad' aspect of the Self seems to be at the bottom of all feelings of guilt, all desire for punishment, and all longings for atonement and reconciliation. The moral complex forms on the basis of an archetypal imperative to learn and maintain the values of the culture into which we happen to have been born. If no such imperative existed, anarchy would be the natural human condition: we should all be psychopaths, incapable of co-operation or mutual trust, and the species could not conceivably exist.

However, the acquisition of a moral complex imposes severe restraints on the Self, much of which is necessarily relegated to the shadow, where it is experienced—when it is experienced—as a threat. To defend ourselves from this threat, and to sustain our peace of mind, we make use of a variety of ego-defence mechanisms, particularly *repression*, *denial*, and *projection*. Not only do we repress the shadow in the personal unconscious, but we deny its existence in ourselves, and project it out on to others. This is done quite unconsciously: we are not aware that we do it. It is an act of ego-preservation which enables us to deny our own 'badness' and to attribute it to others, whom we then hold responsible for it. It explains the ubiquitous practice of *scapegoating* and underlies all kinds of prejudice against people belonging to identifiable groups other than our own. Shadow projection is also involved in the psychiatric symptom of paranoia, when one's own hostile, persecutory feelings are disowned and projected on to others, who are then experienced as being hostile and persecutory towards oneself.

Shadow projection can function, therefore, as a major threat to both social and international peace, for it enables us to turn those whom we perceive as enemies into devils or vermin that it is legitimate to hate, attack, or exterminate. Unscrupulous leaders can manipulate this mechanism in whole populations. Adolf Hitler, for example, repeatedly described the Jews as *Untermenschen* (subhumans) and through the skilful use of propaganda was able to induce enough Germans to project their shadow on to them as to make the holocaust possible. The same mechanism is involved in all pogroms, all 'ethnic cleansing', and all wars.

The most demanding part of a Jungian analysis occurs when the *analysand* (the person undergoing analysis) begins to confront his own shadow. That this should be difficult is not surprising since the whole shadow complex is tinged with feelings of guilt and unworthiness, and with fears of rejection should its true nature be discovered or exposed. However painful the process may be, it is necessary to persevere because much Self potential and instinctive energy is locked away in the shadow and therefore unavailable to the total personality. People suffering from this inner state of Self-division commonly complain of feeling flat and listless, and that life has become meaningless for them. Analytic success in making the shadow conscious and coming to terms with its contents results, after the initial struggle, in a sense of greater vitality, of feeling more vigorous, more creative, and more whole. To own one's shadow is to become responsible for it, so that one's morality is less blind and less compulsive, and ethical choices become possible. Shadow consciousness is important not only for personal development, therefore, but as a basis for greater social harmony and international understanding.

Sex and gender

While Jung acknowledged that environmental factors exert an enormous influence over a person's psychological development, he nevertheless maintained that these influences act by bringing out the 'subjective aptitudes' with which all children are born. He held this to be as true of gender awareness as it is of development of the persona, the shadow, or the psychological type. The specious idea that gender differences are due entirely to culture, and have nothing to do with biological or archetypal predispositions, still enjoys wide currency in our society, yet it rests on the discredited *tabula rasa* theory of human development and is at variance with the overwhelming mass of anthropological and scientific evidence.

Sexual differentiation begins approximately six weeks after conception, when in male children the gonads are formed and begin to manufacture male hormone, which has a profound effect on the future development of the embryo. In the female, on the other hand, the ovaries are not formed until the sixth month, by which time the greater size, weight, and muscular strength of the male is already established. This is the biological basis of the sexual dimorphism apparent in the great majority of societies known to anthropology, where child-rearing is almost invariably the responsibility of women, and hunting and warfare the responsibility of men. These differences have less to do with cultural 'stereotypes' than some fashionable contemporary notions would have us believe. While it is true that at all ages males and females have far more in common than they have differences between them, there can be no doubt that some differences exist which have their roots in the biology of our species. Jung was quite clear about this. Again and again, he refers to the masculine and the feminine as two great archetypal principles, coexisting as equal and complementary parts of a balanced cosmic system, as expressed in the interplay of *yin* and *yang* in Taoist philosophy. These archetypal principles provide the foundations on which masculine and feminine stereotypes begin to do their work, providing an awareness of gender. Gender is the psychic recognition and social expression of the sex to which nature has assigned us, and a child's awareness of its gender is established by as early as eighteen months of age.

Initially, the mother functions as a 'carrier' of the Self, in the sense that the child's Self is unconsciously *projected* on to the mother in a *participation mystique* (a term which Jung borrowed from the anthropologist Lévy-Brühl to denote a relationship in which both partners are so intensely identified with one another as to be unaware of their separate existence). This is true of both boys and girls, and gender awareness has to be superimposed on this original sense of oneness with the mother. For a girl this presents no problem: her gender consciousness is based on *shared* identity with her mother. But for the boy, a transformation has to be achieved to an awareness of an identity based on *difference* from the mother. At this point, the presence of a father-figure can prove crucial, enabling the boy to move from a self-concept based on mother identity to one based on identification-with-father. For the girl, the father's presence is no less important, for it heightens her sense of being female in contrast to the essential 'otherness' of the male, and so profoundly influences how she *experiences* her femininity in relation to men.

In mythology the dawning of consciousness is symbolized by the separation of the world parents, Father Heaven from Mother Earth, and the creation of light out of darkness. Originally, the sky lay flat upon the earth, and so the world parents remained until a hero got between them and gave the sky such an enormous shove that it flew up into the firmament and has remained there ever since. This momentous event was followed by the coming of light—the symbol of consciousness and 'illumination'.

As the parent–child relationship matures within the traditional family setting, there is a growing awareness on the part of the child that father-love differs from mother-love: the father's love is *contingent* love (i.e. it is conditional upon the adoption of certain values, standards, and modes of conduct) while the mother's love is largely *unconditional* (i.e. it is usually sufficient for her that her child *exists*). This distinction accords with the phenomenological differences between the father and mother archetypes as represented in myths, religions, and fairy-tales. While the mother archetype finds universal expression as Mother Nature, Goddess of Fertility, Womb of Life, and Dispenser of Nourishment, the father archetype is personified as Ruler, Elder, King, and Lawgiver. The mother is abundantly endowed with *Eros*, the principle of love, intimacy, and relatedness, while the father is the living embodiment of *Logos*, the principle of reason, judgement, and discrimination. His word is law. Jung wrote:

The archetype of the mother is the most immediate one for the child. But with the development of consciousness, the father also enters the field of

vision, and activates an archetype whose nature is in many respects opposed to that of the mother. Just as the mother archetype corresponds to the
Chinese *yin*, so the father archetype corresponds to the *yang*. It determines
our relation to man, to the law and the state, to reason and the spirit and the
dynamism of nature. (*CW* X, para. 65)

Gender consciousness and an awareness of the characteristics of
the opposite sex, having been established in relation to the parents,
are refined through interaction with the peer group, especially in
play. The roles children adopt in play are, of course, culturally
related, being based on mimicry of the parents and other significant
adults in the community. But, as evidence from widely differing
societies indicates, these cultural influences proceed on the basis
of an archetypal design. Virtually everywhere, it appears that girls
tend to be more nurturant and affiliative than boys in that they are
more prone to seek the proximity of others and to show pleasure in
doing so. Boys, on the other hand, are less interested in social
interaction for its own sake and tend to prefer some form of
physical activity, such as running, chasing, and playing with large,
movable toys. They also tend to be more rowdy and aggressive and
less amenable to control by adults and their peers.

Anima and animus

Just as gender is experienced as an affirmation of the archetypal
principle appropriate to one's sex, so relations with the other sex
rest on an archetypal foundation. Of all the archetypal systems
enabling us to adapt to the typical circumstances of human life,
that involved in relating to the opposite sex is the most crucial.
Jung called this contrasexual archetype the *animus* in women and
the *anima* in men. As the feminine aspect of man and the masculine aspect of woman, they function as a pair of opposites (the
syzygy) in the unconscious of both, profoundly influencing the
relations of all men and women with each other.

Jung also found that in practice both anima and animus act in
dreams and in the imagination as mediators of the unconscious to
the ego, so providing a means for inner as well as outer adaptation.
He described them as 'soul-images' and the 'not-I', for they are
experienced as something mysterious and numinous, possessing

great power. The more unconscious the anima or animus, the more likely it is to be projected—the psychodynamic process responsible for the experience of 'falling in love'. For this reason, Jung called the contrasexual complex the 'projection-making factor'.

'Every man carries within him the eternal image of the woman, not the image of this or that woman, but a definite feminine image. This image is fundamentally unconscious, an hereditary factor of primordial origin . . .' (*CW* XVII, para. 338). 'Woman is compensated by a masculine element and therefore her unconscious has, so to speak, a masculine imprint . . . and accordingly I have called the projection-making factor in women the animus . . . The animus corresponds to the paternal Logos just as the anima corresponds to the maternal Eros' (*CW* IX. ii, para. 28).

As with the shadow, the contrasexual complex possesses qualities opposite to those manifested in the persona, for, even in our egalitarian times, boys are expected to be boys and girls to be girls. Thus, the more a man is incapable of accepting his shadow and the feminine qualities in himself the more he is identified with his persona. Indeed, Jung even goes so far as to declare that 'the character of the anima can be deduced from that of the persona' because 'everything that should normally be in the outer attitude, but is conspicuously absent, will invariably be found in the inner attitude. This is a fundamental rule . . .' (*CW* VI, para. 806).

A self-regulating system

This fundamental rule is the *homeostatic* rule of self-regulation, which Jung borrowed from biology and applied to human psychology. Homeostasis is the means by which all organic systems keep themselves in a state of balance, despite changes in the environment. In fact, homeostatic regulation can be observed at all levels of existence, from molecules to communities, in living as well as non-living systems, and our whole planet is conceivable as one vast homeostatic system. Because the psyche evolved in the context of the world, Jung held that the laws which prevail in the cosmos must also prevail in the psyche. He therefore felt justified in viewing the psyche as a self-regulating system which strives perpetually to maintain a balance between opposing propensities, while, at the same time, seeking its own growth and development.

The psyche is a self-regulating system that maintains its equilibrium just as the body does. Every process that goes too far immediately and inevitably calls forth compensations, and without these there would be neither a normal metabolism nor a normal psyche. In this sense we can take the theory of compensation as a basic law of psychic behaviour. Too little on one side results in too much on the other. Similarly, the relation between conscious and unconscious is compensatory. (*CW* XVI, para. 330)

The principle of compensation is the key concept of Jungian psychodynamics, in that it is central to Jung's understanding of how the psyche adapts and develops in the course of the life cycle.

A programme for life

Jung's approach to developmental psychology was so different from that prevailing throughout his lifetime that it marked him out in the eyes of many as a maverick. In the orthodox behaviourist view the human organism was a mere response system which reacted to outer stimuli to build up a repertoire of behaviours through conditioning and learning. Jung, on the contrary, held that human beings were born with an elaborate programme for life which presupposed the natural life cycle of humanity and was incorporated in the Self. As he wrote:

Behind a man's actions there stands neither public opinion nor the moral code, but the personality of which he is still unconscious. Just as a man still is what he always was, so he already is what he will become. The conscious mind does not embrace the totality of a man, for this totality consists only partly of his conscious contents . . . In this totality the conscious mind is contained like a smaller circle within a larger one. (*CW* XI, para. 390)

As one passes from one stage of the life cycle to the next, new and appropriate aspects of the Self become active and demand expression, and Jung believed that this inner programme imparted to the second half of life a quality quite different from the first. The primary concerns of the first half are biological and social, while those of the second are cultural and spiritual. 'Man has two aims,' he wrote. 'The first is the natural aim, the begetting of children and the business of protecting the brood; to this belongs the acquisition of money and social position.' Only when this aim has been achieved does the new aim—'the cultural aim'—become feasible (*CW* VII, para. 114).

Transition from one stage of the life cycle to the next is a time of potential crisis for everyone and it was in order to assist the individual through these critical period that *rites of passage* evolved in primitive societies. These rites—particularly puberty initiation rites, rites of incorporation into the hunter, warrior, or shamanic role, marriage rites, rites on the birth of children and the death of relations—possessed great value because they provided public affirmation of the fact that a significant transition had occurred and, through the powerful symbolism of the ritual, activated archetypal components in the collective unconscious appropriate to the life stage that had been reached: this archetypal potential was then incorporated in the personal psyche of the initiate.

Archetypal expectations

Maturation is to be conceived, therefore, as proceeding through an innate sequence of archetypal *expectations*, namely, that the environment will provide the following: sufficient *nourishment*, *warmth*, and *protection* from predators and enemies to guarantee physical survival, a *family* consisting of mother, father, and peers; sufficient *space for exploration and play*; a *community* to supply language, myth, religion, ritual, values, stories, initiation, and, eventually, a *mate*; and an *economic* role and/or *vocational status*.

Although these archetypal requirements are the same for everyone, each culture will succeed (or fail) in meeting them in its own way and every individual's experience of living through the sequence will be unique. Thus, the actual qualities of the parents will have a profound influence on a child's development, for they will determine the quality and content of the mother and father complexes in the child's personal psyche, which in turn provide the foundations on which the mature personality is built. However, these complexes are never simple 'video clips' of the actual parents: they are parental *imagos*, the products of a continuous interaction between the personal parents in the environment and the archetypal parents in the collective unconscious. The crucial criterion is that the actual parents should be 'good enough' to actualize the parental archetypes, namely, that they should be sufficiently present (to satisfy the law of *contiguity*) and sufficiently appropriate in their care-giving (to satisfy the law of *similarity*) to approximate to the child's archetypal expectations. Where the parents are not 'good enough' the rest of the programme for life may be distorted and later stages in the archetypal sequence may fail to be realized. Thus, the boy whose father was inadequate or absent may fail to actualize his masculine potential sufficiently to establish the social or vocational role his talents equip him for, or he may be unable to sustain a relationship with a member of the opposite sex long enough for him to become an adequate husband or father himself.

Rites of passage

The archetypal tasks of childhood and adolescence for the male are symbolized in the hero myths which are found in all parts of the world. These tell how the hero leaves home and is subjected to a number of tests and trials, culminating in the 'supreme ordeal' of a fight with a dragon or a sea monster. The hero's triumph is rewarded with the 'treasure hard to attain', i.e. the throne of a kingdom and a beautiful princess as a bride. So it is in actuality: to embark on the adventure of life, a boy has to free himself of his bonds to home, parents, and siblings, survive the ordeals of initiation (which virtually all traditional societies imposed), and win a place for himself in the world (the kingdom). To achieve all this and to win a bride, he must overcome the power of the mother complex still operative in his unconscious (the fight with the dragon). This amounts to a second parturition from the mother, a final severing of the psychic umbilical cord (victory over the dragon-monster often involves the hero being swallowed into its belly from which he cuts his way out in a kind of auto-Caesarian section: as a result, he 'dies' as his mother's son and is 'reborn' as a man worthy of the princess and the kingdom). The ritual of masculine initiation at puberty facilitates this necessary transition. Failure to pass the ordeals of initiation or to overcome the monster, signifies failure to get free of the mother: then the princess (the anima) is never liberated from the monster's clutches. She remains trapped and inert in the unconscious in the custody of the mother complex.

In girls, the transition to womanhood is more readily accomplished since feminine gender consciousness does not demand a radical shift of identification from mother's world to father's world as it does in boys. As a result, female initiation, where it occurs, is (with the exception of the culturally rare and appalling rite of female circumcision) a less demanding and protracted process than for boys, consisting essentially of a ceremonial recognition that a young woman has now entered the reproductive phase of her life. It is as if the ritual were designed to heighten her introverted awareness of herself as a woman *creative on the plane of life itself*, with access to a sacred realm of experience that man can never know. (Man himself recognizes this and is filled with awe: 'The anima', wrote Jung, 'is the *archetype of life itself*' (*CW* IX. i, para. 66); Jung's italics.)

In many cultures there are no female initiation rites, and the task of bringing this new feminine consciousness into being falls to the initiated male. Hence the myths and fairy-tales in which the heroine lies sleeping till a prince comes to awaken her with a kiss (awakening his own anima in the process). She is the Sleeping Beauty surrounded by a thicket, or the slumbering Brünnhilde awaiting the arrival of her Siegfried within the circle of Wotan's fire.

Although our culture no longer provides rites of initiation, there persists in all of us, regardless of gender, *an archetypal need to be initiated*. We can deduce this from the dreams of patients in analysis which become rich in initiatory symbolism at critical periods of their lives—e.g. at puberty, betrothal, marriage, childbirth, at divorce or separation, at the death of a parent or spouse. Attainment of a new stage of life seems to demand that symbols of initiation must be experienced. If society fails to provide them, then the Self compensates for this deficiency by producing them in dreams.

The dynamics of progress

For all young people growth is a hard journey out of the familiar past into an unknown future, and there are times when everyone feels daunted by the precarious uncertainty of the path. Sometimes its challenges may appear so overwhelming that individuals break down, give up, or regress to a previous stage of development, returning to the mother in her archetypal aspect of nurturer and container. In the circumstances, this may well be an appropriate strategy, a *reculer pour mieux sauter* to recover enough strength and determination to encounter the ordeals that lie ahead.

An inherent conflict is apparent at this stage: the archetypal programme decrees that we must separate from the mother and grow away from her but, at the same time, hold on to the love and security she represents: 'Whoever sunders himself from the mother longs to get back to the mother. This longing can easily turn into a consuming passion which threatens all that has been won' (*CW* V, para. 352). It was this threat that rites of passage were meant to overcome, for, as Jung discovered in his confrontation with the unconscious, a dual dynamic is at work in all psychic development. On the one hand, we are driven outwards and onwards into the future; on the other, we are pulled inwards and backwards to the past. Development is never a simple, linear progress: it is a spiral with progressive ascents and regressive descents. But from his own experience, Jung learned that regression can act in the service of growth and that psychiatric illness may represent an effort on the part of the psyche to heal itself.

The period from adolescence to early adulthood is the time when people are most highly motivated to look after 'No. 1', pouring all their energies into job, marriage, home, and children. It is a time of rapid, if one-sided, development, when few people have much time to devote to their inner life. For this reason, Jung maintained that a psychological commitment to the path of individuation was hardly appropriate to this stage. On the contrary, this is the time to pay one's dues to society in order to purchase the right to individuate, which then becomes the task of the second half of life.

Love and marriage

In most people the capacity to relate to the opposite sex matures during adolescence and early adulthood to the point where marriage becomes both possible and desired, should circumstances allow. The experience of 'falling in love' occurs, as we have seen, when one meets a woman or man who, rightly or wrongly, appears to be the living embodiment of one's anima or animus. This profoundly moving experience is an example of what it means to be 'taken over' by the power of an autonomous complex.

Every archetype, once activated, seeks its own fulfilment in life. This is specially true of the animus and anima, for their quest for completion is rendered more imperative by the nagging insistence of sexual desire. Bonding with a partner is more than just a matter of unconscious projection. If the bond is to last long enough for children to be reared, then it has to be sustained by continuing sexual interest, the insistence of the law, and the recognition by each partner of the other as a real person, with qualities over and beyond those that have been projected. Failure to forgive a spouse for *not* living up to his anima or her animus fantasies can lead to heartache, recrimination, and divorce.

Jung was very aware of this from his own experience of marriage. In his essay 'Marriage as a Psychological Relationship', published in 1925, he argues that a marriage can only be a true relationship if it transcends blind mutual animus/anima projections and if both partners become *conscious* of each other's psychic reality. Otherwise it remains a 'medieval marriage', ruled by custom and illusion, a mere *participation mystique* ('one heart and one soul'). In present circumstances, marriage has to be a more conscious, less stereotyped institution, even if this entails feelings of disillusionment as the contrasexual fantasies are withdrawn, and results in an increased incidence of separation and divorce. 'There is no birth of consciousness without pain' (*CW* XVII, para. 331).

If, however, the union survives, then it can become what has been called an 'individuation marriage' (Guggenbühl-Craig, *Marriage, Dead or Alive?* Zürich: Spring Publications, 1977) enabling both personalities to grow through a richer understanding of each other, their marriage, and themselves. 'This is what happens very frequently about the midday of life,' says Jung, 'and in this wise our miraculous human nature enforces a transition that leads from the first half of life to the second. It is a metamorphosis from a state in which man is only a tool of instinctive nature to another in which he is no longer a tool, but himself: a transformation of nature into culture, of instinct into spirit' (*CW* XVII, para. 335).

Jung's views on same-sex love also drew on his animus/anima concepts. The homosexual is one who, in the course of growing up, has identified more closely with the parent of the opposite sex while the same sex potential has remained relatively unconscious and unactualized. As a result, the essential polarity of sexual attraction, the desire for union with the 'unknown other', is experienced in relation to members of the same sex who appear to have those desirable qualities which are felt to be lacking.

Thus, when male homosexuals come into analysis it is often because they have been unable to find what they are questing for, namely, the love partner who is perceived as the embodiment of their own unactualized masculine potential. Analysis can help to make the psychological significance of this quest conscious and pave the way for an 'individuation relationship' with another man, in which each helps the other to find what he has been questing for. Similar considerations apply to the analysis of homosexual women.

These and other implications of Jungian theory for gay psychology are well presented in *Jung, Jungians and Homosexuality* by Robert H. Hopcke (Boston: Shambhala, 1989).

The stroke of noon

Jung's comparison of mid-life with midday is drawn from his metaphor of life as the diurnal course of the sun:

In the morning it rises from the nocturnal sea of unconsciousness and looks upon the wide, bright world which lies before it in an expanse that steadily widens the higher it climbs in the firmament. In this extension of its field of action caused by its own rising, the sun will discover its own significance; it will see the attainment of the greatest possible height, and the widest possible dissemination of its blessings, as its goal. In this conviction the sun pursues its course to the unforeseen zenith—unforeseen, because its career is unique and individual, and the culminating point could not be calculated in advance. At the stroke of noon the descent begins. And the descent means the reversal of all the ideals and values that were cherished in the morning. The sun falls into contradiction with itself. It is as though it should draw in its rays instead of emitting them. Light and warmth decline and are at last extinguished... (*CW* VIII, para. 778)

At the middle of life an *enantiodromia* occurs, carrying with it terse intimations of mortality. For many this is a time of crisis, of

61

self-doubt, and inner questioning. 'What exactly have I achieved with my life?' 'What am I to do with the rest of it?' 'What is there to look forward to but old age, infirmity, and death?' 'The wine has fermented and begins to settle and clear,' comments Jung. '. . . instead of looking forward one looks backward . . . one begins to take stock, to see how one's life has developed up to this point' (*CW* XVII, para. 331*a*). The period from 35 to 45 is one of raised rates of depression, divorce, and suicide. Somewhat later women have to confront the additional problems of menopause. However, as Jung discovered for himself, the mid-life crisis, though traumatic, is also an opportunity to become more conscious and to grow.

Success in the first half of life usually requires channelling one's energies single-mindedly in a specific direction. This results in development of a relatively narrow, 'one-sided' personality and a failure to actualize much Self potential which remains dormant in the unconscious. As Jung emphasized, *'Personality need not imply consciousness. It can just as easily be dormant or dreaming'* (*CW* IX. i, para. 508; Jung's italics). The crisis of mid-life can serve to 'wake up' this dreaming, undiscovered Self and the rest of life can provide the opportunity for its development. With this realization the real work of individuation can begin, for individuation is a process of bringing to conscious awareness the developmental process unfolding within oneself.

The individuation of the Self

Philosophers have shown interest in the *principium individuationis* since Aristotle, but only a handful of developmental psychologists have studied the phenomenon in the present century, using such terms for it as 'self-realization' or 'self-actualization'. Jung's concept went further, however, because he viewed individuation as a biological principle evident in all living organisms and not restricted to human beings. 'Individuation', he wrote, 'is an expression of that biological process—simple or complicated as the case may be—by which every living thing becomes what it was destined to become from the beginning' (*CW* XI, para. 144). As with the archetypes themselves, he eventually came to believe that individuation was at work in inorganic matter as well—as when a crystal forms out of a hidden configuration within its pre-existent liquor.

But as a psychologist what fascinated him was what he saw as the highest achievement of the individuation principle—the human psyche in its fullest possible development. It is a creative act of Self-completion: a progressive integration of the unconscious, timeless Self (which Jung sometimes referred to as 'the two million-year-old man that is in all of us') with the time-bound personality of the contemporary man or woman. How does this extraordinary fusion occur? The answer is that it occurs in our sleep and that the process is immeasurably assisted if we record our dreams, reflect on them, and work on them.

Describing the work of analysis, Jung wrote: 'Together the patient and I address ourselves to the two million-year-old man that is in all of us. In the last analysis, most of our difficulties come from losing contact with our instincts, with the age-old unforgotten wisdom stored up in us. And where do we make contact with this old man in us? In our dreams' (*Psychological Reflections*, 76).

As will be described in Chapter 5, Jung proposed that dreams play an indispensable role in psychic homeostasis, in that they promote adaptation to the demands of life by compensating the one-sided limitations of consciousness. Repeated night after night, and year after year, this compensatory activity makes recurrent contributions to the individuation process, as becomes readily apparent when one examines a long series of dreams from the same person.

Remembering dreams, writing them down, and analysing them enhances this homeostatic function. But dreams continue to do their work whether we remember them or not. After all, the great majority of dreams occur without anyone being consciously aware of them, yet they must have a crucial purpose since virtually all animals dream, and dreaming brains have been around for 135 million years. It would be an extraordinary waste of nature's time if dreams did not contribute in some vitally important way to survival. As it turns out, both ethology and Jungian psychology share a common view of this fascinating phenomenon, though few ethologists (and indeed few Jungians) are aware of the fact. In the ethological view, dreams perform the task of integrating the daily experience of an animal with the programme for life laid down in the genome (the total genetic constitution) of the species. Dreams promote the animal's competence to survive and provide the means by which the basic patterns of the life cycle are realized. This is individuation proceeding at the natural, organic level.

The kind of individuation that was the centre of Jung's concern was the process consciously lived out by men and women actively seeking to become as complete an incarnation of humanity as it was in them to be. Circumstances inevitably impose constraints on personal development, and just as no mother can hope to embody the totality of the mother archetype so no individual can ever hope to incorporate the whole potential of the collective unconscious. However fortunate our upbringing may have been, few of us by middle age can hope to be any more than a 'good enough' version of the Self. One can, nevertheless, follow the Apollonian advice to 'know thyself', heed Pindar's dictum 'Become what thou art', and learn from Plato and Aristotle to discover one's 'true self'—to make explicit what implicitly one already is. In Jungian terms this means overcoming the divisions imposed by the parental and cultural milieu, to divest oneself of 'the false wrappings of the persona' (*CW* VII, para. 269), abandon one's ego-defences, and, rather than projecting one's shadow on to others, strive to know it and acknowledge it as part of one's inner life, come to terms with the contrasexual personality living within the personal psyche, and attempt to bring to conscious fulfilment the supreme intentions of the Self. Complete achievement of these objectives within the compass of one individual lifetime is never possible, of course, but that is not the point. 'The goal is important only as an idea,' wrote Jung; 'the essential thing is the *opus* which leads to the goal: *that* is the goal of a lifetime' (*CW* XVI, para. 400).

To commit oneself to the *opus* is to live fruitfully into old age while discharging the spiritual obligations of late maturity. 'A human being would certainly not grow to be seventy or eighty years old if this longevity had no meaning for the species. The afternoon of life must have a significance of its own and cannot be merely a pitiful appendage of life's morning' (*CW* VIII, para. 787).

To use these years to become as complete a human being as we can within the limitations of our culture is to contribute to the well-being of society as much as to the personal fulfilment of our lives. Well individuated older people are, and always have been, the repositories of wisdom, for they have had time to reflect, to integrate all they have learned with a lifetime of experience. However well educated the young may be, 'book learning' can never rival the inspiration to be gained from someone who *knows* and has *lived*. To individuate is to realize one's personal existence as a unique expression of humanity and, within the frail vessel of one's little psychic world, to distil the essence of creation. In this microcosmic experiment the great cosmos becomes conscious of itself.

4 Psychological types

Jung was concerned with both the universal and the particular in human life. Psychology had to define what psychic structures and functions all people shared in common and then describe how these came to be assembled in the unique combination that makes up the individual personality. *Psychological Types* (*CW* VI), published in 1921, was his first attempt to achieve this dual purpose.

It is a reasonable assumption that all people have broadly the same psychological equipment with which to perceive what is happening outside and inside themselves, to formulate ideas about it, and to determine how to respond to events as they occur. Where people differ is in the way that each of them typically makes use of the equipment; and this typical mode of apperception and responsiveness is what is meant in psychology by their 'type'.

The questions which must exercise the ingenuity of any psychologist attempting to devise a typology are (1) what are the essential components of the equipment, and (2) how do people differ in using these components to form their habitual mode of adaptation to reality? Jung's answers to these questions were (1) that the equipment consists of four psychological *functions*, which he named *sensation, thinking, feeling,* and *intuition,* all of which are available a priori to everybody, and (2) that individuals differ in regard to which of the four functions they use for preference.

A further distinction between people depends on whether they habitually place greater emphasis on the importance of outer objective events or inner subjective ones (i.e. whether their *attitude* to reality is characteristically *extraverted* or *introverted*).

The four functions

In *Psychological Types* Jung describes the different characteristics of the four functions in great detail, but he summed up this information very succinctly in *Man and his Symbols*, published two years after his death: 'These four functional types correspond to the obvious means by which consciousness obtains its orientation to experience. *Sensation* (i.e., sense perception) tells us that something exists; *thinking* tells you what it is; *feeling* tells you whether it is agreeable or not; and *intuition* tells you whence it comes and where it is going' (*Man and his Symbols*, 61).

Jung considered thinking and feeling to be *rational* functions and sensation and intuition to be *irrational* functions. Few people find it hard to agree that thinking, to be effective, needs to be logical and rational; but many have difficulty in conceiving feeling as a rational process. This, says Jung, is because they confuse feeling with *emotion* or *affect*. Feeling, as he used the term, can certainly give rise to emotions but only when the feeling is powerful enough to trigger biochemical or neurological changes in the body; its normal use is to make value-judgements about inner or outer events to determine whether they are pleasant or unpleasant, beautiful or ugly, desirable or undesirable, good or bad, etc. This requires evaluative reflection in the light of past experience and is, therefore, in Jung's view, a rational process. Confusion over this issue is reduced if one thinks of Jung's feeling function as a judgemental process concerned with values: *evaluating* function might be a more appropriate term.

As a psychological function, sensation is the means by which we process in consciousness the evidence of our senses and build up percepts of our world. Intuition is the means by which we make inferences about the possibilities inherent in a situation presented to our awareness at any given moment. To describe these two functions as 'irrational', as Jung does, is unhelpful because it gives the impression that he regarded them as in some way pathological or 'mad'. By 'irrational' he wished to imply that they functioned in a way that had nothing to do with reason. 'Non-rational' would be a better term.

The two attitudes

The way in which each function manifests in the psychology of the individual depends on the characteristic *attitude* adopted by him or her. Whereas the *extravert* is oriented primarily to events in the outer world, the *introvert* is primarily concerned with the inner world. Typically, the extravert has 'an outgoing, candid and accommodating nature that adapts easily to a given situation, quickly forms attachments, and, setting aside any possible misgivings, will often venture forth with careless confidence into unknown situations'. The introvert, on the other hand, has 'a hesitant, reflective, retiring nature that keeps itself to itself, shrinks from objects, is always slightly on the defensive and prefers to hide behind mistrustful scrutiny' (*CW* VII, para. 43).

A pub brawl

An example will help to clarify what Jung meant by these different functions and attitudes. Let us imagine that four people, a sensation type, a thinking type, a feeling type, and an intuitive type, witness the following scene:

Two men come staggering out of a bar. They are shouting and swearing at one another. There is a struggle. One of them falls to the ground and bangs his head on the pavement.

Each witness will respond to these events in a manner typical of his type. We will take each of them in turn.

The sensation type will give the clearest account of what happened. He will have noted the height, build, and general appearance of the two men: one was fat, middle-aged, and bald and had a scar over his left eye; the other younger, fair-haired, more athletic, and had a moustache. Both were dressed casually in T-shirts, jeans, and trainers. It was the fat one who fell and it was his right temple that struck the kerb. There was a crack on impact, etc.

The thinking type interprets the events as they happen, working out what it all means. The two men come staggering out of the bar, so evidently they have been drinking. They are shouting and swearing at one another, so they are having a disagreement. A struggle ensues, so they must feel strongly enough to become physically violent about it. One falls to the ground, so he must be the weaker (or drunker) of the two. The latter cracks his head, so he may be concussed and in need of medical attention, etc.

The feeling type responds to each event in the scene with value-judgements: 'What a sordid episode!' 'What thoroughly objectionable people!' 'That is clearly a bar frequented by louts and not a place to go to if one wants a quiet chat with a friend.' 'The one on the ground may have hurt himself, but it serves him right!' etc. *The intuitive type* 'sees' the whole story: they are football hooligans who support opposing teams. Disgusted by their bad language, the landlord told them to clear off, and this inflamed them to violence. The man who cracked his head is accident prone, and this is just another incident in a lifetime of misfortune. He has fractured his skull and a clot will form on his brain requiring surgery. He will be off work for weeks and his long-suffering wife will once again have to struggle to make ends meet. This is what happens to people from a poor cultural background, who have nothing else to live for but football and drink. Things like this will go on happening and get much worse because we do nothing to change society or improve the educational system, etc.

Similar observations, thoughts, value-judgements, and intuitions to those just described are available to anyone who chanced to witness this episode, but Jung's point is that each of us will characteristically tend to emphasize one functional mode in monitoring the events rather than the other three. Habitual use of this mode is what determines one's functional type. Moreover, how one responds to the episode will also be determined by one's characteristic attitude, an extravert being more likely to intervene, render first aid, drag the assailant off, call for an ambulance, etc., while the introvert will be more prone to observe, record, and inwardly reflect on what has occurred, preferring to leave it to someone else (i.e. an extravert) or an official whose job it is to do something about it.

Eight psychological types

Out of the two *attitude* types and the four *functional* types it becomes theoretically possible to describe eight psychological types: the extraverted sensation type, the introverted sensation type, the extraverted thinking type, the introverted thinking type, and so on. Jung observed that it is rare for people to make exclusive use of one function: they tend to develop two functions, usually one *rational* function and one *irrational* function; one of these becomes the *primary* or *superior* function and the other an *auxiliary* function.

Jung

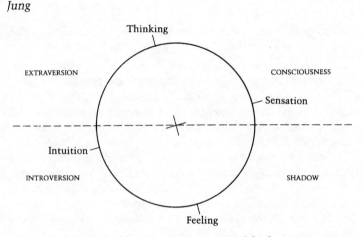

Thinking

EXTRAVERSION

CONSCIOUSNESS

Sensation

Intuition

INTROVERSION

SHADOW

Feeling

FIG. 2. The attitudes and functions in an extraverted thinking-sensation type

The other two functions remain relatively unconscious and associated with the shadow. The more unconscious of these is known as the *inferior* function. Thus, it is unusual to find thinking *and* feeling, sensation *and* intuition, developed in the same person. As a result, the rational functions, thinking and feeling, can be conceived as a pair of opposites, as can the irrational functions, sensation and intuition. An extraverted thinking-sensation type, therefore, would have an introverted feeling-intuitive shadow, and vice versa. This can be represented diagrammatically (Fig. 2).

In *Psychological Types* Jung gives a full and entertaining account of each of the eight theoretical types. Here it is possible to give no more than a thumbnail sketch of each type, together with a brief mention of its shadow opposite (which can be evident to those who have dealings with the person concerned).

Extraverted sensation types

People of this type are primarily concerned with objective reality, with how things really *are*. Essentially down-to-earth and practical, they love details, and have little time for abstractions, values, or meanings. Their constant aim, says Jung, is 'to have sensations and if possible to enjoy them' (*CW* VI, para. 605). They actively seek thrills in dangerous sports and tend to be *bons viveurs* who

70

live in the moment and, like Epimetheus, take little account of the future. As a result they can be excellent company. Their motto is: 'Eat, drink and be merry, for tomorrow we die.' However, they can seem superficial and 'soulless'. If they come to the notice of psychiatrists, it is usually on account of addiction, fetishism, or obsessive-compulsive neurosis.

Shadow: their inferior function is intuition, which, being introverted, is triggered by inner events and not related to outer happenings. When activated, it tends to give rise to negative hunches which are generally off-beam. As a result, people of this type may suddenly become paranoid or hostile for little apparent reason. Their crude, undifferentiated intuition can also carry them off, much to everyone else's surprise, into some esoteric cult such as anthroposophy, or some form of archaic mysticism.

Examples: engineers, business people, builders, racing drivers, jockeys, hang-gliders, mountaineers; Mr Gradgrind in Dickens's *Hard Times*, whose obsessive interest is in 'facts'.

Introverted sensation types

'Whereas the extraverted sensation type is guided by the intensity of objective influences,' says Jung, 'the introverted type is guided by the intensity of the subjective sensation excited by the objective stimulus' (*CW* VI, para. 650). Emma Jung, who considered herself to be of this type, described herself as being like a highly sensitized photographic plate. Every detail of a situation is noticed and can be recalled at will. Such people have vivid memories for sights, colours, passages in books, sounds, conversations, smells, tastes, tactile sensations, and so on.

Shadow: their inferior function is extraverted intuition, which, when activated, is triggered by outer events. Such intuition tends to be essentially negative, in that when introverted sensation types use what little intuition they have they usually pick up what is wrong in a situation: they are forever smelling rats and detecting flies in ointment. Often they are wrong in these hunches, but occasionally they score a bull's eye. 'Whereas extraverted intuition . . . [normally has] a "good nose" for objectively real possibilities, this archaicized intuition has an amazing flair for all the dangerous possibilities lurking in the background' (*CW* VI, para. 654). This can give rise to dark prophetic fantasies about what might happen in the outer world. When people of this type break down they tend to become paranoid.

Examples: the detailed descriptions of people and places in Thomas Mann's novels suggest that he belonged to this type; leading French impressionist painters, who reproduced their vivid inner impressions of reality, probably also tended to be introverted sensation types.

Extraverted thinking types

People of this type base their activities on intellectual considerations guided by external criteria. They are good at solving problems, reorganizing businesses, clarifying issues, and sorting the grain from the chaff. Almost invariably they concern themselves with outer conditions and not with theories or ideas. They love practical rules of thumb which they seek to apply to all situations in which they involve themselves. Because they subordinate feeling to thinking they can seem cold and aloof.

Shadow: introverted feeling. This gives rise to feelings and value-judgements which are crude, inappropriate, and poorly expressed. Extraverted thinkers tend to take their personal relationships for granted and to be unaware of the feelings of people around them. Their archaic feeling function can sometimes lead them into sudden political or religious conversions or equally sudden changes in personal loyalties.

Examples: lawyers, administrative civil servants, management consultants, practical scientists, and technicians; Voltaire, a brilliant thinker and atheist, who was a scourge of the Church throughout his life, was suddenly converted to Catholicism on his death-bed, and demanded extreme unction.

Introverted thinking types

The activities of this type are also based on intellectual considerations but they are guided by internal criteria. They tend to show little interest in events proceeding in the outer world, and are essentially concerned with theories and ideas. When one reads Jung's account of this type, one realizes that he is describing himself: 'What seems to it of paramount importance is the development and presentation of the subjective idea, of the initial symbolic image hovering darkly behind the mind's eye' (*CW* VI, para. 628). In fact, Jung's theory of psychological types is a good example of introverted thinking in action: it is a carefully thought-out system, devised in neat opposites and balances, then imposed, like all typologies, on the psychological data. Preferring to be left alone with their thoughts, people of this type often prefer solitude to company, and, such is their intellectual self-sufficiency, they are little concerned whether their ideas find general acceptance or not.

Shadow: extraverted feeling. This can become active in relation to external objects, but introverted thinkers have great difficulty in recognizing their feelings and in sharing them with others. Since feeling is primitive and largely unconscious it can express itself in quixotic and unpredictable ways: powerful affects can suddenly erupt when people or events do not behave in a way that the introverted thinker believes they 'ought' to behave; attachments can be formed to unsuitable partners—like the professor in *The Blue Angel* who becomes passionately committed to a prostitute— with disastrous consequences.

Examples: philosophers, 'intellectuals', mathematicians, 'pure' scientists; Bertrand Russell.

Extraverted feeling types

The feelings, values, and judgements of this type tend to be conventional and in harmony with those of the company they habitually frequent. As a result, they are affable and easy to get on with. They hate their own company and find introspection morbid and depressing. Popular with friends and work-mates, they can always be relied upon to rally round in times of need. If you are forced to take to your bed with a slipped disc or the flu, the friend who pops in to feed the cat and do the shopping may well be an extraverted feeling type.

Shadow: introverted thinking. Jung: 'the unconscious of this type contains first and foremost a peculiar kind of thinking, a thinking that is infantile, archaic, negative' (*CW* VI, para. 600). Such thinking is narrow, coarse, and cynical. It can find specious application in providing justification for the feeling state of the moment, a tactic which greatly irritates extraverted thinkers. If extraverted feeling types should take up an intellectual system they tend to become fanatical about it because they are unable to think it through. When these types break down they tend to develop either hysteria or mania.

Examples: actors, TV 'personalities', public relations experts; Goethe's Wagner (in *Faust*); Noel Coward, Oscar Wilde, Lady Ottoline Morrell, Mae West, Sir Thomas Beecham, Sarah Bernhardt.

Introverted feeling types

People of this type have a highly differentiated set of values which they tend to keep to themselves. They may have a covert influence on those around them, however, by virtue of the standards they embody in their way of life. They can provide a group with its ethical backbone, not by preaching or lecturing, but just by being there. Jung: 'They are mostly silent, inaccessible, hard to understand . . . harmonious, inconspicuous, giving an impression of pleasing repose . . . with no desire to affect others, to impress, influence, or change them in any way . . . there is little effort to respond to the real emotions of the other person . . . This type observes a benevolent though critical neutrality, coupled with a faint sense of superiority . . .' (*CW* VI, para. 640). With this type it is true that 'still waters run deep'.

Shadow: extraverted thinking. As with extraverted feeling types, this thinking is concrete and primitive, but being extraverted it tends to be slavishly tied to objective facts, and when people of this type do attempt to use their thinking function, they tend to get lost in detail, not being able to see the wood for the trees. Breakdown usually leads to depression.

Examples: Rainer Maria Rilke, who once wrote to a lady: 'I love you, but it's none of your business!' The Mona Lisa gives the impression of belonging to this type.

Extraverted intuitive types

People of this type habitually use their intuition to deal with outer reality. In contrast to sensation types, intuitives are not interested in things 'as they really are' but in what might be done with them. Jung: 'intuition is not mere perception, or vision, but an active, creative process that puts into the object just as much as it takes out' (*CW* VI, para. 610). Extraverted intuitives are quick to see the possibilities inherent in a given situation and are good at predicting future developments. But unless they have thinking as their auxiliary function, they are not good at staying with the projects they initiate and seeing them through to a satisfactory conclusion. Their gift is essentially innovative and they are bored with routine. They will take up new friends, hobbies, or ideas because of their interesting possibilities, and then just as quickly drop them when other possibilities come into view.

Shadow: introverted sensation. Jung: '[the intuitive] does have sensations, of course, but he is not guided by them as such; he uses them merely as starting points for his perceptions' (*CW* VI, para. 611). However, he is often completely unconscious of his sensations and, as a consequence, is prone not to notice when he is tired, cold, or hungry. When his introverted sensation does become active, it can cause him to misinterpret messages arriving from his own sense organs, with the result that he may become hypochondriacal, or indulge in fads about diet and exercise.

Examples: journalists, stockbrokers, entrepreneurs, dealers in 'futures', currency speculators, creative artists and fashion designers who anticipate the *nouvelle vague* before it breaks.

Introverted intuitive types

'[Introverted intuition] does not concern itself with external possibilities but with what the external object has released within' (*CW*

75

VI, para. 656). People of this type are inclined to make use of the mechanism of *reification* (i.e. they treat ideas, images, or insights as if they were real objects). 'For intuition, therefore, unconscious images acquire the dignity of things' (*CW* VI, para. 657). Like Jung himself, who was primarily an introverted intuitive type (with thinking as his auxiliary function), they have difficulty in communicating their ideas simply and in an organized way, for they pursue image after image, idea after idea, 'chasing after every possibility in the womb of the unconscious', as Jung says, while usually overlooking what personal implications these possibilities may have. 'Had this type not existed, there would have been no prophets in Israel' (*CW* VI, para. 658). They may have brilliant insights, which, if they can be bothered or sufficiently organized to communicate them, others proceed to build on.

Shadow: extraverted sensation. Because this is mostly unconscious, they are constantly in danger of losing touch with outer reality, and if they break down they become schizophrenic. Many have schizoid personalities, as did Jung himself as a boy. Vague about practical details and poorly oriented in space and time, they tend to forget appointments, are seldom punctual, and easily get lost in strange places. Their poor relationship to reality, combined with the depth of their insights, causes some to experience themselves as belonging to the 'misunderstood genius' category. Their attitude to sexuality can be crude and inappropriate, and they tend to make poor lovers since they are unaware of what is happening in their own or their partner's body.

Examples: Seers, prophets, poets, psychologists (not experimental or academic ones), artists, shamans, mystics, and cranks; Nietzsche (especially in *Thus Spake Zarathustra*); Swedenborg.

The reader should be warned that the above descriptions are necessarily over-simplified and do less than justice to the detailed exegesis offered by Jung. Those wishing to study the typology in detail are referred to chapter X in volume VI of the *Collected Works*.

Origins

The search for typical psychological characteristics was by no means confined to Jung. Looking for common denominators is the way that the thinking function invariably proceeds when confronted with complex data, and many other typologies have been devised from classical times up to the present. Interestingly, the categories into which these typologies are divided are commonly four in number. It is as if the mind has a natural propensity to orientate itself through a tetrad of paired oppositions. That indispensable instrument of orientation, the magnetic compass, is a case in point. In the fifth century BC, the Greek philosopher Empedocles held that a tetrad of elements—earth and air, fire and water—was ruled by a great archetypal pair of opposites, Love and Strife. At about the same time, four primary qualities were defined—hot and cold, wet and dry—which also made up a tetrad of opposites, as did the four blood types of Aristotle and the four humours of Hippocrates. These ancient classificatory systems found modern expression in Rorschach's *Theory of Types* (1921) and Kretschmer's *Physique and Character* (1921) about the same time as Jung published *Psychological Types*.

Jung's motive in devising his typology was derived only in part from his wish to explain why he and Adler had quarrelled with Freud; it was also, I believe, a further attempt to compensate for his sense of personal oddity and isolation. Just as he had to discover what he shared in common with the rest of humanity, so he had also to explain how he was different.

Accordingly, he embarked on an extensive investigation of some of the great quarrels of history (e.g. those between St Augustine and Pelagius, Tertullian and Origen, Luther and Zwingli) and some of the major categorical distinctions made by philosophers and poets in the past (e.g. Nietzsche's contrast between the Apollonian and Dionysian, Spitteler's between Prometheus and Epimetheus, and Goethe's between the principles of diastole and systole). In all instances, he concluded, the distinctions represented a fundamental difference between extraverted and introverted attitudes.

In addition, he based his presentation on empirically gained insights derived from the observation of many different individuals. He was touchy on this point, for when his typology was attacked by academic psychologists they drew a tart riposte in his preface to the seventh edition of *Psychological Types*: 'my typology is the result of many years of practical experience, and such experience is, of course, not available to the academic psychologist . . .'!

One important source of the two attitude types is, however, conspicuously absent from Jung's extensive review of the literature, and that is the French psychologist Alfred Binet's distinction (made in his *L'Étude experimentale de l'intelligence*, 1903) between two types of intellectual attitude, which he termed 'introspection' and 'externospection'. Introspection he defined as 'the knowledge we have of our inner world, our thoughts, our feelings'; while externospection is 'the orientation of our knowledge toward the exterior world as opposed to the knowledge of ourselves' (Ellenberger, *The Discovery of the Unconscious*, 702–3). Since Binet's distinction, to say nothing of his terminology, is so close to Jung's it is strange that no mention is made of it in *Psychological Types*. The most charitable interpretation of his silence is that, in developing his ideas about the introverted and extraverted attitude types, Jung was experiencing a *cryptomnesia* (lit. hidden memory)—that although he had lost all conscious recollection of Binet's work, it had none the less borne fruit in his personal unconscious.

Use of the typology

Jung's typology is open to the same objection as all other typologies, namely, that it seeks to constrain the apparently infinite variety of human psychological traits within narrow, arbitrarily imposed categories. However, it must be said in his defence that Jung, the great individualist, was intensely aware of this problem, stating his conviction that 'every individual is an exception to the rule'. He goes on:

One can never give a description of a type, no matter how complete, that would apply to more than one individual, despite the fact that in some ways it aptly characterizes thousands of others. Conformity is one side of a man, uniqueness is the other. Classification does not explain the individual psyche. Nevertheless, an understanding of psychological types opens the way to a better understanding of human psychology in general. (*CW* VI, para. 895)

'Pure' types do not exist. No one has just one function and one attitude and nothing else. We are all an amalgam. With some people it is easy to work out which function and which attitude habitually dominates, with others it is virtually impossible. This Jung freely admits: 'it is often very difficult to find out whether a person belongs to one type or the other, especially in regard to oneself.' With regard to the attitude types, he says: 'everyone possesses both mechanisms, extraversion as well as introversion, and only the relative predominance of one or the other determines the type. Hence, in order to throw the picture into the necessary relief, one would have to retouch it rather vigorously, and this would amount to a more or less pious fraud' (*CW* VI, para. 4).

The aspect of Jung's typology which has found widest acceptance is, in fact, his distinction between introverted and extraverted attitude types. Even Professor Hans Eysenck of London University, who has always been hostile to all forms of analysis, has confirmed the existence of an extraversion–introversion axis in the human personality, using the most carefully controlled quantitative techniques. Attempts to establish Jung's four functional types on an empirical basis have been less successful, however.

Jung argued that one's type was as much determined by genetic as by environmental factors, and it would indeed seem likely that both extraverted and introverted attitudes are biologically adaptive. Our predominant position on this planet is the direct result of our ability to adapt to changing environmental conditions on the one hand, and to reflect on ways of effectively meeting them on the other. In so complicated a species as *Homo sapiens* it is appropriate that some individuals should be genetically predisposed to specialize in an extraverted orientation and others to specialize in an introverted one.

Both extraverted and introverted attitudes are necessary for healthy development and all of us alternate in some degree between these two orientations. After all, even the most extraverted people fall every night into a profoundly introverted state when they go to sleep and begin to dream. In the dreaming state one is wholly withdrawn from the outer world and, for as long as it lasts, the dream represents the sum total of one's experience of reality.

In developing the theory of psychological types, Jung realized something extremely important that the academic psychologists tended to overlook, namely, that it is not possible for a psychologist to be entirely objective in collecting and interpreting his data. Unless the observer can know his own 'personal equation' and allow for it in his work, his observations must inevitably be vitiated by bias. Even in physics, it has been found that the scientist affects the phenomena he is observing; how much truer must this be in the study of human psychology and in the practice of analysis. Knowledge of one's type is useful, therefore, in that it enables one to correct in some measure the personal biases one brings to a situation.

On the whole, Jung's typology is best used in the way that one would use a compass: all typological possibilities are theoretically available to the Self, but it is useful to be able to establish those coordinates that one is using to chart one's course through life. Jung accepted that this course is never intractably fixed; it may at any time be subject to alteration. Viewed in this light, awareness of one's psychological type is not a constraint but a liberation, for it can open up new navigational possibilities in life, the existence of which one might otherwise never have discovered.

5 Dreams

The use of dreams is indispensable to classical Jungian analysis. Jung's theoretical approach to the dream was profoundly influenced by Freud's, first as a model for practical therapy, and later as a model to react against, to modify, and to extend. We must, therefore, take Freud's view of dreams as a starting-point.

Freud believed that during sleep forbidden wishes are liberated from their daytime inhibition and seek to gain admission to consciousness. However, the 'forbidden' nature of these wishes means that they are experienced by the ego as disturbing, and are therefore capable of waking one up. It is the function of dreams, in Freud's view, to prevent this from happening: they protect the ego by transforming the unacceptable wish into an acceptable set of images, thus enabling the dreamer to go on sleeping. 'All dreams are in a sense dreams of convenience,' wrote Freud in *The Interpretation of Dreams*: 'They serve the purpose of prolonging sleep instead of waking up. *Dreams are the GUARDIANS of sleep and not its disturbers*' (p. 330; Freud's italics).

The mental institution responsible for performing this protective function is the 'censor' or super-ego, which causes the forbidden wish (the *latent content* of the dream, as Freud called it) to be disguised and appear in a form which will neither disturb the ego nor wake the dreamer. The dream itself is thus the *manifest content* of the disguised wish. In order to disguise the latent content, the censor makes use of a number of techniques, such as *displacement, condensation, symbolization,* and *pictorialization,* and these defensive transformations account for the often bizarre or irrational nature of the manifest dream. Freud even goes so far as to make the circular argument that the bizarre nature of dreams is itself evidence for the existence and function of the censor in disguising the dream's true meaning.

The goal of Freudian dream interpretation is to undo the work of the censor. This is achieved by the technique of free association, whereby one starts with a dream image and allows one's thoughts to associate to it in complete freedom. As Freud put it: 'The restoration of the connections which the dream-work has destroyed is a task which has to be performed by the interpretative process' (ibid. 422). Thus: *'the interpretation of dreams is the royal road to a knowledge of the unconscious activities of the mind'* (ibid. 769; Freud's italics). In other words, the dream is a code to be decoded, a scrambled line to be unscrambled, so that its images can be reduced to their basic meanings.

Freud was satisfied that with these formulations he had solved the riddle that had intrigued mankind since antiquity, namely, how to unravel the meaning of dreams. He became so convinced of this when he was on holiday in Belle Vue Castle near Vienna in 1895 that he had the fantasy that one day a marble tablet would record that *'In this house on July 24th, 1895, the Secret of Dreams was revealed to Dr. Sigmund Freud'*.

Initially, Jung went along with Freud's approach, but he was quick to see its limitations, and his growing reservations were similar to those that he entertained about psychoanalysis as a whole. Freud believed that dreams fashioned their manifest content out of memory residues from two sources: from events of the previous day and from childhood. Jung accepted this, but, as we have seen, he went much further, maintaining that dreams draw on a third, much deeper source, belonging to the evolutionary history of our species, which he called the collective unconscious. Moreover, Freud believed that the forbidden wishes responsible for the production of dreams were predominantly sexual in origin. Jung, on the other hand, was convinced that dreams had their origins in much wider concerns, namely, the basic issues of human existence.

After the break with Freud and his encounter with the unconscious, Jung felt free to develop his own approach to dreams, though, unlike Freud, he was never dogmatic about it. On the contrary, he was capable of undue modesty: 'I have no theory about dreams,' he wrote, 'I do not know how dreams arise. And I am not at all sure that my way of handling dreams even deserves the name of a "method"' (*CW* XVI, para. 86). Having issued this disclaimer, however, he proceeded to reject the basic tenets of Freud's dream theory and replace them with suggestions of his own.

In fact, most of Freud's hypotheses have proved untenable in the light of dream research, while Jung's have stood up to the test of time. For example, the well-established observation that all mammals dream and that human infants devote much of their time to REM (rapid eye movement) dream sleep, both in the womb and post-natally, would seem to dispose of the idea that dreams are disguised expressions of repressed wishes or that their primary function is to preserve sleep. It is more likely that dreams are, as Jung maintained, natural products of the psyche, that they perform some homeostatic or self-regulatory function, and that they obey the biological imperative of adaptation in the interests of personal adjustment, growth, and survival.

Jung's theory of dreams can be summarized under four headings:

1. Dreams are natural, spontaneous events, which proceed independently of conscious will or intention;
2. Dreams are both purposive and compensatory, in that they serve to promote the balance and individuation of the personality;
3. The symbols of dreams are true symbols, not signs, and they possess a transcendent function;
4. The therapeutic power of dreams is better served by the techniques of *amplification* and *active imagination* than by interpretation based on 'free association'.

We shall consider each of these in turn.

Pure nature

Dreams are impartial, spontaneous products of the unconscious psyche, outside the control of the will. They are pure nature; they show us the unvarnished, natural truth, and are therefore fitted, as nothing else is, to give us back an attitude that accords with our basic human nature when our consciousness has strayed too far from its foundations and run into an impasse. (*CW* X, para. 317)

'They do not deceive, they do not lie, they do not distort or disguise ... They are invariably seeking to express something that the ego does not know and does not understand' (*CW* XVII, para. 189). The dream is 'a spontaneous self-portrayal, in symbolic form, of the actual situation in the unconscious' (*CW* VIII, para. 505).

Certainly, it is not a façade designed to conceal what lies behind it:

the so-called façade of most houses is by no means a fake or a deceptive distortion; on the contrary, it follows the plan of the building and often betrays the interior arrangement. The 'manifest' dream-picture is the dream itself and contains the whole meaning of the dream. When I find sugar in the urine it is sugar and not just a façade for albumen. What Freud calls 'the dream façade' is the dream's obscurity, and this is really only a projection of our own lack of understanding. We say that the dream has a false front only because we fail to see into it. (*CW* XVI, para. 319)

Jung was fond of quoting the Talmud to the effect that 'The dream is its own interpretation'. Why then do dreams need to be interpreted? Not because they are *disguises* but because their meanings are formulated in a pictorial 'language' that is rendered comprehensible to the ego only when put into words.

'The whole dream-work is essentially subjective, and a dream is a theatre in which the dreamer is himself the scene, the player, the prompter, the producer, the author, the public, and the critic' (*CW* VIII, para. 509).

The view that dreams are merely the imaginary fulfilments of repressed wishes is hopelessly out of date. There are, it is true, dreams which manifestly represent wishes or fears, but what about all the other things? Dreams may contain ineluctable truths, philosophical pronouncements, illusions, wild fantasies, memories, plans, anticipations, irrational experiences, even telepathic visions, and heaven knows what besides. (*CW* XVI, para. 317)

Compensatory function

Jung's proposition that dreams perform a compensatory function in balancing the one-sided attitudes of ego-consciousness is consistent with his concept of psychic homeostasis. The passage, quoted above on pp. 54–5, in which Jung asserts that 'the theory of compensation is a basic law of psychic behaviour' continues: 'Too little on one side results in too much on the other. Similarly, the relation between conscious and unconscious is compensatory. This is one of the best-proven rules of dream interpretation. When we set out to interpret a dream, it is always helpful to ask: What conscious attitude does it compensate?' (*CW* XVI, para. 330).

Thus dreams 'add something important to our conscious knowledge', and 'a dream which fails to do so has not been properly interpreted' (*CW* XVI, para. 318). Dreams 'always stress the other side in order to maintain the psychic equilibrium' (*CW* VII, para. 170).

In one sense, Jung's compensatory concept may be seen as an extension of Freud's theory of wish-fulfilment, for both conceive dreams as a means of making accessible to consciousness something previously unavailable and unconscious. But whereas Freud held the purpose of the dream to be one of deception so as to outwit the censor and enable the shadow to enter consciousness in disguise, Jung thought its purpose was to serve individuation by making valuable unconscious potential available to the whole personality. In contrast to Freud's causal or reductive approach, which traced dream contents back to their infantile instinctual origins, Jung advocated a constructive, teleological approach which sought to discover where the dream contents might be leading. For Jung, the prospective implications of a dream were more significant for personality development (and for a positive therapeutic outcome) than its possible origins in earlier personal experiences. To plough a symbol back into its past was to deprive the dreamer of its contribution to the present and the future, and to adopt an essentially reductive standpoint was to negate the creative, goal-seeking powers of the psychic system. 'No psychological fact can ever be explained in terms of causality alone; as a living phenomenon, it is always indissolubly bound up with the continuity of the vital process, so that it is not only something evolved but also continually evolving and creative' (*CW* VI, para. 717).

Accordingly, dreams serve the teleological imperative of the Self, which works unceasingly towards its own realization in life. (*Teleo* is a combination word derived from *teleos*, meaning perfect, complete, and *telos*, meaning end; *teleology*, therefore, is about attaining the goal of completeness.)

Symbolism

No area of disagreement between Jung and Freud reflected more clearly the temperamental differences between them than their respective attitude to symbols. To Freud, a symbol was a figurative representation of an unconscious idea, conflict, or wish. It was a substitute-formation which effectively disguised the true meaning of the idea it represented: a sword was a symbol of the penis, its sheath a symbol of the vagina, and pushing the sword into its sheath a symbol of sexual intercourse.

For his part, Jung did not consider the Freudian symbol to be a symbol at all; it was a *sign*, for it regularly referred to something already known or knowable and embodied a meaning that was fixed. Jung's understanding of symbols was quite different. To him symbols were living entities striving to express something previously unknown; they were intuitive ideas that, at the moment of their creation, could not be formulated in any better way (*CW* XV, para. 105). Thus, symbols 'mean more than they say' and remain 'a perpetual challenge to our thoughts and feelings' (*CW* XV, para. 119).

These different approaches to symbolism are a further expression of Freud's reductive orientation on the one hand and Jung's teleological orientation to the psyche and its functions on the other. To Jung, symbols were natural growth factors which made possible the development of the personality, the resolution of conflict, and the transcendence of polar oppositions. For this reason, he held that symbols possessed a *transcendent function*, facilitating all transitions from one psychological state to another. Symbols are, therefore, indispensable to healing and to the individuation of the Self. Human beings owe their pre-eminent status in the world to the fact that they are symbol-making animals.

Consideration of the transcendent function brings us to the heart of Jung's love of paradox and his celebration of the generative power of *opposites*. 'The opposites are the ineradicable and indispensable preconditions of all psychic life,' he wrote (*CW* XIV, para. 206). All opposites are intrinsically irreconcilable: but conflict between any pair of opposites generates tension which motivates the psyche to seek a third possibility that transcends them both. If one can learn to bear the tension that oppositions invariably bring, then the problem is raised to a higher plane: good is reconciled with evil, love with hate, doubt with certainty, and a new synthesis will follow between conscious and unconscious, persona and shadow, ego and Self. Such reconciliations are attained neither rationally nor intellectually, but symbolically, through *the transcendent function of symbols*.

Creative work with symbols is, therefore, the key to successful personal development and therapeutic practice.

Interpretation

In working on a dream the starting-point for Jung was not interpretation but 'amplification'—that is, to enter into the atmosphere of the dream, to establish its mood as well as the detail of its images and symbols, in such a way as to *amplify the experience of the dream itself*. Then its impact on consciousness is enhanced.

Because every symbol encompasses more than can be said about it, it must not be 'reduced' to its origins, but its implications examined in an archetypal light. Instead of breaking the dream down into a series of intellectual formulations, one should *circumambulate* its symbols (lit. walk round about them) allowing them to reveal their different facets to consciousness. Personal associations need to be taken into account, but a full appreciation of the dream's intention cannot stop there if one is to receive all that it has to offer.

Though most remembered dreams are little more than fragments or a few brief episodes, many have a story to tell and take the form of a private drama. In these a definite structure can be perceived, which Jung divided into four stages: (1) the *exposition*, which sets the place and often the time of the action, as well as the dramatis personae involved; (2) the *development* of the plot, in which the situation becomes complicated and 'a definite tension develops because one does not know what will happen'; (3) the *culmination* or *peripeteia*, when 'something decisive happens or something changes completely'; and (4) the *lysis*, the conclusion, the solution, or result of the dream-work (*CW* VIII, paras. 361–4).

An example will help to make these points clear.

[I was] in a mountainous region on the Swiss-Austrian border. It was toward evening, and I saw an elderly man in the uniform of an Imperial Austrian customs official [stage 1: the *exposition*]. He walked past, somewhat stooped, without paying any attention to me. His expression was peevish, rather than melancholic and vexed [stage 2: the *development*]. There were other persons present, and someone informed me that the old man was not really there, but was the ghost of a customs official who had died years ago [stage 3: the *peripeteia*]. 'He is one of those who still couldn't die properly' [stage 4: the *lysis*]. (*MDR* 158)

This is not the end of the dream, however, as the dreamer is transported to another place and a similar narrative structure is repeated: he now finds himself in a city.

The city was Basel, and yet it was also an Italian city, something like Bergamo. It was summertime; the blazing sun stood at the zenith, and everything was bathed in an intense light [*Exposition*]. A crowd came streaming toward me, and I knew that the shops were closing and people were on their way home to dinner [*Development*]. In the midst of this stream of people walked a knight in full armour. He mounted the steps toward me. He wore a helmet of the kind that is called a basinet, with eye slits, and chain armour. Over this was a white tunic into which was woven, front and back, a large red cross [*Peripeteia*]. . . . I asked myself what this apparition meant, and then it was as if someone answered me—but there was no one there to speak: 'Yes, this is a regular apparition. The knight always passes by here between twelve and one o'clock, and has been doing so for a very long time (for centuries, I gathered) and everyone knows about it' [*Lysis*]. (*MDR* 160)

The first thing that strikes one about the dream as a whole is the powerfully arresting quality of its mood and imagery, as well as the stark contrast apparent between the sad, ghostly customs official and the extraordinary, surreal presence of the medieval knight. That the dream opens on the Swiss-Austrian border must carry some significance, as must the dress, appearance, and manner of the customs official. Why should he not be there and why can he not die properly? Why is the knight, who should have died so long age, seen striding through the streets of a modern city? While the former is old and worn out, a has-been, the latter is imbued with the vibrant intensity of an archetypal image—the knight in shining armour. What does this mean?

In Jungian therapy, it is customary to approach a dream in three stages. The first attempts to establish the context of the dream in the life of the dreamer, so as to understand something of its purely personal significance. Next, the cultural context of the dream has to be defined, since it is invariably related to the milieu and time in which is was dreamt. Finally, the archetypal content is explored so as to set the dream in the context of human life as a whole, since at the most profound level dreams link us with the age-old experience of our species.

In practice it is seldom possible to keep these stages separate because, inevitably, the personal, cultural, and archetypal components of experience, as well as interpretations of their meaning, constantly interact. However, in the interests of clarity, we will consider the elements of this dream under three headings, while tolerating the unavoidable overlap between them.

Personal context

Much of the personal context has already been revealed (pp. 12–16 above): the dream was dreamt by Jung shortly before he broke off his friendship with Freud. To be more precise, it occurred while Jung was working on his book *Transformations and Symbols of the Libido* (*CW* V, *Symbols of Transformation*), in which he expressed ideas which he feared would prove unacceptable to Freud. The associations which Jung reports to the dream are brief and to the point, for he did not advocate uninhibited use of free association as did Freud. To Jung, association only facilitated dream interpretation as long as it was confined to the images in the dream. Freudian free association, in Jung's view, carried the dreamer away from the dream and served only to lead him back, time and again, to his childhood complexes, and this defeated the object of the exercise.

With the word *customs* Jung says he at once associated the word 'censorship', and in association with *border* he thought of the border between consciousness and the unconscious on the one hand, and between his views and Freud's on the other.

Of the knight Jung says:

One can easily imagine how I felt: suddenly to see in a modern city, during the noonday rush hour, a crusader coming toward me. What struck me as particularly odd was that none of the many persons walking about seemed to notice him. . . . it was as though he were completely invisible to everyone but me. . . . even in the dream, I knew that the knight belonged to the twelfth century. That was the period when alchemy was beginning and also the quest for the Holy Grail. The stories of the Grail had been of the greatest importance to me ever since I read them, at the age of fifteen, for the first time. I had an inkling that a great secret still lay hidden behind those stories. Therefore it seemed quite natural to me that the dream should conjure up the world of the Knights of the Grail and their quest—for that was, in the deepest sense, my own world, which had scarcely anything to do with Freud's. My whole being was seeking for something still unknown which might confer meaning on the banality of life. (*MDR* 158–61)

Cultural context

A frontier is an agreed line of demarcation separating two states: in terms of dream logic, it makes little difference whether these be nation states or states of mind. What cannot be overlooked is that Freud's state is Austria and Jung's Switzerland; and Freud, in some official 'imperial' role, is patrolling the border between them. At a frontier, one's personal belongings are subject to scrutiny, one's suitcases opened and searched for contraband, and one's passport examined to ensure that one's credentials are in order, and all this is done by a customs officer. Could this be a reference to the subject-matter of psychoanalysis (the borderline between consciousness and the unconscious) and to Freud as the master analyst, peevish, vexed, and sad because he suspects the dreamer is harbouring ideas that are both subversive and objectionable? In reflecting on the dream, Jung certainly made this connection. But why, he asked himself, should he dream of Freud as the ghost of a customs inspector? 'Could that be the death-wish which Freud had insinuated I had felt toward him?' He thought not, for he had no reason for wishing Freud dead. Rather he saw the dream as compensating and correcting his conscious attitude to Freud, which he now perceived as unduly deferential. The dream was recommending a more critical, more robust manner in his dealings with Freud.

The confusion between Basel and Italy in the second part of the dream is probably a reference to the achievement of Jung's fellow Baseler, Jakob Burckhardt, who linked the civilization of their home town with that of the Renaissance in Italy. This Italy is the world of anima and love, of Dante and Beatrice, Petrarch and Laura, of art and the rebirth of the human spirit. That the sun is at its zenith as the people stream home from the shops evokes the enantiodromia of mid-life, as Jung described it (p. 61 above): 'At the stroke of noon the descent begins. And the descent means the reversal of all the ideals and values that were cherished in the morning.' The first half of life is the life of 'getting and spending', but now the shops are shut and this phase is over. What promise does the future bring? The answer appears in the extraordinary figure of the knight, dressed in armour; not a man of the future, but an archetypal figure from the past, the Christian gentleman, the chivalrous warrior. He belongs to the twelfth century, which Jung associates with the beginnings of alchemy and the emergence of the legend of the Holy Grail.

Archetypal context

The archetypal images of greatest significance in this dream are the vessel (the Grail), the knight/warrior, and the cross. These in turn, and by association, bring up the archetypal themes of the old and dying king, the wounded healer, and the shaman/magician.

According to legend, the Grail was the vessel used by Jesus at the Last Supper and later by Joseph of Arimathea to collect and preserve the Saviour's blood after the Crucifixion. It is thus the most precious object in Christendom. The theme of the miraculous vessel is much older than Christianity, however. As Freud would have been the first to agree, the Grail or vessel is a feminine symbol, a womb in which a miraculous, life-giving transformation occurs. The vessel or *vas* was central to the alchemical tradition which began in ancient China and reached Northern Europe, as Jung comments, in the twelfth century. The Gnostics, with whom Jung felt a close affinity, believed that one of the original gods had made a gift to humanity of a *krater*, a mixing vessel, in which those who sought spiritual transformation were immersed. This Gnostic tradition seems to have entered European alchemy through the influence of Zosimos of Panopolis, one of the earliest and most influential alchemists, whose visions were later to be of great interest to Jung. The medieval mystics adopted the vessel as a symbol of the soul, which exists to be filled and replenished endlessly by Divine Grace.

The association of the Grail legend with England and King Arthur's Knights of the Round Table came through the figure of Merlin, the great magician, shaman, and bard of Celtic mythology. Merlin was born of an illicit union between the devil and an innocent virgin and thus emerged as a counterbalance to the figure of Christ. Early in his career, Merlin presides over a dragon fight which results in the deposition of the old usurper King Vertigier and his replacement by King Uter, to whom Merlin confides the secret of the Grail, instructing Uter to set up a Third Table. The

First Table was that of the Last Supper; the Second was the Table on which Joseph of Arimathea had kept the Grail, and it was *square*; the Third Table, which King Uter will provide, must be *round*. This rounding of the square is the very essence of the *mandala* configuration and symbolizes the achievement of wholeness, the complete realization of the Self. The quest for the Holy Grail is the individuation quest undertaken *sub specie aeternitatis*.

The Grail legend fascinated Jung all his life. As a boy he read Malory and Froissart and of all music he loved Wagner's *Parsifal* the most. He would have devoted as much time to the Grail as to alchemy had not his wife expressed a strong wish to do the work herself. As far as the dream is concerned, the most interesting aspect of the legend, apart from the vessel itself, is the theme of the 'old sick king', Amfortas. Like Chiron in Greek mythology, Amfortas suffers from a wound which will not heal; and the fascinating aspect of this wound is its situation: it is in the thigh or genital region. Amfortas's wound is a sexual wound, his problem a sexual problem. He wishes to relinquish his kingly authority and pass it on to Parsifal, much as Freud wished to hand his over to Jung, but he cannot do so until Parsifal questions him about the Grail.

Jung himself did not make this connection between Amfortas and Freud, but he made it with his own father, who was the psychological precursor of Freud in his life: 'My memory of my father is of a sufferer stricken with an Amfortas wound, a "fisher king" whose wound would not heal—that Christian suffering for which the alchemists sought the panacea. I, as a "dumb" Parsifal was the witness of this sickness during the years of my boyhood, and, like Parsifal, speech failed me. I had only inklings' (*MDR* 205).

Freud was no less a 'fisher king', and in his presence Jung was no less incapable of speech than Parsifal, never putting to Freud the question about his service to the god of sex. That is why their relationship lasted as long as it did.

Under the impress of Freud's personality I had, as far as possible, cast aside my own judgements and repressed my criticisms. That was the prerequisite for collaborating with him. I had told myself, 'Freud is far wiser and more experienced than you. For the present you must simply listen to what he says and learn from him.' And then, to my own surprise, I found myself dreaming of him as a peevish official of the Imperial Austrian monarchy, as a defunct and still walking ghost of a customs inspector! (*MDR* 159)

The symbolism of the cross needs little amplification: it indicates the cardinal points of the mandala and is the Christian symbol of wholeness, representing the reconciliation of opposites through suffering, the memorial of Christ's individuation and at-one-ment with God. The cross stands for the path of submission to one's personal destiny as a human being, for the alchemist no less than the Christian.

Submission to the fundamental contrariety of human nature amounts to an acceptance of the fact that the psyche is at cross purposes with itself. Alchemy teaches that the tension is four-fold, forming a cross which stands for the four warring elements. The quaternity is the minimal aspect under which such a state of total opposition can be regarded. The 'cross' as a form of suffering expresses psychic reality, and carrying the cross is therefore an apt symbol for the wholeness and the passion which the alchemist saw in his work. (*CW* XVI, para. 523)

The solitary crusader is the Christian soldier, marching as to war. He has a goal, a destiny which he has no choice but to fulfil. It is an image of what Jung was to become, not as a Christian but as a man. 'If a man knows more than others, he becomes lonely,' he wrote at the end of his life.

There was a daimon in me ... it overpowered me ... I could never stop at anything once attained. I had to hasten on, to catch up with my vision. Since my contemporaries could not perceive my vision, they saw only a fool rushing ahead ... I was able to become intensely interested in people; but as soon as I had seen through them, the magic was gone. In this way I made many enemies. A creative person has little power over his own life. He is not free. He is captive and drawn by his daimon ... This lack of freedom has been a great sorrow to me. Often I felt as if I were on a battlefield, saying, 'Now you have fallen, my good comrade, but I must go on.' (*MDR* 328–9)

Enough has been said for the reader to appreciate that the analysis of a dream in a manner advocated by Jung is a discursive process requiring considerable erudition as well as a gift for symbolic understanding. Much more is involved than a mere interpretation of the basic message, which in this case might be stated simply as, 'Get rid of Freud and go your own way'.

Before becoming a medical student, Jung had toyed with the idea of studying archaeology, and it was a subject which never lost its fascination for him. As he often said, he approached a dream as if it were an undeciphered text and he used all his archaeological instincts in the endeavour. Only when one has excavated the personal, cultural, and archetypal foundations of the dream is one in a position to appreciate its implications. Then, as one strolls round the site of one's excavations the dream's architecture stands revealed, together with a sense of what the architect was seeking to achieve, and where all his creative energy could lead. It is a delicate process of sifting, cataloguing, and comparing, requiring much imaginative flair: the dream must never be excavated to destruction, but its atmosphere savoured and its message left intact.

As Jung discovered, themes which are of great importance in somebody's life tend to repeat, as can be verified by studying a series of dreams from the same dreamer. Jung himself returned to the theme of the Grail in a dream he had in India in 1938 and this, like his dream of the crusader, linked him with his childhood fantasy of the castle on its rocky promontory. In the dream, he found himself, with a number of his Zürich friends and acquaintances, on an unknown island off the south coast of England. It was a long, narrow strip of land and on the rocky coast at its southern end was a medieval castle. 'Before us rose an imposing *beffroi*, through whose gate a wide stone staircase was visible. We could just manage to see that it terminated above in a columned hall. This hall was dimly illuminated by candlelight. I understood that this was the castle of the Grail, and that this evening there would be a "celebration of the Grail" here . . .' (*MDR* 262).

The world of the knight, the Grail, and of Merlin, was not Freud's world but *his* world—the world of the castle on the rock with its copper column and alchemical laboratory. The trouble with the modern world, like the origin of neurosis, was not so much sexual repression as 'loss of soul', a lack of perception of the sacred. Freud's contribution only served to compound the plight of our culture for he struggled to find the sacred in one basic instinct, sex. The knightly ideal, one of the noblest expressions of the European spirit, was being ignored. The knight's Holy Quest was degenerating into the 'waste land' of our post-Christian civilization.

This theme, too, recurred in another dream in which he found himself surrounded by sarcophagi dating from Merovingian times. Then he passed by dead figures from the eighth century and went on until he came to some twelfth-century tombs, where he stopped before the corpse of 'a crusader in chain mail who lay there with clasped hands. His figure seemed carved out of wood. For a long time I looked at him and thought he was really dead. But suddenly I saw that a finger of his left hand was beginning to stir gently' (*MDR* 167).

The knight is still alive in his unconscious, offering him a way forward out of the past, away from the moribund figure of Freud, the vexed customs officer. But it is a future and a past (red cross on the front and on the back of the crusader) that is marked by the Christian symbol for wholeness and redemption, the state of at-one-ment with God. He would have to go on like the knight, his progress ignored by the populace around him, supported only by the flickering of his own 'little light' and by the few congenial souls he was to collect at his own Round Table.

6 Therapy

It is not possible within the confines of one chapter to give an adequate account of the profound transformation that Jungian analysis at its best can bring, or give anything more than a cursory outline of the principles on which its practice is based. However, the task must be attempted since the school of analysis that is carried on in Jung's name is his chief legacy to our culture.

The innovations introduced by Jung have had an influence which extends far beyond his own school, and it is fair to say that this influence has been benevolent and humane. His initial formulations arose mainly out of his own 'creative illness', as we have seen, but they were also a reaction against the stereotype of the classical Freudian analyst, sitting silent and aloof behind the couch, occasionally emitting *ex cathedra* pronouncements and interpretations, while remaining totally uninvolved in the patient's anguish and sufferings. Instead, Jung offered the radical proposal that analysis is a *dialectical* procedure, a two-way exchange between two people, who are equally involved. Although this was a revolutionary idea when he first suggested it, it is a model which has influenced psychotherapists of most schools, though many seem not to realize that it originated with Jung.

Jung's contribution to the practice of psychotherapy can be considered for convenience under four headings: (1) his approach to mental illness, (2) his attitude to patients, (3) the principles and techniques he advocated in treatment, and (4) his views on the role of the therapist.

Illness

In formulating his approach to mental illness, Jung was reacting not only against the concepts of Freudian psychoanalysis but also against the ideas which prevailed, and to a large extent still prevail, in conventional psychiatry. The truth is that Jung's experience was wider and his mentality more far-sighted than was generally the case among practitioners of either of these disciplines. Freud had tested and (to his own satisfaction) confirmed his hypotheses on the basis of his analyses of a small group of upper-middle-class Austrian patients, mostly women suffering from hysteria (a condition much in vogue at the end of the nineteenth century, but seldom diagnosed today). Jung's patients, on the other hand, came, at least initially, from all walks of life and exhibited practically every condition described in Krafft-Ebing's *Textbook of Psychiatry.* Moreover, Jung based his formulations not only on himself and his patients but on an extensive study of myths, comparative religion, and anthropology in a Herculean effort to establish universal truths which would be valid for all human beings, irrespective of their class, race, or creed. Above all, he did his best to remain undogmatic to the end. When his English colleague, E. A. Bennet, told Jung in 1951 that he was writing an article about him for the *British Medical Journal,* he said at once: 'Whatever you say, make it clear that I have no dogma, I'm still open and haven't got things fixed.'

The open-minded humanity of his approach to mental illness was evident from the beginning of his work at the Burghölzli as Bleuler's assistant. Unlike the great majority of psychiatrists at the time, Jung, as we have already noted (p. 12 above), actually listened to what his patients said to him, however deluded or hallucinated they might be. As he wrote much later:

In many cases in psychiatry, the patient who comes to us has a story that is not told, and which as a rule no one knows of. To my mind, therapy only really begins after the investigation of that wholly personal story. It is the patient's secret, the rock against which he is shattered. If I know his secret story, I have a key to the treatment. . . . In therapy the problem is always the whole person, never the symptom alone. We must ask questions which challenge the whole personality. (*MDR* 118)

By attending carefully to what his psychotic patients told him, he says,

I realized that paranoid ideas and hallucinations contain a germ of meaning. A personality, a life history, a pattern of hopes and desires lie behind the psychosis. The fault is ours if we do not understand them. It dawned upon me then for the first time that a general psychology of the personality lies concealed within psychosis, and that even here we come upon the old human conflicts. Although patients may appear dull and apathetic, or totally imbecilic, there is more going on in their mind, and more that is meaningful, than there seems to be. At bottom we discover nothing new and unknown in the mentally ill, rather we encounter the substratum of our own natures. (*MDR* 127)

This was even more true in the case of neurosis: 'The psychic processes of neurotics differ hardly at all from those of so-called normal persons—for what man today is quite sure that he is not neurotic?' (*CW* VIII, para. 667).

Although he learned all about making psychiatric diagnoses at the Burghölzli, he felt the procedure to be of limited usefulness: 'Clinical diagnoses *are* important, since they give the doctor a certain orientation. But they do not help the patient. The crucial thing is the story. For it alone shows the human background and the human suffering, and only at that point can the doctor's therapy begin to operate' (*MDR* 124).

The old pathological approach, which persists in general psychiatry to this day, describes mental illnesses as distinct 'entia', each presenting a specific and clearly defined clinical picture. Jung considered this to be rewarding up to a point, but it had the disadvantage of thrusting all the inessential features of the condition to the forefront, while covering up the one aspect that is essential, namely, 'the fact that this illness is always an intensely individual phenomenon' (*CW* XVII, para. 203).

In very general terms, he believed schizophrenia (psychosis) and hysteria (neurosis) to be extreme expressions of the two basic attitude types—extreme introversion resulting in a withdrawal of libido from outer reality leading into an entirely private world of fantasy and archetypal imagery, and extreme extraversion leading away from a sense of inner integrity to an exaggerated concern with one's influence in the world of social relationships. In other words, schizophrenics live in the unconscious while hysterics live in their persona.

Put in its widest conceptual context, therefore, mental health and mental illness are both functions of homeostatic balance or imbalance between the needs of the individual and the demands of the collective. When people become neurotic it is because divisions have opened up within them, conscious and unconscious processes no longer operate in homeostatic balance. This 'disalliance with the unconscious' is 'synonymous with loss of instinct and rootlessness'. But 'if we can successfully develop that function which I have called transcendent, the disharmony ceases and we can then enjoy the favourable side of the unconscious. The unconscious then gives us all the encouragement and help that a bountiful nature can shower upon a man' (*CW* XIV, para. 502).

It is true that Jung's emphasis is invariably on the intra-psychic life of the individual, but he does not ignore the importance of adaptation to the demands of society:

Thus, from the psychological (not the clinical) point of view, we can divide the psychoneuroses into two main groups: the one comprising collective people with underdeveloped individuality, the other individualists with atrophied collective adaptation. The therapeutic attitude differs accordingly, for it is abundantly clear that a neurotic individualist can only be cured by recognizing the collective man in himself—hence the need for collective adaptation. (*CW* XVI, para. 5)

Jung's view that psychiatric symptoms are persistent exaggerations of natural psychophysiological responses was not only shared by Freud but has been reaffirmed by contemporary psychiatrists who use ethological concepts in their approach to mental illness. For example, Dr Brant Wenegrat of the Stanford University Medical Centre in California sees all psychopathological syndromes, whether psychotic, neurotic, or psychopathic, as statistically abnormal manifestations of *innate response strategies* (his term for archetypes) shared by all individuals whether they are mentally healthy or ill.

Jung carried this insight one very important stage further, arguing that *symptom formation is itself a product of the individuation process*, that illness is an autonomously creative act, a function of the psyche's imperative to grow and develop having to proceed in abnormal circumstances. Neurosis is thus a form of adaptation, albeit 'inferior adaptation', of a potentially healthy organism responding to the demands of life. 'Because of some obstacle—a constitutional weakness or defect, wrong education, bad experiences, an unsuitable attitude, etc.—one shrinks from the difficulties which life brings . . .' (*CW* XIII, para. 472). Individuation is distorted or goes awry because the individual experiences difficulty in achieving a mature adjustment because certain archetypal needs essential to the programme of development have not been met at the appropriate time in the past.

However, this does not mean that Jung agreed with Freud that the origins of a neurosis invariably lie in early childhood. On the contrary, neurosis is caused by a failure to contend with contemporary circumstances. It may occur at any stage of the life cycle as a response to outer events, such as going to a new school, losing a parent, starting a new job, being conscripted into the Army, getting married, bearing one's first child, etc. Earlier traumata may predispose the individual to exhibit neurotic symptoms, it is true, but such traumata are not the *cause* of the neurosis. Neurosis is, therefore, in Jung's view, essentially an escape from a challenging life event which the individual feels unequipped to meet. Consequently, he taught his students, when confronted with a new patient, to ask themselves: 'What task is the patient trying to avoid?'

Not infrequently the patient's difficulty stops short of an incapacitating breakdown, but life is experienced as essentially unfulfilling and pointless.

I have frequently seen people become neurotic when they content themselves with inadequate or wrong answers to the questions of life. They seek position, marriage, reputation, outward success or money, and remain unhappy and neurotic even when they have attained what they were seeking. Such people are usually confined within too narrow a spiritual horizon. Their life has not sufficient content, sufficient meaning. If they are enabled to develop into more spacious personalities, the neurosis generally disappears. For that reason the idea of development was always of the highest importance to me.

Jung's understanding of symptom formation as a creative act is of the highest value for the development of therapeutic optimism in both patient and therapist, for instead of regarding the symptoms as representing a form of futile suffering, they can be seen as the growing pains of a soul struggling to escape fear and find fulfilment, as providing an invaluable opportunity to become conscious and to grow. Neurosis, he said, in the nearest he came to a definitive definition, is the suffering of a soul that has not found its meaning.

The patient

Many patients who consulted Jung have testified to the cordiality, warmth, and courtesy with which they were received. His sense of humour, always in evidence, made it impossible for him to seem pompous or self-important, and he never attempted to disguise his own fallibility as a human being. For example, he greeted one new and deeply worried patient with a reassuring grin, saying, 'So you're in the soup, too!' He believed in treating people as human beings rather than as 'patients' and taught that every appointment was a social occasion as well as a clinical interview. For that reason he never used a couch or any obvious techniques or tricks of the trade, treating everybody as essentially normal and healthy, while accepting, incidentally, that they might have a problem. 'If the person has a neurosis,' he said, 'that is something extra, but people should be regarded as normal and met socially' (Bennet, *Meetings with Jung*, 32).

What struck most of his patients was the extent to which he was *in* the analytic situation, completely *there*: not aloof and out of sight, not a screen for projections, not a transference manipulator, or a clinical manager, but there as a *real* person, wholly involved in the work, respecting the patient as an equal, not as a sick inferior. His keenness to abdicate all idea of personal superiority or of knowing all the answers, went along with a willingness to acknowledge his own vulnerability in the belief that 'only the wounded physician heals'. 'It's very important *not* to know all the answers,' he said. 'Often we *don't* know, and if we did it would be no good, for it is greater value to the patient when he discovers the answers himself' (ibid. 32).

My own analyst, Irene Champernowne, who was herself analysed by Jung, told me that he gave you the feeling that he was there not just because he was your analyst, but because, through you, he was pursuing his own research, that he too was learning from the process. This gave a sense of heightened importance to the proceedings. Jung himself acknowledged this in his autobiography: 'My patients brought me so close to the reality of human life that I could not help learning essential things from them. Encounters with people of so many different kinds and on so many different psychological levels have been for me incomparably more important than fragmentary conversations with celebrities' (*MDR* 143).

Above all, he never forgot that every patient was unique, and that general rules, dogmatic ideas, and universal procedures should never be applied to him. 'Learn your theories,' he taught his students. 'Then, when the patient walks in through the door, forget them.' He was hostile to group therapy and to all mass-produced remedies. 'In dealing with individuals, only individual understanding will do.'

It will be seen that Jung's approach to a patient differed radically from that of the conventional psychiatrist, who applies the 'medical model' to all who consult him, focusing on the signs and symptoms of illness in order to establish 'what has gone wrong', make a diagnosis, and prescribe treatment, while always maintaining clinical distance and professional authority. Jung, on the other hand, approached the patient not from the standpoint of pathology but from an anticipation of health in an effort to establish 'what can go right'; his focus was on symbols and meanings rather than symptoms, discovering what archetypal needs had been frustrated and needed to be met, while relating to the patient through the personal intimacy and 'mutuality' of the analytic situation. The essential difference between the two approaches is that the psychiatrist sees the patient as a victim of illness, the Jungian as a candidate for individuation.

Treatment

The Jungian approach to treatment is, again, very different from conventional psychiatry. The psychiatrist is concerned to reduce suffering through the provision of medicine and support, whereas the Jungian encourages the patient to *participate* in his suffering so as to confront its meaning and mobilize the healing powers of the unconscious. To face the major issues of life can involve much pain but this is a valuable spur to self-examination, an incentive to 'wake up' to one's predicament and grow beyond it. Jung once remarked of a patient, 'Thank God he became neurotic!' For in this case, as in many others, the neurosis was a call to attend to what was lacking or problematic in his life and to embark on the journey of self-discovery and renewal.

To the psychiatrist, overwhelmed as he often is by large numbers of sick patients, mental illness is an enemy (on to which he projects his own sick shadow) to be fought and overcome, a 'devil' to be driven out. To the Jungian the illness is a symbolic communication from the unconscious indicating where the patient has got stuck in his efforts to meet the demands of the archetypal programme for life. In a psychiatric clinic the patient goes through the ritual of consultation, diagnosis, and treatment, colludes with the psychiatrist in becoming detached from his illness, and is encouraged to relinquish responsibility for his plight into the 'capable hands' of the doctor. The Jungian, on the other hand, treats the whole patient, encouraging him to accept full responsibility for his circumstances, and to understand his illness as an expression of his total life experience. He is taught to see his symptoms as arising from an unbalanced mode of existence, which is itself a result of thwarted archetypal intent. Treatment consists of helping him to recognize and find ways of correcting his archetypal frustration, abandoning his one-sidedness, and bringing about a new equilibrium between the opposing forces in his personality as a whole.

To achieve this it is not sufficient to confine himself to dealing with his conscious circumstances. It is essential to know the situation in the unconscious. Here the analysis of dreams and the analysis of the transference become indispensable. The psychiatric approach is quite different: the aim is not to open up the unconscious, or receive the messages it has to convey, but to suppress it, to silence it with drugs. The goal of psychiatry is first aid and 'rehabilitation'—to return the patient to the community. The possibility that a breakdown may be a crisis filled with existential meaning and an opportunity for growth is seldom considered.

In fairness to the psychiatric profession, however, it must be acknowledged that Jung's patients, once he had left the Burghölzli, were hardly the run-of-the-mill intake of psychiatric practice. Most of them were educated, well-off, and in the second half of life. A number of them were psychologically sophisticated in that they had already received some form of psychotherapy before consulting him, and a fair proportion of them had little that was psychiatrically wrong with them. 'About a third of my cases are not suffering from any clearly definable neurosis, but from the senselessness and aimlessness of their lives. I should not object if this were called the general neurosis of our age' (*CW* XVI, para. 83).

To what did he attribute the 'general neurosis of our age'? To a collective 'loss of soul': to a loss of contact with the great mythic and religious symbols of our culture, to the emergence of social institutions which alienate us from our archetypal nature. This is an extension of the view advanced by philosophers such as Diderot and Nietzsche, and later developed by Freud in *Civilization and Its Discontents*, that the benefits of civilization are bought at the cost of natural happiness. Jung believed that the more secular, materialistic, and compulsively extraverted our civilization became, the greater the unhappiness, 'senselessness and aimlessness' of our lives. What was the answer? Not 'a return to the Church', for his own experience had taught him that—unless it came as a gnostic revelation—organized religion meant spiritual death. Again as a result of his own experience, he felt that we had no other recourse than to abandon the exclusively extraverted quest for meaning in the outer world of material objects so typical of our culture and, instead, establish contact with the symbol-forming capacities latent within our own psychic nature. What was needed was hard psychological work to open our minds to the inner wealth of the unconscious in order to realize in actuality our own capacity for wholeness. In the process, meaning and purpose flood back into our lives.

Jung divided analysis into four stages, which inevitably overlap and certainly do not always proceed in a regular order. These are:

(i) *Confession*: this is the stage of initial catharsis when one shares with the analyst the secrets one has been carrying. This is usually associated with feelings of intense relief, of shedding a burden, of discharging a load of poison. Guilty feelings are reduced, as are feelings of being isolated, inferior, and beyond the pale. The integration of the shadow begins.

(ii) *Elucidation*: this is roughly equivalent to Freudian 'interpretive' analysis. Symptoms and transference phenomena are examined and areas of failed development located. Radical transformations are rare at this stage; but serious work with the unconscious has started.

(iii) *Education*: the insights gained in stages (i) and (ii) are now ploughed into life. One begins to experience oneself differently and to explore new modes of existing. This usually goes along with an improved adaptation to the demands of society.

(iv) *Transformation*: work with the unconscious brings one face to face with the shadow, the anima or animus, and other archetypal components which are activated, as a natural homeostatic compensation, for one's previously narrow, neurotic, or one-sided development. At this stage, the transcendent function of symbols comes into its own. The individuation quest is now under way and is associated with coming to 'selfhood', a state reaching beyond mere 'normality' or 'social adaptation' to a full affirmation and acceptance of oneself as a whole entity in one's own right.

Jung elucidated the analytic process in the light of his alchemical studies. He acknowledged that, like alchemy, analysis is not a science but an art, an *ars spagyrica*—a spagyric art. 'Spagyric' is derived from two Greek words, *span* meaning to rend, to separate, to stretch out (i.e. to analyse) and *ageirein*, to collect together or assemble (i.e. to synthesize). The alchemical slogan *solve et coagula* (dissolve and coagulate) precisely expresses these two steps: 'The alchemist saw the essence of his art in separation and analysis on the one hand and synthesis and consolidation on the other' (Foreword to *CW* XIV). The analytic phase corresponds to the reductive method of Freud and the first two stages of Jungian analysis, and the second, synthetic phase to the last two stages.

Whether or not an analysis succeeds in its objectives depends on the raw materials (the alchemical *prima materia*) which patient and analyst bring with them to the analytical situation (the retort; the *vas*) and the transformation that occurs through their interaction. The first requirement is that both accept full responsibility for themselves and their own contributions to the relationship. 'The doctor must emerge from his anonymity and give an account of himself, just as he expects his patients to do' (*CW* XVI, para. 23).

Initially, most patients find it hard to accept responsibility for themselves and for their illness, preferring to hold others responsible and to adopt a passive or dependent attitude to the analyst. But this has to change if the analysis is ever to progress beyond the second stage: 'The real therapy only begins when the patient sees that it is no longer father and mother who are standing in his way, but himself . . .' (*CW* VII, para. 88).

Persuading the patient to be responsible for his illness can require great tact, otherwise he may adopt a moral attitude of self-condemnation because of it. He needs to understand that the illness is not his 'fault' but that he alone can discover its meaning and find a cure. The objective is to encourage a creative relationship both to the illness and to the personality as a whole and not to engender guilt or remorse.

The techniques of Jungian analysis—the two chairs, the dialectical mutuality between equals, the relatively frequent breaks and progressive reduction in the number of sessions, the personal work on dreams and 'active imagination' outside the analytic situation—are all designed to heighten this sense of responsibility in the patient for his own process of growth.

Jung banished the couch from the consulting room for this reason. Because it made the patient passive and dependent it positively encouraged a Freudian regression to the infantile complexes and hindered the onset of the collaborative, prospective adventure that Jung conceived analysis to be. Although Jung took full account of what his patient had been in the past, he was far more interested in what the patient was in the process of *becoming* in the present. Sitting face to face on similar chairs also made it easier for both therapist and patient to experience themselves as colleagues working on a shared task and to test the reality of whatever projections they might make on one another.

With regard to the frequency of sessions, Jung was critical of the Freudian practice of seeing patients intensively over long periods of time.

The psychoanalyst thinks he must see his patient for an hour a day for months on end; I manage in difficult cases with three or four sittings a week. As a rule I content myself with two, and once the patient has got going, he is reduced to one. In the interim he has to work at himself, but under my control. I provide him with the necessary psychological knowledge to free himself from my medical authority as speedily as possible. In addition, I break off the treatment every ten weeks or so, in order to throw him back on his normal milieu. . . . In such a procedure time can take effect as a healing factor, without the patient's having to pay for the doctor's time. With proper direction most people become capable after a while of making their contribution—however modest at first—to the common work. In my experience the absolute period of cure is not shortened by too many sittings. (*CW* XVI, para. 43)

Jung's assertion that the time needed for an analysis is not shortened by maintaining a high number of weekly sessions is supported by research which has failed to demonstrate that five sessions produces results superior to what can be achieved by one or two sessions a week. There are analysts, however, especially Freudians, and also some post-Jungians of the 'Developmental' school, who maintain as an article of faith that *analysis* means four or five sessions a week, 'otherwise it is not analysis'. Jung would have scorned this idea. In any case, the analytic process cannot be hurried. Inevitably the 'spagyric art' requires time for its goals to be accomplished.

Another aspect of Jung's practice which most analysts have chosen to ignore (often out of financial necessity) is his advice to break off the analysis every ten weeks to throw the patient back into life, to discourage reliance on the analyst, and to encourage reliance on the Self. This way the patient does not live to analyse, but analyses to live. This can be of immense benefit to analysts as well as to patients, for it helps prevent the exhaustion that can so easily afflict hard-working therapists and to ensure against their work becoming 'routine' or lifeless. A regular break from clinical responsibilities can enable analysts to follow other pursuits, such as studying, writing, lecturing, painting, pottery, travel, and sport, so that they can recharge their creative energies and strengthen their immunity to those forms of psychic contagion and 'burn out' that are common among therapists, social workers, and psychiatrists.

It must be acknowledged, however, that some patients find it impossible to work this way, especially those who, as a result of defective parenting in childhood, suffer from 'borderline' or 'narcissistic' personality disorders, or from what Bowlby called 'anxious attachment'. Such patients need time to establish with their analyst a working relationship through which they can begin to conceive of themselves as capable of sustaining a lasting bond of intimacy and trust. Only when this has been achieved can they begin to benefit from the kind of imaginative work with the unconscious that Jungians regard as the crux of analysis. Apart from these and some other exceptions, the classical Jungian approach can be applied with benefit to patients with widely differing kinds of personal difficulties and neurotic disorders.

To Jung, work with the unconscious was his way of life, and its objective was quite simply to *be* in the soul (*esse in anima*). This meant being constantly alive to the creative originality of the psyche. 'Being that has soul is living being. Soul is the living thing in man, that which lives of itself and causes life . . .' (*CW* IX. i, para. 59). Things come alive and are touched with soul when they come under the influence of the imagination. 'The psyche creates reality everyday, the only expression I can use for this activity is fantasy' (*CW* VI, para. 78).

The secret, both of analysis and of life, is to participate in this fantasy, both in our sleeping and our waking lives. 'In sleep fantasy takes the form of dreams. But in waking life, too, we continue to dream below the threshold of consciousness' (*CW* XVI, para. 125). The soul accompanies us as a constant companion, but we generally ignore its utterances because we fail to hear them. This can be rectified not only by attending to our dreams but also through the practice of *active imagination*. This is a technique for granting the psyche freedom and time to express itself spontaneously, without the usual interference of the ego. It is 'the art of letting things happen' that he observed in Hélène Preiswerk during her seances and in himself during his confrontation with the unconscious. 'The art of letting things happen, action through non-action, letting go of oneself, as taught by Meister Eckhart, became for me the key opening the door to the way. We must be able to let things happen in the psyche' (Foreword, *The Secret of the Golden Flower*, Richard Wilhelm, Routledge & Kegan Paul, 1962, 93).

Active imagination requires a state of reverie, half-way between sleep and waking. It is like beginning to fall asleep but stopping short before consciousness is lost, and then remaining in that condition, and observing what occurs. It is important to record what has been experienced, so as to make it lastingly available to consciousness: it can be written down, painted, modelled in clay, or even danced or acted.

To begin with one is usually a mere spectator, but if one is to experience the *reality* of the psyche and truly submit to its transformative power then one must enter the fantasy and become a committed participant in the drama:

You yourself must enter into the process with your personal reactions, just as if you are one of the fantasy figures, or rather, as if the drama being enacted before your eyes were real. It is a psychic fact that this fantasy is happening, and it is as real as you—as a psychic entity—are real. If this crucial operation is not carried out, all the changes are left in the flow of images, and you yourself remain unchanged. (*CW* IV, para. 753)

Again, as a result of his own experience, Jung was particularly keen that his patients should paint their psychic images.

The patient can make himself creatively independent through this method, if I may call it such. He is no longer dependent on his dreams or on his doctor's knowledge; instead, *by painting himself he gives shape to himself*. For what he paints are active fantasies.... It is himself in a new and hitherto alien sense, for his ego now appears as the object of that which works within him. (*CW* XVI, para. 106)

Through learning to work on his own dreams and developing the knack of active imagination, the patient increasingly assumes responsibility for his life and for his own individuation.

Hence the interval between consultations does not go unused. In this way one saves oneself and the patient a good deal of time, which is so much money to him; and at the same time he learns to stand on his own feet instead of clinging to the doctor. The work done by the patient through the progressive assimilation of unconscious contents leads ultimately to the integration of his personality and hence to the removal of the neurotic dissociation. (*CW* XVI, paras. 26, 27)

The therapist

Many people, both medically qualified and lay persons, came to Jung saying that they wished to become analysts. He describes one of these applicants in his autobiography: he was a doctor, with an impeccable background, who came with the best recommendations. When he declared his intention of training as an analyst, Jung said him:

'Do you know what that means? It means that you must first learn to know yourself. You yourself are the instrument. If you are not right how can the patient be made right? If you are not convinced, how can you convince him? You must yourself be the real stuff. If you are not, God help you! Then you will lead your patients astray. Therefore you must first accept an analysis of yourself.' (*MDR* 134)

As it happened, Jung turned this man down after listening to his first dream: it revealed a latent psychosis. But his remarks demonstrate the emphasis he placed on the therapist fully undergoing the process which he intended to supervise in others. 'An ancient adept has said: "If the wrong man uses the right means, the right means work in the wrong way." This Chinese saying, unfortunately, only too true, stands in sharp contrast to our belief in the "right" method irrespective of the man who applies it. In reality, everything depends on the man and little or nothing on the method' (*CW* XIII, para. 4).

Not only is it necessary for the analyst to be analysed during his training, but he must continue to work on himself throughout his professional life.

The analyst must go on learning endlessly . . . We could say, without too much exaggeration, that a good half of every treatment that probes at all deeply consists in the doctor's examining himself, for only what he can put right in himself can he hope to put right in the patient. It is no loss, either, if he feels that the patient is hitting him: or even scoring off him: it is his own hurt that gives the measure of his power to heal. This, and nothing else, is the meaning of the Greek myth of the wounded physician. (*CW* XVI, para. 239)

Self-analysis is necessary because of Jung's conception of what the analytic relationship entails, namely, a commitment on the part of the analyst that is at least as great as that of the patient. At the unconscious level both doctor and patient are participating in what the alchemists termed a *coniunctio*: like two chemical substances, they are drawn together in the analytic situation by *affinity*, and their interaction produces change. 'When two chemical substances combine, both are altered. This is precisely what happens in the transference' (*CW* XVI, para. 358).

The term 'transference' was first introduced by Freud to describe the unconscious process by which a patient attributes to the analyst feelings and attitudes that were, in fact, possessed by significant people in his past. This gives rise to the so-called *transference relationship*, which has to be distinguished from the *analytical re-lationship* or the *therapeutic alliance*, which refers to the total relationship between the analyst and patient as actual people.

Jung greatly extended the Freudian view of the transference, for he understood that the doctor–patient relationship is an archetypal relationship which has been with us since the beginning of time. In the course of an analysis archetypal images are stirred up which, when projected on to the person of the analyst, can confer upon him great therapeutic (or destructive) power. In Jung's own experience such archetypal figures as the magician, shaman, witch-doctor, and wise old man were commonly pro-jected. Secondly, and most importantly from the point of view of therapeutic outcome, the analyst can receive the projection of previously unfulfilled archetypal needs. For example, he may be-come the powerful father figure that a patient lacked in childhood, and this was clearly a crucial component of Jung's own transfer-ence on to the person of Freud. Finally, unconscious activity in the patient causes reciprocal activity in the unconscious of the analyst, with the result that the bond between them is transformed into something much more profound than the conventional doctor–patient relationship. It is this aspect of the transference that makes it essential that the therapist should be thoroughly analysed and remain aware of his 'personal equation'. It then becomes possible for the analyst to recognize what is unconsciously projected on to his patient (the so-called *counter-transference*) and to use this constructively in the therapeutic relationship instead of allowing it to become disruptive.

Moreover, in contrast to analysts of other schools, Jung laid stress on the vital importance of *feeling*—not only the patient's feeling for the analyst but also the analyst's feeling for the patient. Feeling provides an invaluable catalyst. It has to be present in the ego's relationship with the unconscious no less than in the analytic relationship itself. This is particularly true when patient and ana-lyst are both men or both women, success depending on each being in a feeling relationship with the other's unconscious. Some over-rational patients 'try to understand with their brains only . . . And when they have understood, they think they have done their full share of realization. That they should also have a *feeling rela-tionship* to the contents of the unconscious seems strange to them

111

or even ridiculous' (*CW* XVI, para. 489). Yet unless feeling is present no growth or transformation will occur.

Thus, in any thorough analysis, the personalities of both doctor and patient are fully engaged. In advancing this deeply committed view of the analytic relationship, Jung was fulfilling the vision of his life's work when, as a medical student, he read Krafft-Ebing's words that mental illnesses are 'diseases of the personality' and that to treat them the doctor must stand 'behind the objectivity of his experiences' and respond 'with the totality of his being'.

7 Jung's alleged anti-Semitism

I began by declaring Jung to be a man of paradox in that he followed a uniquely individual path towards discovery of the universal human being within himself. So true was he to his own 'little light' that many dismissed him as a crank and made little effort to penetrate his prose or make sense of his ideas. A number of those who did try to understand him got hold of the wrong end of the stick and, often unfairly, used it to beat him with. We can understand this in terms of Jung's psychological type. As an introverted thinking-intuitive type he had an extraverted feeling-sensation shadow. This means that he was capable of brilliant intellectual formulations and profound psychological insights, but it follows that both his feeling-based judgements and his relation to outer conditions could be defective. It is not uncommon for such types to feel impelled to state their vision of the truth boldly and uncompromisingly in circumstances where it would be more tactful and more politic to keep silent. Inevitably this earns them enemies as well as friends. Jung was aware of this drawback.

I have offended many people, for as soon as I saw that they did not understand me, that was the end of the matter so far as I was concerned: I had to move on. I had no patience with people—apart from my patients. I had to obey an inner law which was imposed on me and left me no freedom of choice. Of course, I did not always obey it. How can anyone live without inconsistency? (*MDR* 328)

This can be construed as both a strength and a weakness. It enabled him to make discoveries and frame hypotheses that no one else would have dared to discover or propose at the time, thus enabling him to compensate for the anti-psychic, pro-environmentalist biases of behaviourism, for the reductive biases of Freudian psychology, and for the materialistic biases of our culture. On the other hand, it meant that some of his ideas provoked hostile opposition, while others were greeted with incomprehension or indifference. It also meant that he laid himself open to seriously damaging charges, such as the accusation that he was a racist.

113

This is not the place for a detailed examination of this accusation, but since it is repeated from time to time, and argued that all Jung's ideas should be dismissed on account of it, the reader has a right to know the substance of the allegation as well as Jung's side of the story.

Jung's accusers maintain that in the years following Hilter's accession to power in 1933 Jung behaved in such a way as to demonstrate that he was both an anti-Semite and a Nazi sympathizer. They substantiate this allegation on the basis of two pieces of evidence: (1) that he published articles arguing that there were differences between Jewish and Aryan psychology, and (2) that he became President of the (predominantly German) Medical Society of Psychotherapy in 1933, and turned it into an International Society of which he remained President until 1939—years after the German Society had officially 'conformed' (*gleichgeschaltet*) to Nazi ideology.

Jung did not dispute the truth of these statements but strenuously denied that he was either a Nazi or a racist. How then did he justify his behaviour? In the first place, the articles were published in a professional journal for psychotherapists, the *Zentralblatt für Psychotherapie*, many of whose readers were themselves Jews. In the early 1930s the Jewish–Aryan issue was, to put it mildly, much to the fore in peoples' minds. In Jung's view, the problem was largely one of shadow projection, the Aryans projecting their shadow on to the Jews, and vice versa. What was needed was an attempt to make *real* psychological differences between the two groups conscious in the hope that this would reduce shadow projection and make mutual acceptance easier.

When he was attacked for addressing these issues by a Swiss psychiatrist, Dr Gustav Bally, in the *Neue Züricher Zeitung* on 27 February 1934, Jung replied:

Admittedly I was incautious, so incautious as to do the very thing most open to misunderstanding at the present moment: *I have tabled the Jewish question.* This I did deliberately. My esteemed critic appears to have forgotten that the first rule of psychotherapy is to talk in the greatest detail about all the things that are the most ticklish and dangerous, and the most misunderstood. (*CW* X, para. 1024; italics added)

In this and other articles he argued that the difference between Freud's approach and his own had much to do with Freud's Jewish background and his own Christian upbringing:

I suggested years ago that every psychological theory should be criticized in the first instance as a subjective confession . . . This subjective premise is identical with our psychic idiosyncrasy. Idiosyncrasy is conditioned (1) by the individual, (2) by the family, (3) by the nation, race, climate, locality, and history . . . I am proud of my subjective premises, I love the Swiss earth in them, I am grateful to my theological forebears for having passed on to me the Christian premise . . .

Freud's Jewish psychology is similarly conditioned by the history of the Jewish people.

May it not be asked wherein lie the peculiar differences between an essentially Jewish and essentially Christian outlook . . . ? Are we really to believe that a tribe which has wandered through history for several thousand years as 'God's chosen people' was not put up to such an idea by some quite special psychological peculiarity? If no differences exist, how do we recognize Jews at all?

All branches of humanity originate from one stem, but what is a stem without separate branches? 'Why this ridiculous touchiness when anybody dares to say anything about the psychological difference between Jews and Christians? Every child knows that differences exist' (CW X, para. 1029).

Jung ends by denying that he has raised this issue out of sympathy for the Nazi position. He is merely repeating views he has held since 1913. However, 'It is, I frankly admit, a highly unfortunate and disconcerting coincidence that my scientific programme should, without any assistance of mine and against my express wish, have been linked up with a political manifesto.' (CW X, para. 1034)

With regard to the second accusation, that his Presidency of the Medical Society for Psychotherapy coincided with the first six years of Hitler's dictatorship, Jung's defence is that he accepted the Presidency specifically in order to protect the Society's Jewish members. The facts are as follows: the previous President of the Society, Professor Ernst Kretschmer, resigned when Hitler came to power in 1933, presumably because the *Gleichgeschaltung* (literally, 'bringing into step') of the Society was imminent. Jung, who was then Honorary Vice-President, agreed to take his place at the request of its leading members, but he made it conditional on there being radical amendments to the statutes turning the Society into an *international* organization.

This was done, with the result that the old Germany Society now became the *International General Medical Society for Psychotherapy*, made up of a number of different national sections, including Dutch, Danish, Swedish, and Swiss as well as German. The latter (the *Deutsche allgemeine ärtzliche Gesellschaft für Psychotherapie*) was established and 'conformed' in Berlin in September 1933 under the Presidency of the psychiatrist Professor M. H. Göring, cousin of the Reichsmarshall. One of Jung's first official acts as President of the International Society, at a Congress at Bad Nauheim in May 1934, was to stipulate that all German Jewish doctors who had been excluded from their 'conformed' national Society were now entitled to become individual members of the International Society, thus preserving equal social and professional rights. Moreover, at the end of the Congress, Jung issued a circular letter to all members firmly stating the principle that 'The International Society is neutral as to politics and creed'.

These actions hardly point to anti-Semitic or Fascist sympathies on Jung's part. How is it, then, that these charges have a tendency to be repeated? One reason involves an apparently damning piece of evidence which Jung explained, but not to everyone's satisfaction. It arises out of his editorship of the *Zentralblatt für Psychotherapie* and his responsibility for what appeared in it. The *Zentralblatt* was published in Germany, as it had been since the foundation of the original Society. When it became the organ of the International Society, it was edited from Zürich by Jung. In the autumn of 1933, Professor Göring announced his intention of publishing a special supplement to the *Zentralblatt* for members of the German Society, obliging them to abide by the ideology of National Socialism. Jung was powerless to do anything about this because it was an exclusively German matter. However, when the December issue of the *Zentralblatt* appeared, Jung was appalled to discover that the publisher had included Göring's manifesto in the edition intended for international circulation which bore Jung's name as editor. In his 'Rejoinder to Dr Bally' Jung states this was done without his knowledge or approval. His accusers have declined to believe him. However, he publicly declared his innocence in 1934 (not after the war as some have maintained) and, if he was lying, there would have been no shortage of people able to expose him. Moreover, letters have come to light confirming Jung's story. For example, he wrote in March 1934 to Dr Olaf Brüel, a Danish co-founder of the International Society, saying that Göring's manifesto had appeared against Jung's 'express demand' that it should appear in a special issue 'signed by Göring and not by me'. Jung also wrote to the secretary of the Society, Walter Cimbal, protesting against what had occurred, and adding an urgent request that all future issues of the *Zentralblatt* intended for international circulation should be 'unpolitical in every respect'.

Another difficulty for Jung arises from the language used by him in his articles on Aryan and Jewish differences and from the fact that he perceives Freud's attribution of a 'negative value' to the unconscious as a threat to our culture, because it could help to release the destructive forces accumulating in the Aryan psyche.

As a member of a race with a three-thousand-year-old civilization, the Jew, like the cultured Chinese, has a wider area of psychological consciousness than we. Consequently it is *in general* less dangerous for the Jew to put a negative value on his unconscious. The 'Aryan' unconscious, on the other hand, contains explosive forces and seeds of a future yet to be born, and these may not be devalued as nursery romanticism without psychic danger. The still youthful Germanic peoples are fully capable of creating new cultural forms that still lie dormant in the darkness of the unconscious of every individual—seeds bursting with energy and capable of mighty expansion. The Jew, who is something of a nomad, has never yet created a cultural form of his own and as far as we can see never will, since all his instincts and talents require a more or less civilized nation to act as host for their development. (*CW* X, para. 353)

Jung goes on to suggest that the Aryan unconscious has a 'higher potential' than the Jewish because it has 'a youthfulness not yet fully weaned from barbarism', as is evidenced by 'the formidable phenomenon of National Socialism, on which the whole world gazes with astonishment' (*CW* X, para. 354).

The expression of such sentiments as these, in a journal published in Nazi Germany, it has been suggested, puts Jung in the same conceptual frame as Adolf Hitler. This extremely hostile

117

judgement takes little account of the social attitudes prevailing in all European countries at the time. The culture in which Jung grew up was inherently anti-Semitic. By our contemporary standards it was a racist society. Even the best-educated Europeans believed that blacks were inferior and that Jews were a problem. Both propositions were accepted by the majority as self-evident, hard though this is to believe for people born after 1945—that fateful year when a tidal wave of horror engulfed the European spirit and transformed our understanding of what it can mean to belong to a minority group.

By the standards of the first four decades of this century Jung was no racist. On the contrary, he was humane, broad-minded, and liberal. Far from being typical of the Swiss bourgeois his enemies have described, his ideas were highly innovative and far ahead of his time. For example, he advocated the decriminalization of homosexuality soon after the turn of the century, seeing it as both morally acceptable and a useful form of birth control; he risked his professional reputation by joining Freud when the latter was widely execrated for his views on infantile sexuality; and he advanced the deeply subversive idea that inside every man was an intact female personality, and a male personality inside every woman, which ought to be made conscious, integrated, and lived. As he wrote to Freud towards the end of their friendship, 'I should never have joined you in the first place had not heresy run in my blood' (*The Freud/Jung Letters*, 491, March, 1912).

It may be said of Jung that he was both tactless and politically inept to address the question of Jewish–Gentile relations in the way that he did, but Freud has never been attacked for doing the same thing. After their friendship had ended, Freud wrote to Sandor Ferenczi acknowledging that he had failed to unite 'Jews and goyim in the service of psychoanalysis', adding that 'They separate themselves like oil and water'. In another letter to Ferenczi he wrote, 'Certainly there are great differences between the Jewish and the Aryan spirit. We can observe that every day. Hence there would assuredly be here and there differences in outlook on life and art. But there should not be such a thing as Aryan or Jewish science.' This would be true enough of psychoanalysis and analytical psychology if they were indeed sciences (in the sense of physics or chemistry) but since they are not sciences but hermeneutic ('interpretive') disciplines, Jung's view of them both as 'subjective confessions', coloured by the personalities and cultures of their originators, is closer to the mark.

Jung has been much criticized for his argument (quoted above) that Jews needed a 'host' nation in which to develop their instincts and talents, since this could imply that Jews were, as the Nazis obsessively maintained, 'parasites'. Yet Freud is never criticized for using the same terminology. In *Moses and Monotheism*, published in 1938, Freud discusses ways in which Jews differ from non-Jews, acknowledging 'the fact that in some respects they are different from their "host" nations. . . . There is no doubt that they have a particularly high opinion of themselves, that they regard themselves as more distinguished, of higher standard, as superior to other peoples. . . . We know the reason for this behaviour and what their secret treasure is. They really regard themselves as God's chosen people . . .' Freud is allowed to make such statements because he was a Jew. Jung is not because he was a Gentile.

If the charge against Jung of anti-Semitism is unfair, where did it originate? Jung was in no doubt: 'This suspicion emanated from Freud' (*CW* X, para. 166). There is reason to believe this is true. A letter exists which Freud wrote to Jung's first psychoanalytic patient, a Russian Jewess called Sabina Spielrein. It was written in 1913 shortly after she gave birth to a son and just before the psychoanalytic conference in Munich: 'I am, as you know, cured of the last shred of my predilection for the Aryan cause, and would like to take it that if the child turns out to be a boy he will develop into a stalwart Zionist. . . . I shall not present my compliments to Jung in Munich, as you know perfectly well. . . . We are and remain Jews. The others will only exploit us and will never understand or appreciate us.' Freud's biographer, Ernest Jones, was aware of how quick Freud and his Viennese circle were to diagnose anti-Semitism in their opponents. He says he became aware, somewhat to his astonishment, 'of how extraordinarily suspicious Jews could be of the faintest sign of anti-semitism and of how many remarks or actions could be interpreted in that sense'. Freud was no exception. 'He had the common Jewish sensitiveness to the slightest hint of anti-Semitism and he made very few friends who were not Jews.'

As Jung well knew, bitter feelings were engendered in the Freudian camp by his 'defection' and many nefarious motives were attributed to him to account for his behaviour: unfortunately, these prejudices have persisted in some Freudian and Jewish circles to the present day.

The injustice of the charges against Jung has been condemned by the Jews who knew him best. Gerhard Adler, James and Hilda Kirsch, Rivkah Kluger, Sigmund Hurwitz, and Jung's secretary, Aniela Jaffé, have all come staunchly to his defence, describing the generous assistance he gave to Jewish colleagues and their families who were fleeing from Nazi persecution and denying that he ever displayed anti-Semitic or pro-Nazi feelings. As long as he remained President of the International Society for Psychotherapy, Jung continued to uphold the right of Jews to participate fully in the Society's affairs, despite what he called in 1938 'the political psychosis of the day'. He resigned only when the psychosis spilled over into the Second World War. Throughout the war, even in the darkest days when it looked as if the Nazis would triumph, Jung was a fervent supporter of the allied cause, as his own letters and many independent witnesses testify.

At the end of the war, he had a significant interview with Leo Baeck, an eminent rabbi and professor of religion, who had survived three years in Theresienstadt concentration camp. On his arrival in Zürich in 1946, Baeck declined an invitation from Jung, so Jung went to see him at his hotel. They talked for two hours, during which Baeck reproached him with all the accusations that he had heard against him. Jung answered all these to Baeck's satisfaction and they parted on good terms.

In the course of their discussion, Jung admitted that he had 'slipped up' in his initial assessment of the National Socialist phenomenon. What did he mean by this? Like everyone else at the time, he had been impressed by Hitler's meteoric rise to power and recognized that the dictator must have tapped some extraordinary energy in the Teutonic unconscious. However, by the end of 1934, he was as aware as any shrewd observer that this energy was being channelled in evil and pathological directions. The truth is that if National Socialism interested him, it was as a *psychological* rather than a political phenomenon: it was an example of archetypes functioning at a suprapersonal level; it accorded with his observation that repressed archetypal components tend to erupt from the unconscious in primitive and destructive ways.

With extraordinary prescience, Jung actually predicted the Nazi eruption in a paper published as early as 1918:

Christianity split the Germanic barbarian into an upper and a lower half, and enabled him, by repressing the dark side, to domesticate the brighter half and fit it for civilization. But the lower, darker half still awaits redemption and a second spell of domestication. Until then, it will remain associated with the vestiges of the prehistoric age, with the collective unconscious, which is subject to a peculiar and ever-increasing activation. As the Christian view of the world loses its authority, the more menacingly will the 'blond beast' be heard prowling about in its underground prison, ready at any moment to burst out with devastating consequences. (*CW* X, para. 17)

Christianity, combined with the disciplined, hierarchical structure of German society, had repressed the Wotanic elements in the Teutonic unconscious—the passionate, irrational god of storm and frenzy, the god of war whose violent spirit takes possession of the hearts of men and drives them berserk with the lust for blood and destruction. These terrible archetypal vestiges were now on the move. Writing in 1936, he ventured 'the heretical suggestion that the unfathomable depths of Wotan's character explain more of National Socialism' than rational explanations based on economic or political causes (*CW* X, para. 385).

German mythology is unique in that its gods are overthrown by the powers of darkness. The whole mythic drama ends in *Ragnorok* as Valhalla is consumed with flames, like the Third Reich in 1945. In 1936 Jung perceived Hitler to be in the grip of these previously repressed Wotanic elements: 'The impressive thing about the German phenomenon is that one man, who is obviously "possessed" has infected a whole nation to such an extent that everything is set in motion and has started rolling on its course towards perdition' (*CW* X, para. 388).

It is fair to conclude, therefore, that Jung was not a Nazi supporter or an anti-Semite, and one must sympathize with him when he wrote: 'It must be clear to anyone who has read any of my books that I never have been a Nazi sympathizer and I never have been anti-semitic, and no amount of misquotation, mistranslation, or rearrangement of what I have written can alter the record of my true point of view' (*C. G. Jung Speaking*, 193).

Jung was temperamentally incapable of being a Nazi. He was hostile to all mass movements because they negated the primary value of the individual psyche. He loathed 'isms' and distrusted dogma in whatever form it took. Like everyone else, he had a shadow and, growing up in the culture that he did, it would be surprising if there were no Fascist or anti-Semitic attitudes in it. But unlike many of his detractors, one suspects, Jung *worked* on his shadow: 'It is indeed no small matter to know one's own guilt and one's own evil, and there is certainly nothing to be gained by losing sight of one's shadow. When we are conscious of our guilt we are in a more favourable position—we can at least hope to change and improve ourselves' (*CW* X, para. 440). It was in this spirit that he confessed to Leo Baeck that he had 'slipped up'.

In recent years a number of Jungians have raked over the evidence in order to confront these issues as openly as possible, and the results of their deliberations have been published in *Lingering Shadows* (Boston: Shambhala, 1991). Some authors of this collection of essays interpret the available material as indicating that Jung indeed held anti-Semitic views, but theirs is a minority opinion among the Jungian community as a whole. Those who continue to press accusations against Jung (and they are mostly from outside this community) doubtless have reasons for their persistence. One possibility is that they have not worked sufficiently on their own repressed Fascist, anti-Semitic, or anti-Christian shadows, and enjoy the glow of self-righteousness that comes as they project them on to Jung.

8 The summing-up

Had Jung been a Nazi sympathizer would this provide grounds for rejecting analytical psychology *in toto?* Some insist that it would, apparently in the belief that a man's views should conform to contemporary notions of political correctness before serious attention can be granted to his work. Their contention could be justified were it proved that analytical psychology, so closely derived from the psychology of its founder, is imbued with a Fascist spirit. Fortunately, its emphasis on the primary importance of the individual psyche and the personal quest for wholeness, combined with its resistance to dogmatism, collectivism, and social conformity, places analytical psychology in an intellectual position as far removed from Fascism as it is possible to be.

Jung was hostile to all political movements that sought to augment the powers of the state, for they would deprive the individual of his right to become *authentic*—to be true to the law of his own being: 'To the extent that a man is untrue to the law of his own being and does not rise to personality, he has failed to realize his life's meaning' (*CW* XVII, para. 314). Those who toe the party line do not choose their own way but submerge their potential for wholeness in a relatively unconscious existence of collective conformity. The increasing dependence of the individual on the state which characterized the political developments of his time Jung regarded as anything but healthy: 'it means that the whole nation is by way of becoming a herd of sheep, constantly relying on a shepherd to drive them into good pastures. The shepherd's staff soon becomes a rod of iron, and the shepherds turn into wolves' (*CW* X, para. 413).

However, some, for whom Jung's alleged Fascism is not an issue, have found other reasons for rejecting his ideas, arguing that they are too distorted by the typical assumptions of a man born in his time (1875), place (Switzerland), and class (professional 'bourgeoisie') to possess universal validity. For example, the theory of individuation is criticized as being too evidently determined by Jung's introverted psychological type, his therapeutic approach as too

123

focused on inner events and insufficiently concerned with personal relationships, and his spiritual orientation as too influenced by his religious background for his Psychology to have much relevance to the existential problems of people living in the world today.

There must be some truth in these criticisms: everyone, however brilliant, must be born somewhere, at some time, in some community, and must inevitably bear the limitations of that fate. The introverted, individualistic, and spiritual biases of Jungian Psychology are evident and undeniable. But what matters in one who grapples with the crucial issues of human existence is the extent to which he can acknowledge his parochial origins, and, through an effort of intellect and imagination, transcend them. This was, as it happens, one of Jung's most extraordinary—and most paradoxical—gifts: his ability to live *in* his time and, simultaneously, to step out of it, to share an affinity with people of all the times that have ever been. Everything he wrote was touched by this affinity; and it has been justly said of him that his ideas were too fundamental, in a sense, to be modern. Precisely because he was so introverted, imaginative, and in love with introspection, he could peer hard and long into the mirror of his inner Self, and the vision of humanity that he saw there is as penetrating, far-sighted, and comprehensive as any yet described.

Jung's gift for transcending the confines of his own consciousness began, as we have seen, in the fantasy games of his childhood. Perhaps the most significant of these was the game involving the stone in the vicarage garden at Klein-Hüningen (p. 4 above): 'Am I the one who is sitting on the stone, or am I the stone on which *he* is sitting?' This recurrent ritual can be understood as the pathological behaviour of an emotionally deprived child who, lacking 'basic trust', in the world of people, compensates for his social isolation by constructing an imaginary relationship with a stone. However, such a reductive interpretation, though valid as far as it goes, neglects the highly significant consequences of the game for the child and his adult career. In this dialogue with the stone the seeds of Jungian Psychology are already germinating—the principles of duality, opposition, and enantiodromia, the animating power of the imagination which, through projection, quickens the world with life and meaning, the inner dialectic of thesis, antithesis, and synthesis central to psychic balance and growth.

The stone was Jung's first intimate encounter with the unconscious: out of it came his fascination with the unknown and his later understanding, confirmed on the Athai Plains, of the *religious* function of the psyche, that it provides the means through which creation becomes conscious of itself. By projecting his psyche into the stone he gave the stone life, identity, consciousness, doing what the alchemists did as they gazed into the *prima materia* in their retorts. He came to see the imagination as the psychic quicksilver out of which everything of value is created; for the material world of objects is devoid of all meaning save that which we grant it in the psyche.

Insights such as these exposed him to two further criticisms, namely, that his Psychology was essentially egocentric and antisocial, and that it was also unscientific: Jung took insufficient account of the social influences on personality development and his therapeutic procedures were not designed to promote adjustment to the demands of society. There is some justice in these criticisms, as I believe Jung recognized. But so deeply introverted was he that he felt it was only through conscious realization of the inner world that relationship to outer reality was achieved. 'Relationship to the Self is at once relationship to our fellow man, and no one can be related to the latter until he is related to himself' (*CW* XVI, para. 445). Individuation, he declared, has two principal aspects: 'In the first place it is an internal and subjective process of integration, and in the second it is an equally indispensable process of objective relationship' (*CW* XVI, para. 448). 'You cannot individuate on Everest,' he said (Hannah, *Jung: His Life and Work*, 290). Individuation does not shut one out from the world but gathers the world to oneself (*CW* VIII, para. 432).

When he eventually discovered in himself the security that was absent from his childhood environment, the 'inner certainty' this gave him enabled him to go his own way, to stand up to Freud and the academic psychologists, and, like William Blake, another introverted visionary, to live in *compensatory* relationship to his Age. If Freud espoused the principles of causality and psychic determinism, concentrated on the psychopathology of childhood, and damned religion as an infantile desire for parental protection, then Jung countered by adopting a teleological perspective, endorsed the freedom of the will, extended the developmental process beyond childhood to the whole span of life, proposed that illness is itself a form of growth, and saw religion as the fulfilment of a basic human need.

The academic psychologists also drove him into a compensatory position. For most of his life psychology in the universities was dominated by behaviourism, with its dogmatic insistence on rigorous investigation of quantifiable behavioural responses to outer stimuli, banning the psyche and introspective techniques from the psychology laboratory, and denying the influence of innate structures on behaviour. Jung, by contrast, stressed the importance of symbolic experience and inner events, insisted that the psyche and its study through introspection took precedence above all else, and claimed that innate propensities provided the basis of all psychological knowledge and experience.

His cultural role was no less compensatory. Western society, detached from its Judeo-Christian roots, was compulsively materialistic, spiritually impoverished, and technologically obsessed. Collectively we were perpetuating the mistake of the alchemists, projecting our spiritual aspirations into material things in the delusion that we were pursuing the highest value. This had encouraged us to treat each other as economic commodities and exploit the physical resources of the planet while neglecting, to our own detriment, the spiritual resources of the Self. The only remedy for our civilization's 'loss of soul' was a massive reinvestment in the inner life of the individual, so as to re-establish a personal connection with 'the mythic world in which we were once at home by right of birth' (*MDR* 237). Deprived of the symbolism of myth and religion, people were cut off from meaning, and society was doomed to die.

It was for statements such as these that the academics condemned him as 'unscientific'. Jung was unconcerned: 'I cannot experience myself as a scientific problem. Myth is more individual and expresses life more precisely than does science' (*MDR* 17). Not that he was a stranger to scientific method, as his early researches show. But he had to look *beyond* science: 'Science comes to a stop at the frontiers of logic, but nature does not: she thrives on ground as yet untrodden by theory' (*CW* XVI, para. 524). What he refused to tolerate was the prevalent fallacy of *scientism*—the denial of everything that is not susceptible to a scientific explanation. He preferred to give due weight to those irrational, acausal experiences which science declines to consider worthy of its attention. In this sense, he saw 'scientific' psychology as anti-life: 'the more the critical reason dominates, the more impoverished life becomes; but the more myth we are capable of making conscious, the more life we integrate. Overvalued reason has this in common with political absolutism: under its domination the individual is pauperized' (*MDR* 280).

Analytical psychology can make no claim, therefore, to be an experimental science, any more than psychoanalysis: it is best classified as a branch of *hermeneutics*—the art of interpretation in the service of meaning. 'Man', said Jung at the end of a famous BBC television interview, 'cannot stand a meaningless life.' Where does meaning come from? Jung's answer is *through an unequivocal affirmation of the Self*. Being passionately on the side of individuation, the Self seeks growth and development in our lives. Affirmation of the Self liberates its creative energies and brings certain knowledge that the best life is the life lived *sub specie aeternitatis*: 'The decisive question for a man is this: Is he related to something infinite or not?' (p. 28 above). This, the ultimate question for mankind, has given rise to all the myths and religions ever created, each one being a brave attempt on the part of some human group to relate to the infinite, the eternal. The quest for the cosmic connection, the experience of the Sacred and Holy, is a fundamental requirement of the Self. To deny it brings spiritual decay; to embrace it illuminates the soul with meaning. 'I can only gaze with wonder and awe at the depths and heights of our psychic nature. Its non-spatial universe conceals an untold abundance of images which have accumulated over millions of years of development.' It is comparable in magnificence to the starry heavens at night, 'for the only equivalent of the universe within is the universe without' (*CW* IV, para. 331).

This cosmic perspective gave him his reverence for the unconscious and the unknown, for the *numinosity* of symbols, for the magical power of the imagination and the reconciling genius of the transcendent function, for the meaning we attribute to everything about us, for the primacy of the individual psyche as the link between our own lives and the inscrutable intentions of the great universe itself. His emphasis on the priceless value of the individual, his insistence on the supremacy of *gnosis* (knowledge through experience, not through book-learning or belief), his openness to the irrational, the spontaneous, the synchronistic, his celebration of the richly creative purposes of life, his realization of individuation as the goal to which all other goals are subservient, his recognition of dreams and myths as speaking the timeless language of the soul—all were expressions of the cosmogonic inspiration that filled his life.

There can be no doubt that Jung was an odd and unusual man, but his extraordinary achievement would not have been possible had he been any other than as he was. He expressed his credo at many different times in different ways, but there is one passage that sums it up better than any other: 'Personality is the supreme realization of the innate idiosyncrasy of a living being. It is an act of high courage flung in the face of life, the absolute affirmation of all that constitutes the individual, the most successful adaptation to the universal conditions of existence coupled with the greatest possible freedom for self-determination' (*CW* XVII, para. 289).

Though aware that our species and our planet are in grave peril from our own unconsciousness, he remained cautiously optimistic to the end. He believed that nothing essential is ever lost because its matrix is ever present among us and can always be recovered by those 'who have learned the art of averting their eyes from the blinding light of current opinions and close their ears to the noise of ephemeral slogans'. In a letter to M. Serranno (14 September 1960) written during the last year of his life he quoted the consolation given by an old alchemist to his disciple: 'No matter how isolated you are and how lonely you feel, if you do your work truly and conscientiously, unknown friends will come and seek you.' And a Chinese adage: 'The right man sitting in his house and thinking the right thought will be heard a hundred miles distant.'

The conclusion of the same letter provides a fitting epitaph:

I tried to find the best truth and the clearest light I could attain to, and since I have reached my highest point and can't transcend any more, I am guarding my light and my treasure . . . It is most precious not only to me, but above all to the darkness of the creator, who needs Man to illuminate his creation. If God had foreseen his world, it would be a mere senseless machine and Man's existence a useless freak. My intellect can envisage the latter possibility, but the whole of my being says 'No' to it.

Further Reading

In the present text I have endeavoured to define all special terms where they are first introduced, but anyone in need of a glossary will find one at the end of *Memories, Dreams, Reflections*. In addition, Daryl Sharp's *C. G. Jung Lexicon* (Toronto: Inner City Books, 1991), an invaluable primer of terms and concepts, is available in paperback.

Jungian psychology is as much a state of mind as a system of theory and practice. Hence Jung's quip: 'Thank God I'm Jung and not a Jungian,' and his insistence that all analysts must be analysed. The successful outcome of any analysis, whatever the theoretical allegiance of the analyst, depends less on the use of textbook procedures than on the spirit with which these procedures are applied. The spirit that informs the practice of analytical psychology is unequivocally that of its founder. Works by this extraordinary, rich, and complex personality are listed below.

Works by Jung

The Collected Works of C. G. Jung, ed. Herbert Read, Michael Fordham, and Gerhard Adler (20 vols.; London: Routledge, 1953–78). Quotations in the present work are identified by volume and paragraph number (e.g. *CW* VIII, para. 788). Readers with access to *CW* may like to use the quotations as a starting-point for their own explorations. The huge index (vol. XX) is an extremely helpful means of orientation.

Memories, Dreams, Reflections (London: Routledge & Kegan Paul, 1963; cited as *MDR* in this book), one of the most remarkable memoirs to be published this century.

Man and his Symbols (London: Aldus Books in association with W. H. Allen, 1964).

The Tavistock Lectures (*Analytical Psychology: Its Theory and Practice*, London: Routledge & Kegan Paul, 1968).

C. G. Jung: Psychological Reflections: A New Anthology of his Writings 1905–1961, selected and ed. Jolande Jacobi (London: Routledge & Kegan Paul, 1971).

Further Reading

C. G. Jung Letters, selected and ed. Gerhard Adler in collaboration with Aniela Jaffé (2 vols.; London: Routledge & Kegan Paul, 1973, 1976).

The Freud/Jung Letters, ed. William McGuire (London: The Hogarth Press and Routledge & Kegan Paul, 1974).

C. G. Jung Speaking, ed. William McGuire and R. C. F. Hull (London: Thames & Hudson, 1978).

Selected Writings, intro. Anthony Storr (London: Fontana Pocket Readers, 1983), warmly recommended for those not brave enough to tackle the *Collected Works* directly.

In addition there are a number of seminars, recorded by his students, several of which have been published.

Books about Jung

Writing about Jung remains a precarious business because certain crucial documents (e.g. his diaries and some of his letters) are still not in the public domain, and a definitive biography has yet to be written. However, much of significance can be gleaned from the following:

Bennet, E. A., *Meetings with Jung* (London: Anchor Press, 1982).

Brome, Vincent, *Jung: Man and Myth* (London: Macmillan, 1978).

Hannah, Barbara, *Jung: His Life and Work* (London: Michael Joseph, 1977).

Hopcke, Robert H., *A Guided Tour of the Selected Works of C. G. Jung* (Boston: Shambhala, 1989).

Jaffé, Aniela, *From the Life and Work of C. G. Jung* (London: Hodder & Stoughton, 1971).

Stern, Paul J., *C. G. Jung—The Haunted Prophet* (New York: George Brazillier, 1976).

Stevens, Anthony, *On Jung* (London: Penguin, 1990), examines the development of Jung's ideas in the context of his life and in relation to the life cycle of humanity.

Storr, Anthony, *Jung* (London: Fontana/Collins, 1973; Routledge, 1991).

van der Post, Laurens, *Jung and the Story of our Time* (New York: Pantheon Books, 1975).

von Franz, Marie-Louise, *C. G. Jung: His Myth in our Time* (London: Hodder & Stoughton, 1975).

Wehr, Gerhard, *Jung: A Biography* (Boston: Shambhala, 1987).

Post-Jungian Revisions

Papadopoulos, Renos (ed.), *Carl Gustav Jung: Critical Assessments* (London: Routledge, 1992).

Samuels, Andrew, *Jung and the Post-Jungians* (London: Routledge & Kegan Paul, 1985).

The most important developments, in my view, have been the extension of archetypal theory into the realms of childhood development, feminine psychology, religious symbolism, social and political studies, mythology and cultural history. Some key works are cited below under each of these headings.

Childhood development

Fordham, Michael, *Children as Individuals* (London: Hodder & Stoughton, 1969).

Neumann, Erich, *The Child: Structure and Dynamics of the Nascent Personality* (London: Hodder & Stoughton, 1973).

Wickes, Frances G., *The Inner World of Childhood* (New York: Appleton-Century, 1966).

Feminine psychology

Harding, M. Esther, *The Way of All Women* (New York: Harper & Row, 1975).

Wehr, Demaris S., *Jung and Feminism: Liberating Archetypes* (London: Routledge, 1988).

Whitmont, Edward C., *Return of the Goddess: Femininity, Agression and the Modern Grail Quest* (London: Routledge & Kegan Paul, 1983).

Religious symbolism

Edinger, Edward, *Ego and Archetype: Individuation and the Religious Function of the Psyche* (New York: Putnam, 1972).

Hostie, Raymond, *Religion and the Psychology of Jung* (London: Sheed & Ward, 1957).

White, Victor, *God and the Unconscious* (London: Harvill, 1952).

Social and political studies

Bernstein, Jerome S., *Power and Politics* (Boston: Shambhala, 1989).

Further Reading

Odajnyk, Volodymyr Walter, *Jung and Politics* (New York: Harper & Row, 1976).

Progoff, Ira, *Jung's Psychology and its Social Meaning* (London: Routledge & Kegan Paul, 1953).

Mythology and cultural history

Campbell, Joseph, *The Hero with a Thousand Faces* (New York: Pantheon, 1949).

Eliade, Mircea, *Shamanism: Archaic Techniques of Ecstasy* (London: Routledge & Kegan Paul, 1964).

—— *Birth and Rebirth (or Rites and Symbols of Initiation)* (New York: Harper, 1975).

Henderson, Joseph L., *Thresholds of Initiation* (Middletown, Conn.: Wesleyan University Press, 1967).

Neumann, Erich, *The Origins and History of Consciousness* (New York: Pantheon Books, 1954).

—— *The Great Mother: An Analysis of the Archetype* (London: Routledge & Kegan Paul, 1955).

Books by the present author

Archetype: A Natural History of the Self (London: Routledge & Kegan Paul, 1982), a study of the biological foundations of Jungian theory, with particular reference to development in childhood and adolescence.

Withymead: A Jungian Community for the Healing Arts (London: Coventure/Element Books, 1986), a study of a therapeutic community.

The Roots of War: A Jungian Perspective (New York: Paragon House, 1989), on war.

Index

abandonment, fear of 49
active imagination 10, 19, 108–9
adaptation 23, 44, 53, 79, 105
Adler, Alfred 16, 24, 77
adolescence 59
Aeneid 23
aging 28–31
Aion 29
alchemy 26–8, 91, 93, 105, 125, 126
Amfortas 92
analysis 50, 96–112
   stages of 104–5
analytical psychology vii, 118, 123–8
   see also analysis; psychotherapy
anima 17, 21, 53–4, 59–61, 108
animus 53–4, 59–61
Answer to Job 29
anti-Semitism 13, 113–22
anxious attachment 107
archaeology 94
archetype 20, 21, 33–43
   activation of 35–7, 56–9
   archetypal law 40
   archetypal programme 44, 55–9
   archetype-as-such 39
   biological basis of 37
   cultural transmission and 39–41
   evocation of 35
   father archetype 52
   frustration of archetypal intent 103
   masculine and feminine archetypes 51–4
   mother archetype 35–6, 40, 52–3
   psychoid archetype 41
   wise old man 20, 111
   see also anima; animus; persona; Self; shadow
Aristotle 62, 64
association, laws of 35, 56–7
   see also free association
Athai Plains 30, 125
attitude types 66–79

auxiliary function 69, 75

Baeck, Leo 120, 122
Bally, Gustav 114, 116
Basel 2, 5, 88, 90
   Cathedral 6
   University 2, 7–9
basic trust 124
Bateson, Gregory 23
behaviourism 38, 55, 113
Bennet, E. A. 97
Binet, Alfred 78
biology 51, 54, 79
   in relation to spirit 10
Blake, William 125
Bleuler, Eugen 10–12, 20, 97
Bollingen 4, 26, 31
Bowlby, John 3, 15, 107
Breuer, Joseph 16
Brüel, Olaf 117
Brünnhilde 58
Burckhardt, Jacob 90
Burghölzli 10–12, 16, 97–8

censor 81–2
Champernowne, Irene 101
Chiron 92
Chomsky, Noam 37
Christ, Jesus 91
Christianity 115, 121
Cimbal, Walter 117
Civilization and Its Discontents 104
Clark University, Mass. 32
collective unconscious, *see* unconscious, collective
compensation, principle of 7–8, 54–5, 63, 84–5, 125
   see also dream
complex 9, 11, 13, 34–5, 44
   contrasexual complex 53–4
   father complex 56
   mother complex 35–6, 56–7, 59
   shadow complex 48

133

Index

complex (*cont.*):
  see also moral complex; Oedipus
    complex
coniunctio oppositorum 110
consciousness 30, 46, 55, 100
  see also ego-consciousness
cosmology 30, 127–8
counter-transference 111
creative illness 22–4
creativity 87, 107–9, 127
  and symptom formation 99–100
Critique of Pure Reason 7
cross 91–5
cryptomnesia 78
culture 51–2, 56–8, 118

Dante 23, 90
da Vinci, Leonardo 27
death and rebirth 57
deep structures 37
delusions 12, 14
denial 46, 49
depression 62, 74
development, *see* psychology
Discovery of the Unconscious, The
  22, 78
Divine Comedy, The 23
divorce 60, 62
Dorian Gray 48, 49
dragon 57
dreams 27, 47, 58, 81–95
  amplification of 87
  analysis of 103, 108
  compensatory function of 63, 84–5
  and individuation 63
  interpretation of 87–95
  'manifest' and 'latent' content of
    81–2
  as pure nature 83–4
  structure of 87–8
  see also Jung, Carl Gustav

Eckhart, Meister 7, 108
ego 34, 45, 46
  ego-consciousness 46, 84
  ego-defence mechanisms 46, 49
  ego-Self axis 34, 45
Ellenberger, Henri 22
enantiodromia 7

enemy 48
Eros 52
eternal ground 41
ethology 36–9, 63–4
evil 48
extraversion 23, 24, 37, 66–79
  and hysteria 98
Eysenck, Hans 79

fairy-tales 14, 58
fantasy 19, 20
father 52
  see archetype; complex; Jung, Carl
    Gustav
Faust 7
Fechner, Gustav Theodor 23
feeling 66–70
  and analysis 111–12
  feeling types 73–5
femininity 51–4
femme inspiratrice 17
Ferenczi, Sandor 118
Fliess, Wilhelm 16
Flournoy, Theodore 9
free association 23, 81–3
Freud, Anna 46
Freud, Sigmund 11–16, 22–3
  theory of dreams 81–2
  see also Jung, Carl Gustav,
    relations with
Freud/Jung Letters 17, 118
functional types 66–79

Galton, Sir Francis 11
gender 50–4, 57–8
Gilgamesh 23
gnosis 8, 127–8
Gnosticism 8, 91
God 6
Goethe, Johann Wolfgang von 2, 7,
  77
Göring, M. H. 116–17
Grail legend 89–95
growth 28–31, 44, 59, 62
Guggenbühl-Craig, Adolf 60
guilt 49, 50, 104

hallucinations 10, 12, 14
Hannah, Barbara 125

Heracles 19
Heraclitus 7
hero 57
Hitler, Adolf 50, 114–17, 120–1
homeostasis 44, 54–5, 63
and mental illness 98–9
homosexuality 60–1
Hopcke, Robert H. 61
hunting 51
hypnotism 9
hysteria 98

I Ching 28, 42
images 15, 22, 36, 54, 76, 109
primordial image 38
imagination 124–5, 127
see also active imagination
imago 56
incest 15
individuality 99
individuation 10, 16, 25, 45, 62–5,
123, 125
and analysis 63, 109
biological basis of 62
individuation marriage 60–1
and mental illness 100, 102
and symptom formation 99–100
infantile sexuality 13
inferior function 70
infrastructures 37
inheritance of acquired
characteristics 38
initiation 56–9
initiation hunger 58
innate releasing mechanism 36–7,
39
innate response strategies 99
International Psychoanalytic
Association 14, 15, 18
Interpretation of Dreams, The 11, 23
introspection 2
introversion 23, 24, 37, 66–79
and schizophrenia 98
intuition 66–70
intuitive types 75–6
irrational functions 67
see also intuition; sensation

Jahrbuch 14, 15

Jews 50, 114–21
Jones, Ernest 119
Jung, Carl Gustav (paternal
grandfather) 2
Jung, Carl Gustav (1875–1961):
alleged anti-Semitism 113–22
biographical sketch 1–31
Black Book and Red Book 20–1
childhood 2–5
collection of alchemical texts 26
confirmation 6
'creative illness' 22–4, 29
death 31
decision to become a psychiatrist
10
dreams 6, 7, 26; of customs
inspector and knight 87–95; first
dream 6; of Grail castle 94; of
house 32; killing Siegfried
18–20; Liverpool 21–2; of magic
lantern 29; of moribund
crusader 95; revelatory nature
of 6; Spectre of the Brocken 8; of
yogi 29
fainting attacks 4, 7
feelings of isolation 10, 26, 77
introspective genius 2
lecturer at Zürich University 11,
15
marriage 16–18; *see also* Jung,
Emma (née Rauschenbach)
near-death experience 29
No. 1 and No. 2 personalities 5–6,
19, 29, 46
old age 29, 30
personal individuation 25–6
Philemon 20
physical illness 29
psychological type 73, 76, 113, 123
relations with father 2–4, 6–8;
with Freud 12–16, 20, 22–3, 32,
89–94, 111, 118–19; with God 6,
29; with mother 3, 7, 17, 18
stone game 4, 124–5
tower fantasy 5, 26, 94
unconscious, confrontation with
16, 18–22, 25, 29, 59
Zofingia Society 8–9
Jung, His Life and Work 125

Index

Jung, Jungians and Homosexuality 61
C. G. Jung Speaking 121
Jung, Emilie (mother) 2
Jung, Emma (née Rauschenbach) 16–18
  psychological type 71
Jung, Gertrud (sister) 3
Jung, Paul Achilles (father) 2–4, 6–8

Kant, Immanuel 7, 39
Krafft-Ebing, R. von 10, 97, 112
Kretschmer, Ernst 77, 115
Küsnacht 17

Lamarch, Jean-Baptiste 38
learning 55
Lévi-Brühl, Lucien 51
Lévi-Strauss, Claude 37
libidinal development 23
libido 14–15, 23
life cycle 35, 44, 55–65
  and neurosis 100, 103
Lingering Shadows 122
Logos 52
love 52, 59–62
  falling in love 54, 59–60

Man and His Symbols 66–7
mandala 21, 26, 45, 92–5
  Jung's painting of 21
Mann, Thomas 72
marriage 59–62
'Marriage as a Psychological Relationship' 60
Marriage, Dead or Alive? 60
masculinity 51–4
Mayer, Robert 15
Mechanisms of Ego-Defence 46
Medical Society for Psychotherapy 114–17
Memories, Dreams, Reflections 2
menopause 62
mental illness, Jungian approach to 96–100
  see also depression; guilt; neurosis; psychosis
Merlin 91, 94
Meynert, Theodor 16

mid-life crisis 61–2, 90
Miller, Miss 23
Monod, Jacques 39
moral complex 49
Moses and Monotheism 119
mother 51–2
  mother–child bond 35–6
  see also archetype; complex
Muller, Catherine, *see* Smith, Helen
mysterium coniunctionis 29
mysticism 41
myth 14, 39, 57–8, 126–7
mythology 13, 121
mythopoiesis 19, 39

Nekya 23, 25
neurosis 22–3, 98–100, 102
  general neurosis of our age 104
Nietzsche, Friedrich 23, 76, 77, 104
normality 1, 101
numinosity 127

objective psyche 30
Odysseus 19, 23
Oedipus complex 15, 24
old age 28, 29, 31, 64–5
On the Psychology and Pathology of So-Called Occult Phenomena 9
opposites 29, 54–5, 77, 86, 93
Orpheus 19

paranoia 49, 71, 97
parapsychology 42
parents 52–3, 56–7
Parsifal 91–2
participation mystique 51, 60
patterns of behaviour 37
Pauli, Wolfgang 28, 41
peer group 53
persona 47, 48, 54
personal equation 80, 111
personality 62, 97, 100, 123, 128
  disorders of 107
  integration of 109
Philemon 20
physics 15
Physique and Character 77
Plato 35, 64
play 53

Preiswerk, Hélène 9–10, 11, 19, 23, 108
Preiswerk, Samuel 2
projection 4, 27, 29, 46, 49, 51, 122
projection-making factor 54
psyche 23
Jung's model of (diagram) 34
reality of 20, 25, 108–9
as self-regulating system 54–5
psychiatry 96–112
psychic energy 14, 15
psychoanalysis vii, 13–16, 23
Psychological Reflections 63
psychological types 66–80
diagram 70
Psychological Types 23, 24, 77, 78
psychology, academic vii, 78, 80, 126–7
developmental 25, 28, 55–9
see also analytical psychology
Psychology and Alchemy 28
Psychology of Dementia Praecox, The 12
psychopathology 28, 99
psychopathy 99
psychosis 12, 16, 19, 20, 22, 97–9, 110
psychotherapy 96–112
see also analysis; analytical psychology

quarternity 93

rational functions 67
see also feeling; thinking
rationalization 46
reaction formation 46
regression 23, 58–9
Reich, Wilhelm 16
reification 76
religion 13, 28, 104, 125–8
REM sleep 83
repression 12, 23, 46, 47, 48, 49
resistance 14
Rilke, Rainer Maria 75
rites of passage 56–9
romanticism 24
Rorschach, Hermann 77
Round Table, Knights of the 91–5

Salome 19
Satan 48
scapegoating 49
schizophrenia 10–12, 13, 14, 40, 76, 98
Schopenhauer, Arthur 7
science 126–7
Secret of the Golden Flower, The 26, 108
Self, the 21, 25–6, 29, 33, 44–6, 126–7
actualization of 55–9
and individuation 62–5
self-regulation 54–5
sensation 66–70
sensation types 70–2
Serranno, M. 128
sex 14, 50–4
sexual theory 14, 15
shadow 47–50, 54, 103–4, 114, 122
and inferior function 70–6
shaman 23, 111
sign stimulus 37, 39
Silberer, Herbert 16
Sleeping Beauty 58
Smith, Helen (Catherine Muller) 9, 23
social relationships 98–9
society 125
sociobiology 37–9
somnambulism 9
soror mystica 27
soul 9, 108, 127
loss of 94, 126
soul image 53
spagyric art 105, 107
Spielrein, Sabina 17, 119
spirit 10, 41, 45
spiritualism 2
'Stages of Life, The' 44
Steiner, Rudolf 23
Stekel, Wilhelm 16
Steps to an Ecology of Mind 23
Strange Case of Dr Jekyll and Mr Hyde, The 49
stranger anxiety 48
Studies in Word-Association 12
suicide 62
super-ego 49, 81

Index

super-ego (*cont.*):
  see also moral complex
superior function 69
symbolism 27, 85–7, 126
symbols 14, 15
Symbols of Transformation 89
symptom formation 99–100
synchronicity 28, 42
syzygy 53

tabula rasa theory 36, 38, 51
Talmud, the 84
Taoism 26, 51
Tausk, Victor 16
teleology 85
testosterone 51
tetrad 77
Textbook of Psychiatry (Krafft-
  Ebing's) 10, 97
Theory of Types (Rorschach's) 77
thinking 66–70
  thinking types 72–3
trance 19
transcendent function 46, 86, 105,
  127
transference 27, 103, 110–11
  see also counter-transference
transformation 27, 105, 109
*Transformations and Symbols of the
  Libido* 15, 23, 38, 89
treatment, *see* analysis; analytical
  psychology; psychotherapy

UFOs 28

unconscious 25, 103, 125
  collective 14, 33–43, 121
  personal 14, 33–5
unus mundus 41

Virgil 23
Voltaire 72

war 50, 51
warrior 91
Weimar Conference 18
Wenegrat, Brant 99
Wilhelm, Richard 26, 108
Wolff, Antonia 17–18
word-association test 11–13
World as Will and Idea, The 7
world parents 52
Wotan 58, 121
wounded healer 91–2, 110
Wundt, Wilhelm 11

xenophobia 48

yang 51
yin 51

Zarathustra 15
*Zentralblatt für
  Psychotherapie* 114–17
Ziehen, Theodor 11
Zosimos 91
Zürich 18
  University of 10–11